Teacher's Resources

Working with Young Children

Dr. Judy Herr
Associate Dean, College of Human Development
University of Wisconsin-Stout
Menomonie, Wisconsin

Publisher
The Goodheart-Willcox Company, Inc.
Tinley Park, Illinois

Contents

Introduction

Working with Young Children is a comprehensive text designed to make students competent early childhood caregivers and teachers. In addition to the text, the *Working with Young Children* learning package includes these products: the *Student Activity Guide,* the *Teacher's Resource Guide,* the *Teacher's Resource Binder,* the *Test Creation Software, The Observation Guide,* and *Mastering CDA Competencies.* Using these products can help you develop an effective early childhood program tailored to your students' unique needs.

Using the Text

The text for *Working with Young Children* provides a step-by-step approach to the everyday care and teaching of young children. You will find that students are willing to read and study the text because the written material applies directly to students' child care and teaching experiences.

Encourage students to read and study the many charts in addition to reading the text materials. Many charts summarize information in a way that students will find most useful in classroom situations. Others contain countless ideas for activities and learning experiences that are both beneficial and enjoyable for children.

You can help students get the most from each chapter by explaining how the chapter organization is designed to help them learn. Each chapter begins with learning objectives. These allow students to understand what they will be expected to learn and how they will benefit from mastering the material. Related terms are also listed at the beginning of each chapter. Chapter summaries, review questions, and suggested activities and discussion topics follow each chapter. These components allow students to review and expand on the knowledge gained from reading. The glossary at the back of the book helps students learn terms related to early childhood education. A complete index can be used by students to quickly and easily refer to information they need.

Objectives

A set of behavioral objectives are found at the beginning of each chapter. These are performance goals that students will be expected to achieve after studying the chapter. Review the objectives in each chapter with students to help make them aware of the skills they will be building as they read the chapter material.

Terms to Know

Vocabulary words appear at the beginning of each chapter under the heading "Terms to Know." This list is designed to help students identify important terms from the chapter. Terms are listed in the order in which they appear in the chapter. These terms are in bold type in the text where they are defined so that students can recognize them while reading. Discussing these words with students will help familiarize them with concepts to which they are being introduced. To be sure students are familiar with these important terms, you may want to ask them to

- look up, define, and explain each term.
- relate each term to the topic being studied.
- match terms with their definitions.
- find examples of how the terms are used in current newspaper and magazine articles, reference books, and other related materials.

Review and Reflect

The questions at the end of each chapter under the heading "Review and Reflect" cover the basic information presented in the chapter. The review section for each chapter consists of a variety of true/false, completion, multiple choice, short answer, and essay questions. These review questions are designed to help students recall, organize, and use the information presented in the text. Answers to these questions appear in the *Teacher's Resource Guide* and the *Teacher's Resource Binder.*

Apply and Explore

The activities in this section give students opportunities to increase their knowledge through firsthand experiences. These activities allow students to apply many of the concepts learned in the chapter to real-life situations. Suggestions for both individual and group work are provided in varying degrees of difficulty.

Therefore, you may choose and assign activities according to students' interests and abilities.

Using the Student Activity Guide

The *Student Activity Guide* designed for use with the text *Working with Young Children* helps students recall and review concepts presented in the text. It also helps students apply what they have learned to classroom situations.

The activities in the guide are divided into chapters that correspond to the chapters in the text. By reading the text first, students will have the information they need to complete the activities. (Some activities may also be used as pretests to spark interest in the chapter and should be done before reading. These activities are noted in the "Introductory Activities" sections of the *Teacher's Resource Guide* and the *Teacher's Resource Binder.*) Students should try to do the activities without looking in the book. Then they can use the text to check their answers and to answer the questions they could not complete.

The pages of the *Student Activity Guide* are perforated so students can easily turn completed activities in to you for evaluation. They are also drilled so that students can keep completed activities in a file for easy reference.

The activity guide includes a number of types of activities. Some of them have objective answers. Students can use these activities to review as they study for tests and quizzes. Answers to these activities are given in the *Teacher's Resource Guide* and the *Teacher's Resource Binder.* Other activities help students apply and expand on the information provided in the text. Responses to these activities cannot be judged as "right" or "wrong." These activities allow students to form their own ideas about information presented in the text by considering alternatives and evaluating situations thoughtfully. These activities can often be used as a basis for classroom discussion by asking students to defend, explain, and justify their answers and conclusions.

Each activity in the activity guide is described in the *Teacher's Resource Guide* and the *Teacher's Resource Binder* as a teaching strategy under the related instructional concept and is identified as an activity in the *Student Activity Guide.*

Using the Teacher's Resource Guide

The *Teacher's Resource Guide* for *Working with Young Children* suggests many methods of presenting the concepts in the text to students. The individual and group activities will allow students to apply the concepts learned to realistic situations. Like the *Student Activity Guide,* the *Teacher's Resource Guide* is divided into chapters that match the chapters in the text. Each chapter contains the following:

- *Behavioral Objectives.* These are the objectives that students will be able to accomplish after completing the chapter activities.
- *Teaching Materials.* A list of all materials available to supplement each chapter in the text is conveniently located at the beginning of each chapter. The list includes the names of all activities contained in the *Student Activity Guide.* It also lists reproducible masters and transparency masters provided in the *Teacher's Resource Guide* and the color transparencies provided in the *Teacher's Resource Binder.*
- *Introductory Activities.* These motivational activities are designed to stimulate your students' interest in the chapter they will be studying. These activities encourage a sense of curiosity that students will want to satisfy by reading the chapter.
- *Instructional Concepts and Student Learning Experiences.* A variety of student learning experiences are described for teaching each of the major concepts discussed in the text. Each of the major concepts is listed in this guide in bold type. The student learning experiences for teaching each concept follow. Activities that are found in the accompanying *Student Activity Guide* are also described for your convenience in planning daily lessons. These are identified with the letters SAG following the title and letter of the activity.
- *Additional Resources.* This section lists resources available outside the classroom that can be used to help students relate information to their own environment. Guest speakers that might be invited into your classroom are suggested and ideas for panel discussions are presented. Field trips to sites located in your community are also listed. These activities are listed separately because they require advance planning and preparation. It is easy for you to look ahead to the "Other Resources" section of future chapters and make any necessary arrangements in advance.
- *Research Topics.* This section lists activities that involve in-depth research techniques such as literature review, interviewing, and experimentation. The activities also require more advanced writing and presentation techniques. These activities may be used to stimulate and challenge the gifted and highly motivated students in your classroom.
- *Answer Keys.* This section contains the answers for the "Review and Reflect" questions at the end of each chapter in the text. Answers to the learning experiences in the activity guide are provided. It

also includes any answers needed for the reproducible masters and answers for the chapter tests.

- *Reproducible Masters.* Several reproducible masters are included for each chapter. These masters are designed to enhance the presentation of concepts. Some of the masters are designated for use as *transparency masters* with an overhead projector. These are often charts or graphs that can be used as a basis for class discussion of important concepts. They can also be used as student handouts. Some of the masters are designed to be used as *reproducible masters.* Each student or group can be given a copy of the activity or informational handout. These items encourage individual creative and critical thinking. They can also be used as a basis for class discussions. Some masters provide material not contained in the text that you may want students to know.
- *Chapter Test Masters.* Individual tests with clear, specific questions that deal with topics presented in each chapter are provided. Multiple choice, true/false, and matching questions are used to measure student learning about facts and definitions. Essay questions are also provided in the chapter tests. Some of these require students to list information, while others allow students to express their opinions and creativity. You may wish to modify these tests to tailor the questions to your classroom needs.

Using the Teacher's Resource Binder

The *Teacher's Resource Binder* for *Working with Young Children* includes all of the materials from the *Teacher's Resource Guide* plus one or more color transparencies for each chapter of the text. These materials are included in a convenient three-ring binder. Reproducible materials can be removed easily. Handy dividers included with the binder help you organize materials so you can quickly find the items you need.

The color transparencies are designed to illustrate concepts more clearly, reinforce and expand upon text information, review text material, and promote critical thinking skills. Each transparency includes a brief description and several suggestions on how it can be used in the classroom.

Using the Test Creation Software

In addition to the printed supplements designed to support *Working with Young Children,* you may choose to acquire the available *Test Creation Software.* The database for this software package includes all the questions from the chapter test masters in the *Teacher's Resource Guide/Binder.* You can choose the EasyTest option to have the computer generate a test for you with randomly selected questions. You can also opt to choose specific questions from the database and, if you wish, add your own questions to create customized tests to meet your classroom needs. You may want to make different versions of the same test to use during different class periods. Answer keys are generated automatically to simplify grading.

Using the Observation Guide

Even the most complete textbook cannot prepare students for all of the experiences they will encounter as early childhood teachers. Careful observation of a variety of children and settings will help give students a more comprehensive education.

The Observation Guide provides forms and instructions so that students can gain the most from their observations. Like the *Student Activity Guide* and *Teacher's Resource Guide, The Observation Guide* is divided into chapters that match the chapters in the text. Early observations are designed to help students become familiar with observation and recording techniques. As the chapters progress, student involvement in observations becomes more advanced. In later chapters, students are expected to plan their own activities to lead and evaluate.

Each observation experience begins with objectives for the observation. These help students focus on the specific goals for each observation. Instructions for any preparation needed are given. Space to record information on the setting and activities of the observation are provided as well. Questions are also provided to help students summarize and interpret their evaluations.

The Observation Guide should be used to supplement learning from textbook reading and classroom lecture. Students should have a good basic understanding of chapter information before conducting the observation activities. The observations can then be used as bases for discussions on how the text material applies to actual classroom situations.

Using Mastering CDA Competencies

The students in your program may be planning on obtaining their Child Development Associate Credential. The CDA program represents a national effort to credential qualified caregivers who work with children from birth to age five. *Mastering CDA Competencies* can help students earn their CDA Credential. The CDA program uses six statements of skill called Competency Goals to establish the framework for caregiver behavior. These goals are divided into 13 Functional Areas, which describe major tasks caregivers must accomplish to satisfy the Competency Goals.

Mastering CDA Competencies is used with the text *Working with Young Children*. Each chapter of this book corresponds to the same chapter in the text. The chapters begin by listing CDA Competency Goals and Functional Areas that the reading and exercises address. Each chapter of *Mastering CDA Competencies* is divided into the following four parts:

- Read from *Working with Young Children*
- Review What You Have Read
- Observe What You Have Learned
- Apply What You Have Learned

Mastering CDA Competencies prepares students to become competent caregivers and will benefit anyone involved in training for the CDA program.

Using Hands-On Experiences

Most students interested in becoming early childhood teachers tend to learn best by doing. Therefore, you should use as many hands-on experiences as possible to teach these students. In addition to observations, students should be given opportunities to make their own classroom materials, write and follow through on their own lesson plans, and do evaluations of themselves.

Throughout the text, instructions, recipes, and other guidelines for making materials and conducting activities are given. Additional instructions and guidelines are offered in the *Teacher's Resource Guide/Binder*. You will enhance student learning by offering materials, time, and encouragement for student involvement with these hands-on activities. Making fingerpaint, creating and using puppets, and writing stories will all help to increase students' enthusiasm and build confidence in their teaching skills.

Bulletin Boards

Creating attractive, interesting visual materials will be an important part of your students' roles as teachers. One method of building student skill in this area is to assign bulletin boards to them throughout the class year. You may create a schedule at the beginning of the year by assigning weeks to each student or allowing each student to choose a week for his or her bulletin board.

If time allows, or if you have several bulletin boards with which to work, you may have students work in pairs on a first bulletin board. Then after all student teams have completed bulletin boards, you may have each student design and make a bulletin board individually.

Students should be assigned topics that coordinate with the current subject matter being studied in the class. This will challenge students to create bulletin boards to match a variety of topics rather than simply using topics they find easy to illustrate.

The bulletin boards should be appealing to, and developmentally appropriate for, young children. The reproducible master, *Evaluating Bulletin Boards,* can be used by students to plan appropriate bulletin boards. (You can use the same form for grading the finished bulletin boards.) This master is located at the end of the introduction.

Planning Lessons and Activities

To prepare your students for the classroom setting, make planning lessons and activities regular assignments for the students. Methods of developing activities and themes are thoroughly discussed in Chapter 17 of the text, "The Curriculum."

The reproducible masters, *Theme Development Form* and *Block Plan Form,* are included at the end of the introduction. These forms may help students develop uniform planning methods. They may also help you evaluate students' plans consistently.

Using Other Resources

Much student learning in this class can be reinforced and expanded by exposing your students to a variety of viewpoints and teaching methods. Your providing guest speakers, panel presentations, field trip experiences, and access to media resources related to child care can greatly enhance student learning.

Current magazines and journals are good sources of articles on various aspects of early childhood education. Having copies in the classroom will encourage students to use them for research and ideas as they study early childhood education. Information can also be obtained from the Internet and the World Wide Web.

The following magazines and journals may be helpful to your students:

The American Montessori Society Bulletin
American Montessori Society (AMS)
150 Fifth Avenue
New York, NY 10011

The Black Child Advocate
Black Child Development Institute
1463 Rhode Island Avenue NW
Washington, DC 20001

Child and Youth Quarterly
Human Sciences Press
72 Fifth Avenue
New York, NY 10011

Child Development and Child Development
  Abstracts and Bibliography
Society for Research in Child Development
5801 Ellis Avenue
Chicago, IL 60637

Childhood Education
Association for Childhood Education
International (ACEI)
11141 Georgia Avenue, Suite 300
Wheaton, MD 20902

Child Health Alert
P.O. Box 388
Newton Highlands, MA 02161

Child Welfare
Child Welfare League of America, Inc.
  (CWLA)
440 First Street, NW
Washington, DC 20001

Children Today
Superintendent of Documents
U.S. Government Printing Office
Washington, DC 20402

Day Care and Early Education
Human Sciences Press
72 Fifth Avenue
New York, NY 10011

Developmental Psychology
American Psychological Association
1200 17th Street, NW
Washington, DC 20036

Dimensions of Early Childhood
Southern Association for Children Under Six
Box 5403 Brady Station
Little Rock, AK 72215

Early Child Development and Care
Gordon and Breach Science Publishers
One Park Avenue
New York, NY   10016

Early Childhood News
330 Progress Road
Dayton, OH 45499

Early Childhood Research Quarterly
National Association for the Education
of Young Children
Ablex Publishing Company
355 Chestnut Street
Norwood, NJ 07648

Early Childhood Today
Scholastic
Office of Publication
2931 East McCarty Street
P.O. Box 3710
Jefferson City, MO 65102-3710

Education Leadership
Association for Supervision and Curriculum
Development (ASCD)
125 North West Street
Alexandria, VA 22314-2798

Educational Research
American Educational Research Association
(AERA)
1230 17th Street, NW
Washington, DC 20036

ERIC/EECE Newsletter
805 West Pennsylvania Avenue
Urbana, IL 61801

Exceptional Children
Council for Exceptional Children
1920 Association Drive
Reston, VA 22091

Gifted Child Quarterly
National Association for Gifted Children
4175 Lovell Road, Suite 140
Circle Pines, MN 55014

Instructor
P.O. Box 6099
Duluth, MN 55800

Journal of Family and Consumer Sciences
American Association of Family and Consumer
Sciences (AAFCS)
1555 King Street
Alexandria, VA 22314

Journal of Research in Early Childhood
  Education International
11501 Georgia Avenue, Suite 315
Wheaton, MD 20902

Multicultural Leader
  Educational Materials and Service Center
  144 Railroad Avenue, Suite 107
  Edmonds, WA 98020

Report on Preschool Education
  Capital Publications, Inc.
  2430 Pennsylvania Avenue NW, Suite G-12
  Washington, DC 20037

Young Children
  NAEYC
  1509 16th Street NW
  Washington, DC 20036-1426

The following magazines are written for school-age children:

Cricket
  Box 7433
  Red Oak, IA 51591-2433

Highlights for Children, Inc.
  Box 269
  Columbus, OH 43216-0269

Ladybug
  P.O. Box 7436
  Red Oak, IA 51591-2436

Ranger Rick
  National Wildlife Federation
  P.O. Box 777
  Mount Morris, IL 61054-8276
  web site: http://www.nwf.org/nwf

Sesame Street
  P.O. Box 55518
  Boulder, CO 80328-5518

Spider
  Box 7435
  Red Oak, IA 51591-2435
  (800) 827-0227

Stone Soup
  Children's Art Foundation
  Box 83
  Santa Cruis, CA 95063
  (408) 426-5557
  FAX: (408) 426-1161
  E-Mail: editor@stonesoup.com; URL:
  hht//www.stonesoup.com

Turtle
  Benjamin Franklin Literary and Medical Society, Inc.
  Box 567
  1100 Waterway Blvd.
  Indianapolis, IN 46206
  (317) 636-8881
  FAX: (317) 684-8094

Your Big Back Yard
  National Wildlife Federation
  1400 16th Street NW
  Washington, DC 20036
  (202) 797-6800

U.S. Kids
  Children's Better Health Institute
  1100 Waterway Blvd.
  Box 567
  Indianapolis, IN 46202
  (317) 636-8881
  FAX: (317) 684-8094

Other information may be obtained through various professional organizations. The following may be able to provide you with some resources:

American Association for Gifted Children
  15 Grammercy Park
  New York, NY 10003

American Child Care Services
  P.O. Box 548
  532 Settlers Landing Road
  Hampton, VA 23669

American Educational Research Association (AERA)
  1230 17th Street NW
  Washington, DC 20036

American Association of Family and Consumer Sciences (AAFCS)
  1555 King Street
  Alexandria, VA 22314

American Montessori Association (AMS)
  150 Fifth Avenue
  New York, NY 10011

Association for Childhood Education International (ACEI)
  11141 Georgia Avenue, Suite 200
  Wheaton, MD 20902

Canadian Association for the Education of
Young Children (CAYC)
    252 Bloor Street, Suite 12-115
    Toronto, Ontario
    Canada M5S 1V5

Children's Defense Fund
    122 C Street, NW
    Washington, DC 20001

Child Welfare League of America
    440 First Street, NW
    Washington, DC 20001

Council for Exceptional Children
    1920 Association Drive
    Reston, VA 22091

Daycare and Child Development Council of America
(DCCDCA)
    1401 K Street, NW
    Washington, DC 20005

International Reading Association
    800 Barksdale Road
    P.O. Box 8139
    Newark, DE 19714

Association for Supervision and Curriculum
Development (ASCD)
    125 North West Street
    Alexandria, VA 22314-2798
    (703) 549-9110

National Association for the Education of
Young Children (NAEYC)
    1509 16th Street, NW
    Washington, DC 20036-1426
    (800) 424-8777

National Association for Gifted Children
    4175 Lovell Road, Suite 140
    Circle Pines, MN 55014

National Black Child Development Institute (NBCDI)
    1463 Rhode Island Avenue, NW
    Washington, DC 20005
    (202) 387-1281

National Committee on the Prevention
of Child Abuse
    332 South Michigan Avenue, Suite 950
    Chicago, IL 60604-4357

National Education Association (NEA)
    1201 16th Street, NW
    Washington, DC 20036

Society for Research in Child Development
    5801 Ellis Avenue
    Chicago, IL 60637

Southern Early Childhood Associates
    Box 5403 Brady Station
    Little Rock, AR 72215
    (501) 227-6404

Gopher and World Wide Web Sites

The Gophers and Web sites in the following lists contain the full texts of materials of interest to the early childhood community on a variety of topics. The sites are organized by menus or by hypertext links (words highlighted on the computer screen). Choosing a menu item or link takes you to another screen of information.

Name of Site	Address of Site	Contents
ERIC/EECE	gopher://ericps.ed.uiuc.edu http://ericps.ed.uiuc.edu/ericeece.html	ERIC/EECE digests, publications, services, routes to searching the ERIC database.
NPIN	gopher://ericps.ed.uiuc.edu http://ericps.ed.uiuc.edu/npin/npinhome.html	Information for parents and educators.
NCCIC	http://ericps.ed.uiuc.edu/nccic/nccichome.html	National Child Care Information Center publications and directories.
US DE	gopher://gopher.ed.gov http://www.ed.gov	U.S. Department of Education publications and announcements.
DHHS	gopher://gopher.dhhs.gov http://www.acf.dhhs.gov	U.S. Department of Health and Human Services publications, program descriptions, and services.

Name of Site	Address of Site	Contents
CYFERNET	gopher://gopher-cec.mes.umn.edu	Children, youth, and family information: includes ADOPTINFO, FATHERNET, and PAVENET (Partnerships Against Violence).
MCHNet	gopher://mchnet.ichp.ufl.edu	Information on health and young children.
FAMILY WORLD	http://family.com	Electronic magazine from Parent Publications of America, Inc.

Internet Discussion Groups

Discussion Address	Topic	For More Information
ECENET-L@vmd.cso.uiuc.edu	Young children, birth to age 8	ericeece@uxl.cso.uiuc.edu
ECEOL-L@maine.bitnet	Early childhood educators on-line	bonnieb@maine.bitnet
REGGIO-L@vmd.cso.uiuc.edu	The Reggio Emilia (Italy) approach to early education	ericeece@uxl.cso.uiuc.edu
SAC@uxl.cso.uiuc.edu	School-age care	ericeece@uxl.cso.uiuc.edu
PARENTING@postoffice.cso.uiuc.edu	Parenting of children from infancy through adolescence	ericeece@uxl.cso.uiuc.edu
ECPOLICY@uxl.cso.uiuc.edu	Early childhood policy issues	ericeece@uxl.cso.uiuc.edu
CYE-L@cunyvms.1.gc.cuny.edu	Children, Youth, and Environment	ssi@cunyvmsl.gc.cuny.edu
MULTIAGE@Services.dese.state.mo.us	Mixed-age grouping	catchley@mail.coin.missouri.edu

Databases

ERIC Database	Several options are available on the ERIC/EECE gopher (gopher://ericps.ed.uiuc.edu) Or, telnet to ericir.syr.edu; log in as gopher; press ENTER at password prompt Web version is available at http://ericir.syr.edu/ERIC/eric.html
ETS Test Collection	Gopher to gopher.cua.edu and choose Special Resources For Web access, go to http://www.cua.edu/www.eric_ae

Planning Your Program

Working with Young Children is divided into five parts with a total of 32 chapters. The chapters are presented in a logical progression of topics related to early childhood education.

Your program may be organized in a manner that does not coordinate with the sequence of chapters in *Working with Young Children.* For instance, you may have students working in groups, with some having laboratory time, others planning activities and creating materials, and others spending time with text material. You will find that the chapters of *Working with Young Children* are easily adapted to different sequences. References to knowledge needed from previous chapters are made within chapters where applicable.

Therefore, students will be able to refer to those chapters if they feel they need background information to better understand the assigned text.

Scope and Sequence Chart

In planning your program, you may want to use the *Scope and Sequence Chart* on the pages following the introduction. This chart identifies the major concepts presented in each chapter of the text. Refer to the chart to select for study those chapters that meet your curriculum needs. Bold numbers indicate chapters in which concepts are found.

Teaching Techniques

A main goal of this *Teacher's Resource Guide/Binder* is to help you provide students with learning experiences that will enable them to comprehend the material in the text. The students should be able to retain what they learn and apply it to new and varied situations. An important aspect of this goal is to help students achieve personal success and satisfaction in their experiences as early childhood teachers.

You can make the study of child care exciting and relevant by using a variety of teaching techniques. Below are some principles that will help you choose and use different teaching techniques in your classroom.

- *Make learning stimulating.* One way to do this is to involve students in lesson planning. When possible, allow students to select the modes of learning that they enjoy most. For example, some students will do well with oral reports; others prefer written assignments. Some learn well through group projects; others do better working independently. You can also make courses more interesting by presenting a variety of learning activities and projects from which students may choose to fulfill their work requirement. This will increase their interest in the topics under discussion and motivate them to continue learning.
- *Make learning realistic.* You can do this by relating the subject matter to issues that concern students. Students gain the most from their learning when they can apply classroom information to real-life situations. Case studies, role-playing, and drawing on personal experiences all make learning more realistic and relevant.
- *Make learning varied.* Try using several different techniques to teach the same concept. Make use of outside resources and current events as they apply to material being presented in class. Students learn through their senses of sight, hearing, touch, taste, and smell. The more senses that students use, the easier it will be for them to retain information. Bulletin boards, films, tapes, and transparencies all appeal to the senses.
- *Make learning success-oriented.* Experiencing success increases students' self-esteem and helps them mature. Guarantee success for your students by presenting a variety of learning activities. Key these activities to different ability levels so that each student can enjoy both success and challenge. You also will want to allow for individual learning styles and talents. For instance, creative students may excel at designing projects, while analytical students may be more proficient at organizing details. Build in opportunities for individual students to work in ways that let them succeed and shine.
- *Make learning personal.* Students need to interact with each other to derive the greatest benefit from the study of early childhood education. Establishing rapport between yourself and your students will help them feel comfortable about sharing their feelings in group discussions and activities.

A variety of teaching techniques may be used in your class. Types of techniques may be grouped according to different goals you have for your students. Keep in mind that not all techniques work equally well in all classrooms. A technique that works beautifully with one group of students may not be as successful with another group. Which techniques you choose will depend on the topic, your teaching goals, and the needs of your students.

One final consideration should be noted when choosing teaching techniques. Some activities that ask about personal home situations may violate students' rights to privacy. You can maintain a level of confidentiality by having students turn in their papers unsigned. Students can also be encouraged to pursue some of these activities at home for personal enrichment without fear of evaluation or judgment.

The following are techniques that you may use to meet various goals with your students.

Helping Students Gain Basic Information

Many teaching techniques can be grouped according to different goals you may have for your students. One group of teaching techniques is designed to help you meet the goal of conveying information to your students. Two of the most common techniques in this group are reading and teacher presentation. Using a number of variations can make these techniques seem less common and more interesting. For instance, students may enjoy taking turns to read aloud as a change of pace from silent reading. Presentations can be energized through the use of flip charts and overhead transparencies. Classroom discussions of different aspects of the material being presented get students involved and help impart information.

Other ways of presenting basic information include the use of outside resources. Guest speakers, whether speaking individually or as part of a discussion panel, can present classroom material. Guest lectures can be videotaped to show again to other classes.

Helping Students Question and Evaluate

A second group of teaching techniques helps students develop analytic and judgmental skills. These techniques aid you in meeting your goal to help your students go beyond what they see on the surface. As you employ these techniques, encourage your students to think about points raised by others. Have them evaluate how new ideas relate to their attitudes about various subjects.

Discussion is an excellent technique for helping students consider an issue from a new point of view. To be effective, discussion sessions require a great deal of advance planning and preparation. The size of the group being taught and the physical arrangement should be carefully considered. Students may be less likely to contribute in a large group, causing the discussion to become more of a lecture. Discussion will be enhanced by having the room arranged so that students can see each other.

Discussion can take a number of forms. Large group discussions involve the entire class and should be reserved for smaller classes. Buzz groups usually consist of two to six students. They discuss an issue among themselves and then appoint a spokesperson to report back to the entire class.

Debates are a type of discussion involving a two-sided issue. The class is divided into two groups on opposing sides of the issue. Each group then selects a panel of three or four students to present the points of their side.

Helping Students Participate

Another group of teaching techniques is designed to promote student participation in classroom activities and discussion. Discussion is a good technique only when students are willing and able to participate. Sometimes, students have limited knowledge or feel awkward about discussing issues in personal terms. In these cases, you may need to encourage their discussion through other means.

A number of techniques can be used to foster ideas and encourage students to interact. Case studies, surveys, stories, and pictures can all be used to promote discussion. These techniques allow students to react to or evaluate situations in which they are not directly

involved. Open-ended sentences can also be used to stimulate discussion. However, this technique must be used with discretion. Students should not be asked to complete sentences dealing with confidential issues in front of their classmates.

The *fishbowl* is another method for stimulating class discussion. In this method a small interactive group of about five to eight students is encircled by a larger observation group. It is useful for discussing controversial issues due to the rule that observers cannot talk during the fishbowl. Positions can be reversed after an initial discussion period allowing some of the observers to become the participants.

One of the most effective forms of small group discussion is the *cooperative learning group*. The teacher has a particular goal or task in mind. Small groups of learners are matched for the purpose of completing the task or goal, and each person in the group is assigned a role. The success of the group is measured not only in terms of outcome, but in the successful performance of each member in his or her role.

In cooperative learning groups, students learn to work together toward a group goal. Each member is dependent upon others for the outcome. This interdependence is a basic component of any cooperative learning group. The value of each group member is affirmed as learners work toward their goal.

The success of the group depends on individual performance. Groups should be mixed in terms of abilities and talents so that there are opportunities for the students to learn from one another. Also, as groups work together over time, the roles should be rotated so that everyone has an opportunity to practice and develop different skills.

The interaction of students in a cooperative learning group creates a tutoring relationship. While cooperative learning groups may involve more than just group discussion, discussion is always part of the process by which cooperative learning groups function.

Helping Students Apply Learning

Some techniques are particularly good for helping students use what they have learned. Simulation games and role-playing allow students to practice solving problems and making decisions under nonthreatening circumstances. Role-playing allows students to examine others' feelings as well as their own. They can thus determine how they might react or cope when confronted with a similar situation in real life.

Role-plays can be structured, with the actors given written scripts, or they may be improvised in response to a classroom discussion. Students may act out a role as they see the role being played, or they may attempt to act out the role as they presume a person in that position would behave. Roles are not rehearsed and lines are composed on the spot. The follow-up discussion should focus on the feelings and emotions felt by the participants, and the manner in which the problem was resolved. The discussion should help students consider how they would apply the information to similar situations in their lives.

Helping Students Develop Creativity

Some techniques can be used to help students generate new ideas. For example, brainstorming encourages students to exchange and pool their ideas and to come up with new thoughts and solutions to problems. Students are encouraged to spontaneously express any thoughts or reactions which come to mind. No evaluation or criticism of ideas is allowed. The format lets students be creative without fear of judgment.

Helping Students Review Information

Certain techniques aid students in recalling and retaining knowledge. Games can be used to drill students on vocabulary and factual information. Review games are available commercially or you and your students may want to devise your own. The use of crossword puzzles, word puzzles, and mazes, several of which are found in the *Student Activity Guide* and *Teacher's Resource Guide,* can make the review of vocabulary terms more interesting for students. Structured outlines of subject matter can also be effective review tools. Open-book quizzes, bulletin board displays, and problem-solving sessions all offer ways to review and apply material presented in the classroom.

Teaching Students of Varying Abilities

The students in your classroom room represent a wide range of ability levels. Students with special needs who are being mainstreamed will require special teaching strategies in order to meet their learning requirements. On the other hand, students who are gifted must not be overlooked. Their needs must also be met in the same classroom setting. It will be a challenge for you to adapt your daily lessons to meet the needs of all of these students.

To help you meet these needs, consider the following strategies when working with mainstreamed and lower-ability students:

- Before assigning a chapter in the text, ask students to look up the definitions of the words listed in the "Terms to Know" section at the beginning of each chapter. These terms are defined in the glossary at the back of the text. Have your students write out the definitions. Then have them take turns reading the definitions out loud. Have

students tell what they think the definitions mean in their own words. At other times you might want to ask your students to guess what they think the words mean before they look up the definitions. You also might ask students to use the new words in sentences, or point out sentences in the text where the new terms are used.

- When introducing a new chapter, review previously learned information students need to know before they can understand the new material. Review previously learned vocabulary terms they will encounter again.

- Utilize the motivational activities described in the "Introductory Activities" section in this guide for each chapter. Students who have difficulty reading need to be provided with a reason for reading the material. These introductory activities will often provide the necessary motivation. Students will want to read the material to satisfy their curiosity.

- Break the chapters up into smaller parts. Have students read only one section at a time. Define the terms, answer the "Review and Reflect" questions, and discuss the concepts presented in that section before proceeding to the next. It often helps to rephrase questions and problems in simple language and to repeat important concepts in different ways. Also assign activities from the *Student Activity Guide* that relate to that section to reinforce the concepts presented. Many of these activities are designed to improve reading comprehension.

- Have students, individually or in pairs, answer the "Review and Reflect" questions given at the end of each chapter in the text. This will help students focus on the essential information contained in the chapter.

- Use the buddy system. Pair nonreaders with students who read well. Use student aides to give more individual help to students who need assistance, or find a parent volunteer.

- Select a variety of educational experiences to reinforce the learning of each concept. Choose experiences that encourage active participation and involvement. Also select activities that will help slow learners relate the information to real-life situations. Aim for overlearning.

- Give directions orally as well as in writing. Explain all assignments thoroughly and as simply as possible. Ask questions to be certain your students understand what they are to do. Encourage your students to ask for help if they need it. You will also want to follow up as assignments proceed to be sure no one is falling behind on required work.

- Use the overhead projector and the transparency masters included in this guide. A visual presentation of concepts will increase your students' ability to comprehend the material. Also develop your own transparencies for use in reviewing key points covered in each chapter.

If you have students who are advanced or gifted in your class, you should also provide opportunities that will challenge them. These students should be given more assignments that involve critical thinking and problem solving. Because these students are more capable of independent work, they can use the library to research topics in greater depth. Learning experiences listed in the "Research Topics" sections of this guide are most appropriate for these students.

Evaluation Techniques

Because of the active nature of early childhood education classes, objective evaluation methods are limited in testing students' skills and learning. You will find observation and subjective methods most helpful in evaluating students and helping them improve their skills.

Consistency is sometimes difficult in evaluating students using subjective methods. You may find the reproducible masters, *Laboratory Evaluation Form* and *Evaluation of Student Teacher Performance,* useful in providing consistent, constructive evaluation of your students. The first master may be used throughout the year to evaluate specific student teaching experiences. You may discuss the evaluations with each student and focus on areas of improvement. The second master may be used for an overall midpoint and final evaluation of class performance.

Communicating with Students

Communicating with students involves not only sending clear messages to students, but also receiving and interpreting feedback from them. The following are some suggestions for productive communication with your students:
- Recognize the importance of body language and nonverbal communication in presenting material and interpreting student responses. Eye contact, relaxed but attentive body position, natural gestures, and alert facial expression all make for a presentation of material that will command attention. The same positive nonverbal cues from students are an indication of their response and reactions. Voice is also an important nonverbal communicator. Cultivating a warm, lively, enthusiastic speaking voice will make classroom presentations more interesting. By your tone, you can convey a sense of acceptance and expectation to which your students will respond.
- Use humor whenever possible. Humor is not only good medicine, it opens doors and teaches lasting lessons. Laughter and amusement will reduce tension, make points in a nonthreatening and memorable way, increase the fun and pleasure in classroom learning, and break down stubborn barriers. Relevant cartoons, quotations, jokes, and funny stories all bring a light touch to the classroom.
- Ask questions that promote recall, discussion, and thought. Good questions are tools that open the door to communication. Open-ended inquiries that ask what, where, why, when, and how will stimulate thoughtful answers. You can draw out students by asking for their opinions and conclusions. Questions with yes or no answers tend to discourage rather than promote further communication. Avoid inquiries that are too personal or that might put students on the spot.
- Rephrase students' responses to be sure both you and they understand what has been said. Paraphrasing information students give is a great way to clarify, refine, and reinforce material and ideas under discussion. For example, you might say "This is what I hear you saying...correct me if I'm wrong." Positive acknowledgment of student contributions, insights, and successes encourages more active participation and open communication. Comments such as "That's a very good point. I hadn't thought of it that way before" or "What a great idea" will encourage young people to express themselves.
- Listen for what students say, what they mean, and what they do not say. Really listening may be the single most important step you can take to promote open communication. As students answer questions and express their ideas and concerns, try not only to hear what they say, but to understand what they mean. What is not said can also be important. Make room for silence and time to think and reflect during discussion sessions.
- Share your feelings and experiences. The measure of what students communicate to you will depend in part on what you are willing to share with them. Express your personal experiences, ideas, and feelings when they are relevant. Don't forget to tell them about a few of your mistakes. Sharing will give students a sense of exchange and relationship.
- Lead discussion sessions to rational conclusions. Whether with an entire class or with individual

students, it is important to identify and resolve conflicting thoughts and contradictions. This will help students think clearly and logically.

- Create a nonjudgmental atmosphere. Students will only communicate freely and openly in a comfortable environment. You can make them comfortable by respecting their ideas, by accepting them for who they are, and by honoring their confidences. It is also important to avoid criticizing a student or discussing personal matters in front of others.
- Use written communication to advantage. The more ways you approach students, the more likely you are to reach them on different levels. Very often, the written word can be an excellent way to connect.
- Be open and available for private discussions of personal or disciplinary problems. It is important to let students know they can come to you with personal concerns as well as questions regarding course material. Be careful not to violate students' trust by discussing confidential matters outside a professional setting.

Promoting Your Program

Not everyone is aware of the importance of child care classes. You can make people more aware through good public relations. Good public relations can increase your enrollment, gain the support of administrators and peers, and achieve recognition in the community. It can also work to improve the image of your program and your department. The following are some suggestions for promoting your program:

- Create opportunities for peers, administrators, and board members to become more aware of what you are offering. Talk to teachers and administrators about your program's benefits at appropriate meetings and in less formal settings. Invite them to visit your class. Consider attending faculty meetings of other departments and board of education meetings to let these groups know

what you are doing. Let them know that you are interested in what they are doing as well.

- Provide services related to your program for other students or the community. Many activities related to your text can be done as services for other classes or for community groups. These projects increase public awareness while creating a spirit of mutual support. Examples of services include informational brochures and videos, how-to presentations, and hosting of guest speakers.
- Contact local media for coverage of newsworthy projects. Newsworthy projects include those that are unusual or that spotlight outstanding individuals or groups. Submit press releases for upcoming events. Have students submit articles to any school newspapers.
- Display student work in school showcases or display areas. Include a description of your program with the display.
- Work with parents and other community resources. Invite them to be guest speakers for your class. Send them newsletters to let them know what is happening in your classes. Contact parents through phone calls or letters when their children have made positive progress. Likewise, ask for their support in solving problem situations.
- Work with other faculty members on interdisciplinary projects. For instance, you may work with a health teacher to present information on child health and safety, or you may work with a science teacher to cover science activities for children.
- Advertise your class on school bulletin boards, in flyers, and in student publications. Ask your students what they feel they have gained by taking the class. Use some of their ideas in your advertisement. (If you decide to use direct quotes, be sure to get permission from your students.)

We appreciate the contribution of the following Goodheart-Willcox author in this introduction: "Teaching Techniques" from Changes and Choices, by Ruth E. Bragg.

Evaluating Bulletin Boards

Name _____ **Date**_____ **Period** _____

Use this form to plan appropriate bulletin boards for use in a child care facility. As you look at a finished bulletin board, or a sketch of a planned bulletin board, ask yourself the questions below. Choose the column that best describes your answer to each question. Jot a few words in the appropriate column about how each point could be improved or what makes it acceptable or commendable.

	Needs Improvement	Acceptable	Commendable
1. Is the bulletin board placed at the child's eye level?			
2. Does the bulletin board complement the classroom activities?			
3. Does the board motivate action or stimulate children's curiosity?			
4. Does the board contribute to the children's development?			
5. Are the concepts taught worth knowing?			
6. Is the board free from unnecessary detail?			
7. Does the board attract and hold attention?			
8. Is the organization of materials clear and simple?			
9. Is the board in good taste both in design and material?			
10. Can the figures be easily seen from a distance?			
11. Are the figures realistic in proportion to each other?			
12. If human figures are used, do they represent different races?			
13. Are the figures in proportion to the size of the bulletin board?			
14. Are safe materials and attachments used?			
15. Does the addition to the classroom justify the time, effort, and expense (if any) involved?			

Theme Development Form

Name _____ **Date** _____ **Period** _____

Use this form to plan activities that center around a theme for children in a child care facility. Write your theme in the rectangle below. Create a flowchart by drawing boxes that branch off of the main theme. In each box, list the concepts and subconcepts you want to cover in this unit. On the following page, identify the goals you have for children participating in this unit. Then describe the various activities you will use to help children accomplish these goals. (Refer to pages 266 to 267 in the text for information and examples showing how flowcharts can be used to develop themes.)

Theme: _____ **Week of:** _____

Flowchart

(continued)

Goals

Activities for Meeting Goals

Block Plan Form

Name _____ **Date** _____ **Period** _____

Use this form to help you plan a balance of activities throughout the week using all curriculum areas. Keep your theme and the children's developmental needs and interests in mind as you write activities in the boxes. Use your completed block plan to help you schedule the time periods during which the various activities will be offered each day. (Refer to pages 267 to 268 in the text for information and examples of how block plans are to be prepared.)

Theme: _____ **Week of:** _____

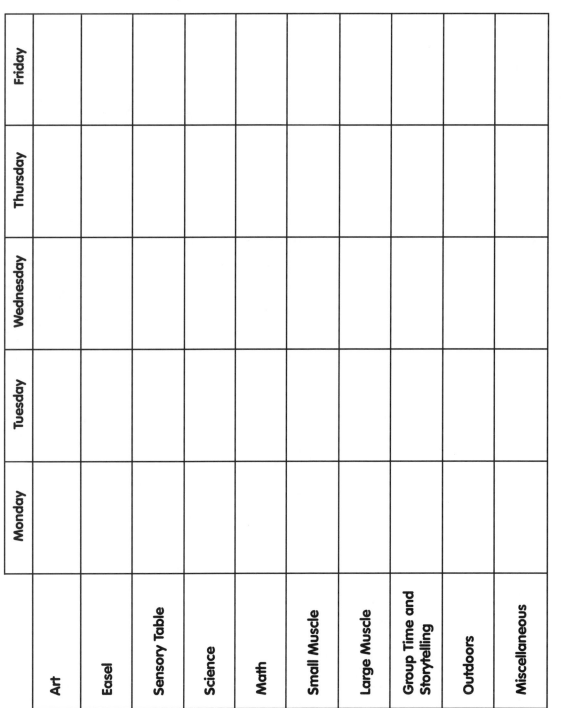

	Art	Easel	Sensory Table	Science	Math	Small Muscle	Large Muscle	Group Time and Storytelling	Outdoors	Miscellaneous
Monday										
Tuesday										
Wednesday										
Thursday										
Friday										

Laboratory Evaluation Form

Student _____ **Instructor** _____

Lesson _____ **Date** _____

Use this form to evaluate students in specific laboratory experiences throughout the year.
Rate each item as follows:

5—Exceptional
4—Very Good
3—Good
2—Average
1—Needs Improvement

	Rating
Lesson Planning	
A. Lesson plan was handed in on time.	
B. Evaluation was handed in on time.	
C. Lesson plan was completed and well written.	
D. Learning activities were developmentally appropriate for the group of children.	
E. Appropriate teaching methods and instructional skills were used.	
Interactions	
A. Demonstrated effective relationships with children.	
B. Applied sound child guidance techniques.	
C. Worked cooperatively with other adults.	
D. Initiated interactions with individuals and small groups of children.	
Professional Behavior	
A. Was present during planning sessions and teaching days.	
B. Contributed ideas during planning sessions.	
C. Arrived for class on time.	
D. Demonstrated an enthusiastic, positive, responsive attitude toward learning.	
E. Accepted and utilized constructive criticism.	

Comments:

Evaluation of Student Teacher Performance

Student _____ **Date** _____ **Period** _____

Use this form as a midpoint and/or final evaluation of a student's performance in your class.
Rate each area as follows:

5—Exceptional
4—Very Good
3—Good
2—Average
1—Needs Improvement

	Midpoint	Final
Curriculum Planning and Preparation		
A. Demonstrates broad knowledge of all content areas and understanding of significant or key concepts within these areas.		
B. Integrates various content matter areas of the curriculum.		
C. Chooses developmentally appropriate and interesting experiences and activities.		
D. Coordinates lesson plans with short and long range goals.		
E. Prepares appropriate daily lesson plans that are detailed and comprehensive.		
F. Arranges for local excursions, field trips, or resource persons that are coordinated with the curriculum.		
Preparation and Management of Classroom Environment		
A. Designs and implements an effective teaching-learning environment.		
B. Develops, as appropriate, activity centers, interest centers, learning centers/stations, displays, and bulletin boards supportive of children's learning.		
C. Assumes responsibility for contributing daily and weekly to the classroom environment.		
D. Varies and extends materials in interest centers and learning centers.		
E. Displays children's work neatly and aesthetically.		
F. Demonstrates an understanding of cultural diversity.		
Application of Child Development Principles		
A. Plans developmentally appropriate learning experiences.		
B. Uses the child's ideas, interests, needs, and social experiences as resources for planning and organizing content.		
C. Provides supplemental materials such as props, block accessories, games, and manipulatives at appropriate times.		
D. Demonstrates flexibility in adopting a learning experience based on the children's response.		

(continued)

Assessment and Evaluation of Children's Learning

	Midpoint	Final
A. Utilizes assessment and evaluative criteria.		
B. Maintains accurate records and samples of children's work.		
C. Discusses each child's involvement or progress with the cooperating teacher.		

Insight and Rapport with Children

A. Demonstrates an awareness of individual children in the classroom.		
B. Demonstrates the ability to listen to the children effectively.		
C. Demonstrates affectionate, sympathetic, and empathetic responses when appropriate.		
D. Develops and maintains effective relationships with young children.		

Child Guidance Strategies

A. Demonstrates principles of adult-child interaction.		
B. Demonstrates room awareness by adjusting teaching behavior accordingly.		
C. Modifies the teaching-learning environment depending upon the children's needs and behavior.		
D. Establishes and follows through with developmentally appropriate limits.		
E. Anticipates and responds to possible conflict situations.		
F. Adjusts voice to meet the situation.		
G. Provides appropriate, timely recognition and feedback for individual and group accomplishments.		
H. Interprets and sensitively responds to children's aggressive behavior.		
I. Recognizes and attends to children's physical-social-emotional needs for nurturance.		
J. Fosters pro-social interactions such as consideration and cooperation, and helping behaviors between and among children.		

Teaching Strategies

A. Adjusts and varies children's groupings to meet individual and group instructional needs.		
B. Uses a rich variety of approaches to learning experiences such as discovery approach, demonstration/presentation, activity approach, discussion, learning centers, and stations.		
C. Demonstrates various methods and instructional skills suited to curricular areas.		
D. Designs individualized learning experiences.		
E. Helps individual children with exceptional learning needs.		
F. Utilizes children's time in an effective manner.		
G. Uses various motivational techniques.		
H. Utilizes unexpected events that arise during class time for incidental learning.		
I. Plans for smooth, effective transitions.		
J. Demonstrates effective language facilitation techniques such as questioning, expansion, feeding-in, restatement, and prompting.		
K. Incorporates elements of surprise, humor, and fantasy when appropriate.		

(continued)

Communication Skills: Oral and Written		
A. Expresses and communicates ideas clearly in written form.		
B. Gives clear, simple directions.		
C. Communicates effectively with parents, staff, and community.		
D. Establishes eye contact and models appropriate nonverbal behaviors, such as facial expressions, with parents, colleagues, and other professionals.		

Utilization of Materials and Resources		
A. Previews and adapts A-V materials and other learning resources to program objectives.		
B. Plans and makes arrangements for local excursions, field trips, or resource persons as they relate to the curriculum.		
C. Uses a variety of media from libraries and other related resources such as pictures, charts, flannel board, puppets, equipment, videos, and artifacts.		
D. Operates and maintains equipment including tape recorders, record players, CD players, and VCRs.		
E. Designs and constructs innovative materials such as a prop box and instructional games that are not readily available for classroom use.		
F. Makes intelligent use of available resources such as time and money.		

Maintenance of Classroom Environment		
A. Maintains a clean, orderly, and comfortable teaching environment consistent with the expectations of the cooperating teacher.		
B. Manages routine housekeeping activities consistently and effectively.		
C. Maintains an environment that contributes to the child's safety and health.		

Self-Evaluation of Teaching		
A. Demonstrates self-evaluation skills.		
B. Utilizes evaluative feedback to reformulate plans.		
C. Accepts and utilizes constructive criticism.		

Professional Behavior		
A. Develops and maintains ethical and professional attitudes toward children, teachers, staff, parents, and administrators.		
B. Exhibits a responsive attitude in learning to teach, such as being willing to experiment, trying another way, using suggestions, etc.		
C. Maintains punctuality and regularity in attendance.		
D. Demonstrates an even temperament, poised, and polite.		
E. Maintains a professional appearance in grooming and dress.		

Scope and Sequence

In planning your program, you may want to use the *Scope and Sequence Chart* below. This chart identifies the major concepts presented in each chapter of the text. Refer to the chart to find the material that meets your curriculum needs. Bold numbers indicate chapters in which concepts are found.

Part 1   The Children and You

Careers and Professionalism
1: Social changes and child care; The teacher's responsibilities; Characteristics of successful teachers
2: Family child care; Child care centers; Montessori schools; Head Start

Child Growth and Development
3: Assessment; Assessment tools; Portfolios; Guidelines for Observing Children
4: Child development; Physical, cognitive, and social-emotional development in the first two years
5: Physical, cognitive, and social-emotional development of two-year-olds; Physical, cognitive, and social-emotional development of three-year-olds
6: Physical, cognitive, and social-emotional development of four- and five-year-olds
7: Physical, cognitive, social-emotional, and moral development of school-age children

Guidance and Discipline
5: Teaching two-year-olds; Teaching three-year-olds
6: Teaching four- and five-year-olds

Health, Safety, and Nutrition
7: Health concerns

Curriculum Development
3: Assessment; Assessment tools; Portfolios; Guidelines for observing children

Parent/Teacher and Community Relationships
2: Parent cooperatives; Sponsorship of programs; Selecting a child care program

Part 2   Creating a Safe and Healthy Environment

Guidance and Discipline
10: Safety guidelines

Health, Safety, and Nutrition
9: Selecting safe toys; Reporting unsafe products
10: Liability; Safety guidelines; Child abuse
11: Nutrition; Planning meals and snacks; Serving meals
12: Objectives for guiding health; Health policies; Controlling diseases transmitted by foods; First aid; Special health concerns

Physical Space and Equipment

Part 3   Guiding Children

Guidance and Discipline

Health, Safety, and Nutrition

Part 4   Learning Experiences for Children

Guidance and Discipline

Health, Safety, and Nutrition

Physical Space and Equipment

Physical Development

Cognitive Development

18: Painting activities; Molding; Collages
21: Early experiences in writing
22: Mathematical activities
23: Developing the child's understanding of senses
25: Cooking experiences
26: Music activities

Social-Emotional Development

19: Selecting stories for children; Reading aloud to children; Achieving variety in storytelling
20: Socio-dramatic play; Puppetry
24: Building social studies concepts; Governmental concepts; Ecology, change, geography, community, current events, and holiday concepts
25: Setting the table

Curriculum Development

17: Responsibility for curriculum; Developing program goals; Assessment in curriculum planning; Activities; Written plans
20: Scheduling socio-dramatic play
21: Objectives for writing
22: Goals of early math experiences; Assessing math ability; Integrating computers in child care centers
23: Planning science activities
24: Importance of social studies; Develop the curriculum
26: Benefits of music experiences; Scheduling music
27: The importance of field trips; Selecting trips; Planning a field trip

Parent/Teacher and Community Relationships

24: Multicultural concepts; Intergenerational concepts; Community concepts
25: Working with parents
27: Adult-child ratio; Parent preparation

Part 5   Other People You Will Meet

Careers and Professionalism

28: Teacher characteristics for infant-toddler programs; Record keeping
29: Characteristics of staff
32: Ranking job preferences; Resumes; Avenues for seeking employment; Preparing for an interview; The interview; On the job

Guidance and Discipline

28: Guidelines for infant-toddler care; Caring for infants and toddlers
29: Using positive guidance
30: Teachers' roles in guiding children with special needs

Health, Safety, and Nutrition

28: Handling routines; Illness policies; Toy safety
30: Speech and language disorders; Vision disorders; Physical disorders; Health disorders

Physical Space and Equipment

28: Infant and toddler environment; Toys

29: The environment

Curriculum Development

28: Infant-toddler curriculum

29: Planning curriculum

30: Individualized Educational Plans; Integrating children with special needs; Children who are gifted

Parent/Teacher and Community Relationships

28: Parent involvement in infant-toddler programs

31: Written communication; Class videos; Parent-teacher conferences; Discussion groups; Other methods of involvement; Volunteers

You: Working with Young Children

Objectives

After studying this chapter, students will be able to

- explain how social and economic changes will increase the need for child care services.
- describe career opportunities in the early childhood field.
- describe the CDA Credential.
- list responsibilities of the early childhood teacher.
- explain how certain characteristics can promote the success of early childhood teachers in caring for and educating young children.

Teaching Materials

Text, pages 13–26
Terms to Know
Review and Reflect
Apply and Explore
Student Activity Guide
  A. *Truths About Early Childhood*
  B. *Comparing Teaching to Other Careers*
  C. *Pleasures and Problems in Teaching*
  D. *Characteristics for Working with Children*
Teacher's Resource Guide/Binder
  Is Teaching Really for Me? reproducible master, 1-1
  Career Match, reproducible master, 1-2
  CDA Competency Goals and Functional Areas,
    transparency master 1-3
  Characteristics of a Successful Teacher,
    transparency master, 1-4
  Chapter Test
Teacher's Resource Binder
  The Teacher's Responsibilities, color
    transparency, CT-1
The Observation Guide
Mastering CDA Competencies

Introductory Activities

1. Ask students to list their reasons for wanting to work with young children. Discuss the reasons in class.

2. Ask students to list and describe qualities that they believe a teacher working with young children should possess.
3. *Is Teaching Really for Me?* reproducible master 1-1. Have students write answers to the questions and discuss their answers in class. Once students have studied the chapter, have them reevaluate their answers in terms of whether or not they feel teaching young children is for them.

Instructional Concepts and Student Learning Experiences

Social and Economic Changes _____

4. Have students write a two-page paper on changes in the family.
5. Have students discuss advantages of employer-sponsored child care.
6. Have students state reasons why a greater allocation of resources is going to early childhood.

Job Opportunities in Early Childhood _____

7. Have students discuss the different job possibilities for people studying early childhood.
8. Have students discuss the role of the nanny and the au pair.
9. Have students call several nanny employment agencies and find out what services they provide and what fees they charge. Display this information on a poster or bulletin board in your room.
10. Have students conduct a research project to find out how many early childhood teachers were hired in your community last year. Child care centers are listed in the Yellow Pages of the telephone directory. Students should give a brief oral report on their findings to the class.
11. Have students prepare a poster or bulletin board using the title, "A Director . . ." Students should complete the title using phrases that describe the role of a director. Examples might include: recruits children, collects fees, hires staff, etc.
12. *Career Match,* reproducible master 1-2. Have

students complete the statements by writing the letter of the correct job possibility in the blanks.

13. *Truths About Early Childhood,* Activity A, SAG. Have students indicate whether the statements about early childhood are true or false.

14. Have students look through the want-ads of a major newspaper and list jobs in which early childhood training would be valuable.

15. In small groups, have students brainstorm the pros and cons of entrepreneurship. Also have them list possible entrepreneurial businesses related to the field of child care. What local businesses can they classify as entrepreneurships?

16. *CDA Competency Goals and Functional Areas,* transparency master 1-3. Explain the CDA Credential to students and go over the Competency Goals and Functional Areas listed on this transparency. The CDA program uses six statements of skill called Competency Goals to establish the framework for caregiver behavior. These goals are divided into 13 Functional Areas, which describe major tasks caregivers must accomplish to satisfy the Competency Goals.

17. Have each student select a child care job and research the amount of training required to obtain such a job. Share findings with the class.

The Teacher's Responsibilities

18. *The Teacher's Responsibilities,* color transparency CT-1, TRB. Use this transparency to introduce the responsibilities of a child care teacher:
    A. Have students brainstorm a list of a child care teacher's major responsibilities.
    B. Discuss the direct and indirect influences that a teacher has on the children.
    C. Ask the students to explain why child development knowledge is essential for developing an appropriate curriculum.
    D. Ask students to identify pleasant and unpleasant tasks associated with teaching young children.

19. Have students describe the ways a teacher may need to be a friend, colleague, janitor, nurse, and cook.

20. Have students discuss how the role of an early childhood teacher can be challenging and rewarding.

21. Have students name and give examples of the four types of development that are emphasized in the early childhood curriculum.

22. Have students explain why a thorough knowledge of child development is important to being an early childhood teacher.

23. Have students discuss why the preparation of the environment is a large part of the teaching process.

24. Have students list ten ways of providing support to coworkers.

25. Have students differentiate between important and urgent tasks.

26. Have students interview an early childhood teacher and find out ways of continuing to learn and keep updated in the field of early childhood. Students should report their findings to the class.

27. Have students develop a list of resources that teachers could use to continue their education in early childhood. Discuss how the Internet can be a valuable resource for teachers.

28. *Comparing Teaching to Other Careers,* Activity B, SAG. Have students use the chart to compare the responsibilities of being a teacher in early childhood to the responsibilities of another career.

29. *Pleasures and Problems in Teaching,* Activity C, SAG. Have students determine whether the items listed would be pleasures or problems for them if they were teaching in early childhood.

Characteristics of Successful Teachers

30. Have class members work with partners to discuss their teaching strengths.

31. Have students discuss ways young children can raise their self-esteem.

32. Have students define the following terms in their own words: compassionate, dependable, reliable, friendly, flexible, knowledgeable, and spontaneous.

33. Have each student write a one-page paper on why he or she wants to teach children.

34. Have students survey early childhood teachers, asking them to share the advantages and disadvantages of teaching. Students should share their findings in class.

35. *Characteristics of a Successful Teacher,* transparency master 1-4. Use this master to review with students characteristics that are often found in a successful early childhood teacher.

36. Have students list some of their interests, feelings, and satisfactions. Students should then write a short evaluation of how their interests, feelings, and satisfactions relate to a desire to be an early childhood teacher.

37. Have students design a bulletin board displaying the characteristics of a successful teacher.

38. Have students interview an early childhood teacher about the joys and rewards of working with young children. Students should use information from the interview to write an article on the subject.

39. *Characteristics for Working with Children,* Activity D, SAG. Have students use the form to rate themselves in terms of characteristics for working with young children. Students should

then have a friend or family member rate them using a second form.

Additional Resources

40. Invite a child care teacher to discuss his or her job with the class. Have students prepare questions in advance.
41. Invite a child care licensing specialist to class. Ask him or her to share with the class the qualifications needed for this position.
42. Invite a director of a child care center to discuss with the class what qualities he or she looks for when hiring teachers.

Research Topic

43. Have the student take a survey of five parents of young children. The student should find out what qualities these parents value in early childhood teachers. The student should compare the parents' lists with the qualities discussed in class. Have the student write a paper discussing the similarities and differences between parent and classroom lists, giving possible reasons for differences.

Answer Key

Text

Review and Reflect, page 26

1. early childhood
2. true
3. Offering child care services has been found to have positive effects on recruitment, morale, productivity, and absenteeism. Child care services have also had positive influences on turnover, public relations, taxes, scheduling, and the quality of the work force.
4. nannies
5. licensing specialist
6. (Student response. See pages 17–18.)
7. Those who have this national credential have taken postsecondary courses in child care education and have demonstrated their ability to work with young children.
8. The arrangement of space and selection of materials in a classroom has a direct influence on a child's physical, intellectual, emotional, and social development. A well-designed environment encourages children to experiment, explore, and manipulate objects. It also encourages children to interact with each other in positive ways.
9. time management
10. C
11. false
12. (Student response. See pages 22–25.)

Student Activity Guide

Truths About Early Childhood, Activity A

1. T	10. F
2. T	11. T
3. F	12. F
4. F	13. T
5. T	14. F
6. F	15. T
7. T	16. T
8. T	17. F
9. T	18. T

Teacher's Resource Guide/Binder

Career Match, reproducible master 1-2

1. D	10. R
2. K	11. C
3. O	12. E
4. L	13. M
5. A	14. P
6. H	15 I
7. G	16. F
8. Q	17. B
9. N	18. J

Chapter Test

1. B	17. F
2. A	18. F
3. D	19. T
4. C	20. F
5. A	21. F
6. C	22. T
7. D	23. D
8. D	24. A
9. B	25. C
10. A	26. C
11. F	27. C
12. T	28. D
13. T	29. D
14. T	30. A
15. F	31. D
16. T	32. B

33. (Describe five. Student response.)
34. A nanny provides care for a child in the child's home. Some nannies may live in the child's home. They receive meals and housing as part of their wages. An au pair is a person from a foreign country who lives with a family and performs tasks similar to a nanny in exchange for room, board, and transportation.
35. (Describe five. Student response.)

Is Teaching Really for Me?

Name _____ **Date** _____ **Period** _____

State your interests, feelings, and satisfactions by completing the following statements.

1. My greatest interests include:

2. My feelings toward teaching young children are:

3. The greatest satisfactions I obtain in life are from:

4. I think I should be a teacher of young children because:

Career Match

Name _____ **Date** _____ **Period** _____

Complete the statements by writing the letter of the correct job title in the blank to the left of the number.

_____ 1. An individual who assists a teacher in the public school is called a(n) _____.

_____ 2. An early childhood _____ may be employed by corporations to provide sick child care.

_____ 3. A(n) _____ instructor teaches children creativity.

_____ 4. A toy _____ is responsible for developing new toys.

_____ 5. A _____ specialist ensures that state rules and regulations are followed.

_____ 6. A children's _____ takes children's pictures.

_____ 7. A(n) _____ educator helps parents become more competent in raising their children.

_____ 8. A(n) _____ provides care in the child's home.

_____ 9. _____ teachers are employed in both public and private schools.

_____ 10. Because of the rapid increase in child care services, more child care _____ will be needed.

_____ 11. Knowledge of child growth and development is important for the community _____ director, who organizes and leads activities for area children.

_____ 12. A(n) _____ teacher covers for a teacher who is on vacation, at a conference, or ill.

_____ 13. The child care _____ is responsible for managing the center.

_____ 14. A(n) _____ specialist provides parents with lists of child care providers, maps, and brochures.

_____ 15. A(n) _____ education director may be employed by a church.

_____ 16. A children's _____ is responsible for the children's book collection.

_____ 17. A(n) _____ is a person from a foreign country who lives with a family and provides child care.

_____ 18. A(n) _____ is someone who operates his or her own business.

A. licensing
B. au pair
C. recreation
D. aide
E. substitute
F. librarian
G. parent
H. photographer
I. religious
J. entrepreneur
K. specialist
L. designer
M. director
N. kindergarten
O. art
P. referral
Q. nanny
R. teachers

CDA Competency Goals and Functional Areas

I. To establish and maintain a safe, healthy learning environment
   1. Safe
   2. Healthy
   3. Learning Environment

II. To advance physical and intellectual competence
   4. Physical
   5. Cognitive
   6. Communication
   7. Creative

III. To support social and emotional development and provide positive guidance
   8. Self
   9. Social
   10. Guidance

IV. To establish positive and productive relationships with families
   11. Families

V. To ensure a well-run, purposeful program responsive to participant needs
   12. Program Management

VI. To maintain a commitment to professionalism
   13. Professionalism

Characteristics of a Successful Teacher

- Has a positive attitude
- Is fond of children
- Relates easily and spontaneously to others
- Is a patient, confident, and caring individual
- Is a positive, happy individual
- Is dependable and reliable
- Makes friends easily
- Possesses a sense of humor
- Is flexible and adapts well to the requirements of others
- Is compassionate, accepting children's strong emotions such as anger, love, and wonder
- Takes initiative in the classroom
- Has knowledge in curriculum, child growth and development, and child guidance
- Keeps abreast of changes in the field by reading, attending conferences, seminars, and courses
- Desires continuous learning
- Enjoys challenge and problem solving
- Can juggle several activities at one time
- Feels rewarded by progress even if it is minimal
- Provides interesting materials

38

You: Working with Young Children

Name _____

Date _____ **Period** _____ **Score** _____

Matching: Match the following terms and identifying phrases. (Terms are used more than once.)

_____ 1. Refers to the expression of feelings.

_____ 2. Refers to body growth.

_____ 3. Refers to thinking skills.

_____ 4. Refers to the ability to get along with others.

_____ 5. Refers to coordination.

_____ 6. Involves interacting with others.

_____ 7. Involves problem solving.

_____ 8. Is enriched through hands-on activities.

_____ 9. Involves self-knowledge.

_____ 10. Refers to stamina.

A. physical development
B. emotional development
C. social development
D. cognitive development

True/False: Circle *T* if the statement is true or *F* if the statement is false.

T F 11. Early childhood covers a period from birth to five years of age.

T F 12. Social changes will create a need for more child care services.

T F 13. The number of dual-worker families is increasing.

T F 14. The traditional family accounts for a small percentage of the population.

T F 15. The number of single parents is decreasing.

T F 16. Early childhood teachers usually feel useful, needed, and important.

T F 17. A family child care home provides child care for children in the child's own home.

T F 18. Entrepreneurs usually work for large companies.

T F 19. The materials that teachers provide in the classroom have a strong effect on children's learning.

T F 20. Most preschool teachers have limited contact with parents.

T F 21. Teachers who shame children are usually successful.

T F 22. Being an early childhood teacher places high demands on a person's energy.

(continued)

Multiple Choice: Choose the best answer and write the corresponding letter in the blank.

_____ 23. Currently, compared to the past, women are _____.
   A. less educated
   B. having larger families
   C. staying home
   D. working more for economic reasons

_____ 24. The need for early childhood teachers is expected to _____.
   A. increase
   B. decrease
   C. remain the same
   D. become nonexistent

_____ 25. Tangible payoffs for companies providing child care include _____.
   A. greater absenteeism
   B. increased taxes
   C. increased productivity
   D. greater turnover

_____ 26. A _____ ensures that the rules and regulations established by the state are followed by making on-site visits to assigned centers.
   A. nanny
   B. child care director
   C. licensing specialist
   D. child care advocate

_____ 27. A(n) _____ provides in-home care for children.
   A. nanny
   B. au pair
   C. Both of the above.
   D. Neither of the above.

_____ 28. The Child Development Associate (CDA) Credential _____.
   A. is a bachelor's degree program
   B. is an associate's degree program
   C. requires a minimum of two years of college
   D. requires a minimum number of hours of child care experience and some postsecondary coursework in child care education

_____ 29. Child care center directors generally need at least _____.
   A. a high school diploma
   B. a CDA Credential
   C. an associate's degree
   D. a bachelor's degree

_____ 30. An appropriate developmental curriculum _____.
   A. emphasizes all areas of development
   B. must be developed by child care directors
   C. should be designed for the teacher and parents
   D. emphasizes cognitive and physical growth

_____ 31. The most important trait of an early childhood teacher is _____.
   A. commitment to the profession
   B   a high energy level
   C. knowledge of child development
   D. a fondness of children

(continued)

_____ 32. A compassionate teacher is _____.
       A. a spectator
       B. nurturing
       C. withdrawn
       D. detached

Essay Questions: Provide complete responses to the following questions or statements.

33. Describe five ways companies are benefiting by providing child care benefits.

34. Compare the jobs of a nanny and an au pair.

35. Describe five characteristics of successful early childhood teachers.

Types of Early Childhood Programs

2

Objectives

After studying this chapter, students will be able to

- list and describe the various types of early childhood programs available to parents and their children.
- explain the advantages and disadvantages of each type of program.
- name the three types of center sponsorship.
- explain steps a parent may take in choosing quality child care.
- list the components of center accreditation.

Teaching Materials

Text, pages 27–28
  Terms to Know
  Review and Reflect
  Apply and Explore
Student Activity Guide
  A. *Early Childhood Fill-In*
  B. *Types of Programs*
  C. *Choosing a Program*
  D. *Evaluating Early Childhood Programs*
Teacher's Resource Guide/Binder
  Child Care Program Comparison,
    reproducible master, 2-1
  Standards of Quality for Child Care,
    transparency master, 2-2
  Chapter Test
Teacher's Resource Binder
  Types of Early Childhood Programs,
    color transparency, CT-2
The Observation Guide
Mastering CDA Competencies

Introductory Activities

1. Ask students to identify differences in early childhood programs that they are familiar with.
2. Have students discuss possible advantages and disadvantages of having different types of early childhood programs available to parents.

3. *Early Childhood Fill-In,* Activity A, SAG. As students read the chapter, have them find the words that complete the given statements.

Instructional Concepts and Student Learning Experiences

Family Child Care

4. Have students discuss reasons why some parents may prefer family child care.
5. Have students discuss possible problems that may occur with family child care.
6. Have students discuss how family child care differs from child care centers.
7. Have students visit a family child care home and interview the caregiver about his or her program. Students should discuss their findings in class.

Child Care Centers

8. Have students discuss and debate their concepts of an ideal child care program.
9. Have students observe a child care program and note the features that make it a good environment for the children.
10. Have students research the Yellow Pages of the phone book to find out how many child care centers are located in your community.
11. Have students interview a child care director, asking the director to compare his or her program to other programs such as family child care, Montessori schools, kindergartens, etc. Students should report their findings to the class.

Montessori Schools

12. Have students explain the Montessori philosophy.
13. Have students describe the teacher's role in a Montessori program.
14. Have students discuss their reactions to the Montessori philosophy—whether they feel it is better than, worse than, or equal to other preschool programs; whether they like or dislike various aspects of the curriculum.

Head Start

15. Have students discuss the purpose of Head Start.
16. Have students compare the program in a Head Start center to a typical child care center program.
17. Have students explain the importance of involving parents in the Head Start program.

Kindergarten

18. Have students explain the history of kindergartens.
19. Collect schedules from half-day, full-day, and full-day/alternating day kindergartens. Have the class compare the schedules and discuss the similarities and differences.
20. Have students list the goals for a kindergarten program and discuss the value of those goals.
21. Have students conduct a survey of local child care centers. Students should find out how many conduct private kindergarten programs.

School-Age Child Care

22. Have students find articles on and discuss current trends in school-age child care programs.
23. Obtain curriculum plans from school-age child care programs and have the class study and discuss them.

Parent Cooperatives

24. Have students explain how a parent cooperative operates.
25. Have students discuss the advantages and disadvantages of teaching in a parent cooperative.
26. Have students write a few paragraphs on why they would or would not like to be a teacher in a parent cooperative.

Laboratory Schools

27. Have students describe the purpose of laboratory schools.
28. Have students discuss possible benefits and disadvantages of enrolling children in laboratory schools.

High School Child Care Programs

29. Have students explain the purpose of high school child care programs.
30. *Types of Early Childhood Programs,* color transparency CT-2, TRB. Use this transparency as you review the different types of child care programs:
    A. Ask the students to explain the advantages and disadvantages of each type of program.
    B. Discuss criteria for selecting quality child care.
    C. Have students compare the services provided by family day care as opposed to a child care center.
    D. Have students explain how each type of sponsorship may affect the goals and philosophy of the program.
31. *Types of Programs,* Activity B, SAG. Have students match the statements to the types of programs they best describe.

Sponsorship of Early Childhood Centers

32. Have students compare and contrast public and private sponsorship of child care programs.
33. Have students discuss possible advantages and disadvantages of teaching in chain child care centers.
34. Have students explain the purpose and types of employer-sponsored child care.

Selecting a Child Care Program

35. Have students list questions parents need to seek answers to when choosing child care.
36. Have students discuss the value to teachers of understanding how to evaluate and choose child care programs.
37. Have students discuss the selection process that most parents use to choose a child care program.
38. *Choosing a Program,* Activity C, SAG. Have students read the situations and determine the type of child care program that would work best for each situation.
39. *Evaluating Early Childhood Programs,* Activity D, SAG. Have students visit two centers and evaluate them using the form provided.
40. *Child Care Program Comparison,* reproducible master 2-1. Have students complete the chart to help them compare the different types of early childhood programs.

Center Accreditation

41. Discuss the purpose of center accreditation with students. Have students identify the component areas of quality early childhood programs.
42. Have students conduct a community survey to determine how many centers are accredited.
43. Have students explain the purpose of a self-study.
44. *Standards of Quality for Child Care,* transparency master 2-2. Review the standards of quality for child care with students. Discuss the meaning and importance of each item when evaluating a program.

Additional Resources

45. Panel discussion. Invite a panel of directors or teachers of different types of programs to discuss their programs' philosophy, program goals, and curriculum.

46. Field trip. Arrange for students to visit a Montessori school and view the materials and methods used there.

47. Panel discussion. Invite several parents to discuss their considerations for choosing a child care program.

Research Topic

48. Have the student choose a type of child care program and research its philosophy, program goals, and curriculum. The student should give an oral report with visual aids for the class.

Answer Key

Text

Review and Reflect, page 38

1. family child care
2. true
3. active
4. instances in which children learn to be independent by doing for themselves
5. to strengthen the academic skills of children from low-income homes
6. true
7. full-day, half-day, full-day/alternating day
8. (List five:) respect for the contributions, property, and rights of other children; appreciation of objects of beauty; growth in creative skills; achievement of problem-solving and cognitive skills; development of a positive self-concept; growth in language, social, and physical skills; development of positive feelings about school
9. Caregivers call their assigned children at home to make sure they have arrived home safely. Children do not go to the caregivers' homes.
10. parent cooperatives
11. to train future teachers and to serve as a place to conduct research
12. federal, state, or local governments
13. (Student response.)
14. friends
15. A high staff turnover can cause morale problems among teachers. In order to feel secure, children need consistent, predictable care.
16. Being accredited certifies that a set of standards has been met by a child care center. Parents are assured of a high-quality program for their children.

Student Activity Guide

Early Childhood Fill-In, Activity A

1. location
2. Checking-in services
3. Practical life experiences
4. referral
5. Montessori
6. employers
7. Head Start
8. friends
9. custodial care
10. Publicly sponsored
11. social
12. privately owned center
13. family child care
14. parents cooperative
15. Independence

Types of Programs, Activity B

1. C   12. F
2. G   13. H
3. B   14. B
4. A   15. A
5. G   16. H
6. I   17. F
7. E   18. C
8. I   19. G
9. D   20. B
10. S   21. H
11. C   22. E

Teacher's Resource Guide/Binder

Chapter Test

1. C   15. T
2. G   16. T
3. B   17. T
4. A   18. F
5. F   19. T
6. H   20. T
7. D   21. F
8. E   22. F
9. T   23. D
10. T   24. C
11. T   25. C
12. F   26. C
13. T   27. D
14. F   28. A
29. (Describe three. Student response.)
30. (List five. Student response.)
31. (Student response.)

Child Care Program Comparison

Name _____ **Date** _____ **Period** _____

Use the text and local resources to complete the chart below.

Program	Philosophy	Goals	Teacher Roles	Local Programs of this Type
Family Child Care				
Child Care Centers				
Montessori Schools				
Head Start				

(continued)

Program	Philosophy	Goals	Teacher Roles	Local Programs of this type
Kindergarten				
School-Age Child Care Programs				
Parent Cooperatives				
Laboratory Schools				
High School Programs				

Standards of Quality for Child Care

A quality program provides

- ♦ A nurturing, educationally qualified staff.
- ♦ A multi-sensory environment that is safe and affirming.
- ♦ Curriculum that celebrates diversity and supports "best practices."
- ♦ A curriculum that supports children's individual rates of development.
- ♦ Developmentally appropriate teaching strategies.
- ♦ A regular assessment of children's growth and development—emotional, social, physical, and cognitive.
- ♦ Communication and partnerships among center staff and parents.
- ♦ Learning opportunities developed with community and supportive agencies.
- ♦ A continuous staff development program.

Types Of Early Childhood Programs

Name _____

Date _____ **Period** _____ **Score** _____

Matching: Match the following statements and programs.

_____ 1. All children who attend are provided with a comprehensive health plan.

_____ 2. Emphasis is on self-education.

_____ 3. Child care that is often unlicensed.

_____ 4. These offer child care during more hours of the day and night.

_____ 5. These programs are usually provided after school.

_____ 6. These programs are formed and directed by parents.

_____ 7. Many of these programs are now a part of the public school system.

_____ 8. These programs are located on post-secondary or college campuses.

A. child care centers
B. family child care
C. Head Start
D. kindergartens
E. laboratory schools
F. school-age child care programs
G. Montessori schools
H. cooperatives

True/False: Circle *T* if the statement is true or *F* if the statement is false.

T F 9. During the first five years of life, children develop rapidly.

T F 10. Differences between early childhood programs are normal.

T F 11. Family child care programs vary according to the skills of the caregiver.

T F 12. Most child care centers provide care 24 hours daily.

T F 13. Montessori's goal was to "learn how to learn."

T F 14. Montessori schools have a rather unstructured approach where sequence does not matter.

T F 15. In Montessori schools, children learn from sensory training.

T F 16. Curriculum provided in the Head Start center should reflect the child's cultural and ethnic background.

T F 17. Nutrition is an important part of a Head Start program.

T F 18. Studies have demonstrated that Head Start has not been a successful program.

T F 19. Parent cooperatives offer developmental experiences for adults as well as children.

T F 20. A major disadvantage for the teacher in a parent cooperative is lack of control.

(continued)

T   F   21. The largest group of privately sponsored child care programs are those operated by churches.

T   F   22. Typically, teachers plan their own curriculum in child care chains.

Multiple Choice: Choose the best response. Write the letter in the space provided.

_____ 23. The most common type of child care in the United States is _____.
A. parent cooperatives
B. school-age child care programs
C. Head Start
D. family child care

_____ 24. The common focus in _____ is custodial care.
A. Head Start programs
B. kindergartens
C. family child care
D. parent cooperatives

_____ 25. In her first schools, Montessori stressed _____.
A. color recognition
B. intellectual development
C. diet, cleanliness, and manners
D. social development

_____ 26. A trait that is important for the children to develop in Montessori schools is _____.
A. creativity
B. disobedience
C. independence
D. dependence

_____ 27. The first kindergarten focused on _____.
A. intellectual development
B. social development
C. social-emotional development
D. play

_____ 28. A sign of a quality early childhood program is _____.
A. staff concern for the feelings and rights of others
B. high staff turnover
C. at least 20 feet of free indoor play space for each child
D. a loose, unplanned schedule

Essay Questions: Provide complete responses to the following questions or statements.

29. Describe three ways employers can provide child care assistance for their employees.

30. List five questions parents should ask when selecting a child care program.

31. Explain the purpose of the voluntary accreditation system that is administered by the National Academy of Early Childhood Programs.

Observing Children: A Tool for Assessment  3

Objectives

After studying this chapter, students will be able to
- list purposes of assessment.
- contrast initial assessment and on-going assessment.
- list the factors to consider in choosing a method of assessment.
- list the advantages and disadvantages of various assessment tools.
- compile a list of contents for a child's portfolio.
- summarize guidelines for observing children.

Teaching Methods

Text, pages 39-50
  Terms to Know
  Review and Reflect
  Apply and Explore
Student Activity Guide
  A. *Check Your Understanding*
  B. *Assessment Tools Summary*
  C. *Interpreting the Data*
  D. *Designing an Assessment Tool*
Teacher's Resource Guide/Binder
  Appropriate Assessment, transparency master, 3-1
  Descriptive or Interpretive, reproducible master, 3-2
  Reviewing Assessment Date, transparency master, 3-3
  Guidelines for Observing Children,
    transparency master, 3-4
  Chapter Test
Teacher's Resource Binder
  Assessment Is an On-Going Process,
    color transparency, CT-3
The Observation Guide
Mastering CDA Competencies

Introductory Activities

1. Have the students give their definitions of the term *assessment*. Then ask them to explain how the term *assessment* differs from *evaluation*.
2. Have the students brainstorm reasons for observing children and using assessment tools.

Instructional Concepts and Student Learning Experiences

Assessment

3. *Check Your Understanding,* Activity A, SAG. This activity can be used as a pretest to see what students know about assessment, or it can be used as a study guide as they read about assessment and the various assessment tools.
4. Have the students discuss the areas of development that assessment should address.
5. Have the students survey local early childhood teachers to find out how they use assessment.
6. Have the students discuss how assessment information can be useful during parent conferences.
7. *Appropriate Assessment,* transparency master 3-1. Use this master to review with students the purposes of assessment.
8. Have the students discuss the importance of an initial assessment.
9. Have the students interview early childhood teachers to find out how they have used information from home background forms in the initial assessment.
10. Have the students explain why it is important to do ongoing assessments.
11. *Assessment Is an On-Going Process,* color transparency CT-3, TRB. Use this transparency to:
    A. Illustrate how assessment is done initially when a child is enrolled in a program, and continues throughout the child's time at the center.
    B. Review the various types of assessment that might take place during a child's attendance at the center.
    C. Discuss what assessment tools might be used during the initial assessment.
    D. Review what might be included in a child's portfolio at the time he or she "graduates" from the program.
12. Have the students give examples of why an alliance with parents is important.
13. Have the students name ways assessment data can be collected in the classroom.

14. Have the students describe the two different methods of observation—formal and informal.

15. Have the students discuss why preschool teachers usually use informal observation methods to collect data.

16. Have the students identify the three considerations for choosing a method of assessment.

17. Have the students discuss why teachers usually use a variety of methods for gathering information about children.

Assessment Tools

18. Have the students list seven types of assessment tools that are used in early childhood programs.

19. *Assessment Tools Summary,* Activity B, SAG. Have students use this activity to identify the advantages and disadvantages of the various assessment tools described in this chapter. They are also to give an instance when each tool can effectively be used. The text will provide much of the information for the chart, but they will need to use other references as well, or give their own opinions in order to complete the chart. You might want the students to complete the summary as a group activity.

20. Have the students describe the two tests a statement must pass to be objective.

21. *Descriptive or Interpretive?* reproducible master 3-2. Have students take this simple test to see if they can identify those statements that describe observable behaviors and those that interpret behavior. Go over the answers together and discuss. Note: This test also appears as a self-test in the front matter of *The Observation Guide,* which accompanies this text.

22. Have the students discuss why an observation itself serves no purpose without the interpretation of behavior to give meaning to the data.

23. *Interpreting the Data,* Activity C, SAG. Students are to read the incident recorded on the anecdotal record shown in Figure 3-6 of the text. They are to then "interpret" the date by answering the questions. To illustrate how people can interpret data differently, students are then asked to compare their interpretations with classmates' interpretations and to note the differences. Use this activity to discuss the difficulty in making accurate interpretations of behavior.

24. Have the students prepare a list of advantages and disadvantages of using anecdotal records.

25. Have the students discuss the advantages and disadvantages of checklists.

26. Have the students design a participation chart. After the chart is developed, have them use it as a tool while observing a group of preschool children.

27. Have the students discuss the advantages and disadvantages of rating scales.

28. *Designing an Assessment Tool,* Activity D, SAG. Students are asked to create their own assessment tool—a checklist, participation chart, or rating scale. They can use the Appendix of the text to make the chart or scale, and will also want to refer to the samples shown in the text.

29. Videotape a child telling a story. Play the videotape for your students. Ask them to share how the information may be helpful.

Portfolios

30. Have the students describe the contents of a portfolio.

31. Have the students discuss how the information included in a portfolio can be used.

32. *Reviewing Assessment Data,* transparency master 3-3. This transparency shows how on-going assessment data is used in evaluating children's progress. It identifies the questions to ask concerning the child's progress, strengths, abilities, and development. It then lists what should be included in summary statements about each child. Discuss what should then be done with this information.

Guidelines for Observing Children

33. *Guidelines for Observing Children,* transparency master 3-4. Use this master as you review the key points students should keep in mind when observing children in a child care center or classroom.

34. Have the students explain why the information they gather about children should be kept confidential.

35. Have the students discuss methods for protecting confidentiality.

36. Have the students discuss why coats, books, and other personal belongings should not be brought into the classroom while observing.

37. Have the students reflect on the contents of this chapter. Have them discuss the most practical on-going assessment tools.

38. Have two students observe the same child for a period of 30 minutes and write down what the child did and said. Then have them compare their written notes and identify what one had noticed and the other did not.

Additional Resources

39. Panel discussion. Invite a panel of preschool parents to share why parent-teacher alliances are important for assessment.

40. Panel discussion. Invite a panel of preschool teachers to describe how they use observation as a tool for assessment. Have them also reflect on how assessment is an integral part of teaching.

41. Guest speakers. Invite a parent and a teacher to reflect on how parent-teacher communication can be an important assessment vehicle.
42. Field trip. Arrange for the students to visit a local early childhood program to practice writing anecdotal records.

Research Topic

43. Have the student research assessment methods. Find various forms that are used for assessment. Use the forms when observing a child. Write a report on the advantages and disadvantages of using each type of form, and draw conclusions about their use.

Answer Key

Text

Review and Reflect, page 50

1. (List three:) Information collected is used in planning developmentally appropriate curriculum; individual and classroom problems can often be identified; allows you to identify those children who might have special needs; can find out where children are in their development; can see how each child is progressing in his or her development; information can be useful during parent conferences; hHelpful in evaluating your program.
2. An initial assessment is made of all children when they enter a program, but on-going assessment continues as long as a child remains enrolled in a program.
3. B
4. The method chosen depends on the type of behavior you want to assess and the amount of detail you need. It depends on whether the information needs to be collected for one child or the entire group. The amount of focused attention required by the observer needs to be considered.
5. A, B
6. Anecdotal records do not require charts or special settings. They can be recorded in any setting and require no special training. All you need is paper and a writing tool.
7. rating scale
8. (List one advantage and one disadvantage. Student response.)
9. photographs, sketches, diagrams
10. (List five. Student response.)
11. (Name three. Student response.)

Student Activity Guide

Check Your Understanding, Activity A

1. F	11. F
2. T	12. T
3. T	13. T
4. T	14. T
5. T	15. F
6. F	16. T
7. F	17. T
8. T	18. T
9. F	19. F
10. T	20. T

Teacher's Resource Guide/Binder

Descriptive or Interpretive? reproducible master 3-2

1. D	7. I
2. I	8. I
3. D	9. D
4. I	10. D
5. D	11. D
6. D	12. I

Chapter Test

1. B	14. T
2. E	15. T
3. I	16. C
4. C	17. D
5. A	18. D
6. G	19. C
7. D	20. A
8. F	21. B
9. F	22. A
10. T	23. D
11. F	24. D
12. F	25. A
13. T	

26. (List three. Student response.)
27. Method chosen depends on the type of behavior you want to assess and the amount of detail needed. Another consideration is whether the information needs to be collected for one child or the entire group. The amount of focused attention required by the observer needs to be considered.
28. It must describe only observable action. The recorded information must be nonevaluative.

Appropriate Assessment

Assessment should:

✓ Focus on the "whole child"— physical, cognitive, social, and emotional development.

✓ Help teachers identify each child's developmental needs and learning styles.

✓ Evaluate each child's progress and performance over time.

✓ Be used to determine progress of the class as a whole.

✓ Identify those children who have special needs.

✓ Include a variety of methods.

✓ Involve parents, teachers, children, and other professionals.

✓ Give parents understandable information about their child's progress.

✓ Identify and help solve any classroom problems.

✓ Be used to evaluate teaching effectiveness.

✓ Be used in planning developmentally appropriate curriculum.

✓ Be used in evaluating the program's effectiveness in meeting its goals and objectives.

Descriptive or Interpretive?

Name _____ **Date** _____ **Period** _____

To help you learn to write an objective narrative, or anecdotal record, complete the following exercise. Read each statement. Place a *D* in front of those statements that are descriptive. Place an *I* in front of those statements that are interpretive. Write your own examples at the bottom of the page.

_____ 1. Jose opened the door and ran outside.

_____ 2. Mark left the blockbuilding area because he wasn't interested.

_____ 3. Mrs. Devery, the teacher, called each child's name.

_____ 4. When the bunny was taken out of the box, the children were so excited that they screamed.

_____ 5. The teacher aide said, "I like how quietly you are sitting."

_____ 6. The volunteer asked each child to name one color.

_____ 7. May cried because she could not speak English.

_____ 8. Kris hit Kelsi because she was in his way.

_____ 9. Wendy tipped over her glass of milk.

_____ 10. Maurice put the rabbit in the cage, shut the door, and closed the lock.

_____ 11. Tunde walked across the room and sat next to Judy.

_____ 12. Sandy was confused by the teacher's directions so she took another cookie.

Write three statements that contain only observable behavior:

1. _____

2. _____

3. _____

Write three statements that contain interpretive information:

1. _____

2. _____

3. _____

Reviewing Assessment Data

I. Questions to ask when reviewing the assessment data:
   ♦ What evidence of progress is shown?
   ♦ What are the child's strengths and abilities?
   ♦ Are there concerns about the child's development?
        social development
        emotional development
        physical development
        cognitive development
   ♦ Are there concerns about the child's health?
   ♦ Are there any behavior problems?
   ♦ Does the child show a lack of self-esteem?

II. Summary statements to be formulated:
   ♦ Evidence of progress
   ♦ Strengths and abilities
   ♦ Development
   ♦ Behavior
   ♦ Health
   ♦ Self-esteem

Guidelines for Observing Children

- ◆ The information you collect must be kept confidential.
- ◆ Do not discuss a child's behavior outside the classroom.
- ◆ Use first names only in classroom discussions.
- ◆ Do not bring personal belongings into the classroom when you observe.
- ◆ Avoid talking to the children, other observers, or the staff when you observe.
  - ◆ Sit away from the action so you don't interfere or cause a disruption by your presence.
    - ◆ If a child asks you what you are doing, answer in a matter-of-fact manner.

Observing Children: A Tool for Assessment

Name _____

Date _____ Period _____ Score _____

Matching: Match the following terms and identifying phrases.

_____ 1. One of the oldest and best methods for learning about young children.

_____ 2. The process of observing, recording, and documenting children's growth and behavior in order to make decisions about their education.

_____ 3. Characteristics and behaviors typical of children in specific age groups.

_____ 4. Designed to record the presence or absence of specific traits or behaviors.

_____ 5. The activity preferences during self-selected play can be recorded on it.

_____ 6. Used to indicate the degree to which a quality or trait is present.

_____ 7. Contains a brief narrative account of a specific incident.

_____ 8. Takes place continually over a period of time.

A. participation chart
B. observation
C. checklists
D. anecdotal record
E. assessment
F. on-going assessment
G. rating scale
H. portfolio
I. developmental norms

True/False. Circle *T* if the statement is true or *F* if the statement is false.

T F 9. Assessment information is confidential and should not be shared with parents.

T F 10. The assessment method chosen depends upon the type of behaviors you want to assess and the amount of detail needed.

T F 11. A checklist is the simplest form of direct observation.

T F 12. A single assessment will provide an exact assessment of a child's ability or performance.

T F 13. You can write down notes on individual children during free-choice activities.

T F 14. A portfolio should be a summary of the child's development.

T F 15. Dictated stories, photographs, and checklists can all be included in portfolio contents.

Multiple choice: Choose the best response. Write the letter in the space provided.

_____ 16. The process of reviewing information and finding value in it is called _____.
A. observation
B. assessment
C. evaluation
D. documentation

(continued)

_____ 17. A child's development is impacted by diversity in _____.
  A. culture
  B. economic status
  C. home background
  D. All of the above.

_____ 18. Formal methods of observation include _____.
  A. anecdotal records
  B. interest surveys
  C. checklists
  D. standardized tests

_____ 19. To collect data, preschool teachers usually use _____.
  A. research instruments
  B. standardized tests
  C. informal observation
  D. developmental norms

_____ 20. Since it requires no special setting or time frame, the easiest method of assessment is the _____.
  A. anecdotal record
  B. checklist
  C. rating scale
  D. participation chart

_____ 21. A(An) _____ requires you to make a judgment about behavior.
  A. checklist
  B. rating scale
  C. participation chart
  D. anecdotal record

_____ 22. A(An) _____ indicates the presence or absence of a trait.
  A. checklist
  B. rating scale
  C. participation chart
  D. anecdotal record

_____ 23. Samples of children's products do *not* include _____.
  A. artwork
  B. records of conversations
  C. child-dictated stories
  D. rating scales

_____ 24. A portfolio contains _____.
  A. art projects
  B. child-dictated stories
  C. summaries of parent conferences
  D. All of the above.

_____ 25. The most important guideline when observing children is to _____.
  A. keep the information you collect confidential
  B. keep your personal belongings out of the observation area
  C. avoid talking to the children
  D. avoid talking to the teacher in charge

(continued)

Essay Questions: Provide complete responses to the following questions or statements.

26. List three purposes of assessment.

27. What are the three considerations for choosing an assessment method?

28. To be objective, a statement must pass two tests. Name these two tests.

Understanding Children from Birth to Age Two 4

Objectives

After studying this chapter, students will be able to
- describe the areas and characteristics of development.
- chart the physical development of children in the first two years after birth.
- describe how children develop cognitively in the first two years after birth.
- explain how children in the first two years after birth develop socially and emotionally.

Teaching Materials

Text, pages 51–65
  Terms to Know
  Review and Reflect
  Apply and Explore
Student Activity Guide
  A. *Types of Development*
  B. *Reflexes*
  C. *Understanding Development*
  D. *Encouraging Development*
Teacher's Resource Guide/Binder
  Characteristics of Development,
    transparency master, 4-1
  Motor Sequence for Infants, transparency master, 4-2
  Social and Emotional Development,
    reproducible master, 4-3
  Developmental Review, reproducible master, 4-4
  Chapter Test
Teacher's Resource Binder
  Progression of Large Motor Development,
    color transparency, CT-4
The Observation Guide
Mastering CDA Competencies

Introductory Activities

1. Have several students bring in series of pictures of themselves at various ages between infancy and age five. Display the pictures and lead a class discussion on how children change as they grow.

2. Have students discuss the meaning of the term *development*. Students should try to explain how and why the term is used to describe the growth of children.

Instructional Concepts and Student Learning Experiences

Child Development _____

3. Have students explain the differences among the areas of development.
4. *Types of Development,* Activity A, SAG. Have students identify the types of development described in each sentence.
5. Have students explain the following concepts in their own words: cephalocaudal principle, principle of proximodistal development, and maturation.
6. *Characteristics of Development,* transparency master 4-1. Use the master to review and discuss the characteristics of development with the class.
7. Have students describe the purpose of developmental scales.
8. Have students discuss reasons why developmental scales might be helpful. Students should also discuss possible disadvantages to using developmental scales.
9. Obtain some developmental checklists from a child care program or resource book. Have students use one of the checklists to observe one area of development in a child.

Physical Development in the First Two Years ___

10. *Reflexes,* Activity B, SAG. Have students describe the reflexes listed.
11. *Progression of Large Motor Development,* color transparency CT-4, TRB. Use this transparency to introduce the responsibilities of a child care teacher.
    A. Stress that children master motor tasks in a predictable sequence.
    B. Have students describe what muscles need to mature to accomplish each motor task.
    C. Stress the principle that growth and development proceed from the head downward.

D. Remind students that children move through the growth processes at their own rate.

12. Have students research to find out what reflexes adults have. Students should write a short paper comparing infant reflexes to adult reflexes and explaining why these reflexes might differ.

13. *Motor Sequence for Infants,* transparency master 4-2. Have the class try to determine the sequence in which infants develop the skills listed. Use the blanks to number the skills in the appropriate order.

14. Have students interview teachers to find out what methods they use to support motor development in infants and one-year-olds. Students should share their findings in class.

15. Have students list classroom equipment that promotes motor development and explain how it promotes motor development.

Cognitive Development in the First Two Years

16. Have students describe two ways that infants show individual preferences.

17. Have students explain why understanding object permanence is important to learning.

18. Have students interview teachers, asking them to share examples they have observed of toddlers acting out deferred imitation. Students should write an article based on their interviews.

19. Have students bring in magazine articles describing ways of supporting cognitive development in the first two years. Students should share their articles with the class.

20. Have students list classroom equipment that promotes cognitive development, and explain how it promotes cognitive development.

Social-Emotional Development in the First Two Years

21. Have students discuss situations that might promote or deter the development of attachment behaviors.

22. *Social and Emotional Development,* reproducible master 4-3. Have students try to number the skills listed in the order they occur. Then have students check their answers using the developmental charts in the Appendix of the text.

23. Have students discuss ways that teachers can promote the social-emotional development of children in the first two years.

24. Have students list classroom equipment that promotes social-emotional development and explain how it promotes social-emotional development.

25. *Developmental Review,* reproducible master 4-4. Have students complete the statements with the appropriate terms.

26. *Understanding Development,* Activity C, SAG. Have students complete the statements with the given terms.

27. *Encouraging Development,* Activity D, SAG. Have students describe ways of encouraging each area of development in children in the first two years. They will need to talk to an early childhood teacher in order to complete the activity. Have students share their findings with the class.

Additional Resources

28. Field trip. Arrange for students to visit a child care center that cares for infants. Students should observe and note the differences in physical abilities, cognitive abilities, and social-emotional characteristics among the infants.

29. Panel discussion. Invite a child care teacher, a child psychologist, a child care director, and a parent of a child under two years of age to discuss concerns related to separation anxiety in children and ways of handling separation anxiety in the child care center.

Research Topic

30. Have the student research various theories of development by such experts as Erikson, Havighurst, and Maslow. The student should write a research paper based on his or her findings and give a presentation on the paper to the class. The student should prepare and use visual aids in the presentation.

Answer Key

Text

Review and Reflect, page 65

1. physical development
2. false
3. Cephalocaudal principle: the child first gains control of the head, then the arms, then the legs. Principle of proximodistal development: the spinal cord develops before outer parts of the body. Maturation: a sequence of biological changes in the brain, nervous system, and other areas of a child's body that must occur before children can gain certain skills.
4. true
5. Crawling requires mainly arm strength, while creeping requires arm and leg strength. According to the cephalocaudal principle, the arms develop before the legs.
6. C
7. (Student response. See pages 59–60.)
8. deferred imitation
9. Two-word phrases used by toddlers. (Example is student response.)

10. Passivity: how actively involved a child is with his or her surroundings. Irritability: the tendency of a child to feel distressed. Activity patterns: levels of movement in children.
11. false
12. (Student response.)

Student Activity Guide

Types of Development, Activity A

1. social-emotional	11. cognitive
2. cognitive	12. physical
3. cognitive	13. cognitive
4. cognitive	14. physical
5. physical	15. social-emotional
6. social-emotional	16. cognitive
7. cognitive	17. physical
8. cognitive	18. cognitive
9. physical	19. social-emotional
10. social-emotional	20. physical

Reflexes, Activity B

1. Infants turn their heads toward anything that brushes their faces.
2. Occurs when a baby is startled by a noise or a sudden movement. The infant flings the arms and legs outward and then quickly draws the arms together, crying loudly.
3. When you touch the infant's palms, the hands will grip tightly. This is also seen when you place a rattle or other object across the palm.
4. This occurs when stroking the sole of the infant's foot on the outside from the heel to the toe. When this is done, the infant will fan the toes out and curl, and the foot twists in.
5. If you hold an infant so that the feet are flat on a surface, the infant will lift one foot after another in a stepping response.

Understanding Development, Activity C

1. reflex	9. temperament
2. infant	10. physical
3. object permanence	11. motor sequence
4. separation anxiety	12. preschooler
5. deferred imitation	13. fine motor
6. gross motor	14. toddler
7. attachment	15. cognitive
8. social-emotional	

Teacher's Resource Guide/Binder

Motor Sequence for Infants, transparency master 4-2

standing with help—6
walking alone—10
head control—1
hitching—4
rolling over—2
walking with help—8
creeping—5
crawling—3
standing holding on to furniture—7
standing alone—9

Social and Emotional Development, eproducible master 4-3

A— 2	H—10
B—13	I— 5
C— 7	J— 8
D— 4	K—11
E— 9	L— 6
F— 1	M— 3
G—12	N—14

Development Review, reproducible master 4-4

1. development	9. attachment
2. social	10. reflexes
3. physical	11. doubled
4. motor	12. survival
5. mental	13. movement
6. cognitive	14. grasping
7. maturation	15. stepping
8. temperament	16. judgment

Chapter Test

1. E	16. F
2. B	17. T
3. D	18. F
4. C	19. T
5. A	20. T
6. G	21. F
7. F	22. B
8. T	23. B
9. T	24. B
10. F	25. D
11. T	26. C
12. F	27. C
13. F	28. A
14. T	29. A
15. T	

30. Show the child an interesting toy. Then cover the toy with a towel or blanket. If the child attempts to uncover the toy, he or she has at least some understanding of object permanence.
31. Deferred imitation is watching another person's behavior and then acting out that behavior later. A young toddler's pretending is often a form of deferred imitation.
32. (Student response.)

Characteristics of Development

- ◆ Development proceeds in a predictable manner.

- ◆ Development is dependent on maturation.

- ◆ Growth and maturation proceed from the head down.

- ◆ Growth and maturation occur from the center of the body outward.

- ◆ Children move through the growth processes at their own rates.

Motor Sequence for Infants

_____ Standing with help

_____ Walking alone

_____ Head control

_____ Hitching

_____ Rolling over

_____ Walking with help

_____ Creeping

_____ Crawling

_____ Standing holding on to furniture

_____ Standing alone

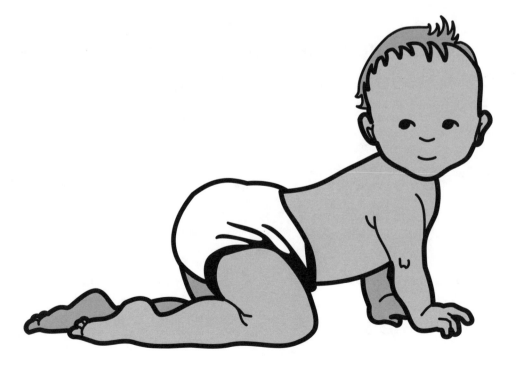

Social and Emotional Development

Name _____ **Date** _____ **Period** _____

Rank these social-emotional skills in the order they occur in the development of a child. Begin by writing the number 1 beside the first skill that the child develops. Check your answers by referring to the development scales listed in the Appendix of the text.

_____ A. Can quiet self by sucking.

_____ B. May become possessive about toys, hiding them from others.

_____ C. Begins to have sense of humor.

_____ D. Enjoys social aspects of feeding time.

_____ E. Shows interest in play activities of others.

_____ F. Recognizes a parent's voice.

_____ G. Shows increased negativism.

_____ H. Is more aware of and sensitive toward other children.

_____ I. May be able to play peek-a-boo game.

_____ J. Likes to explore new places but wants to be able to return to caregiver.

_____ K. May not always want to be cooperative.

_____ L. Desires constant attention from caregiver.

_____ M. Shows feelings of security when held or talked to.

_____ N. Engages in imaginative play related to parents' actions.

Developmental Review

Name _____ **Date**_____ **Period** _____

Read the following definitions and write the corresponding terms in the blanks.

_____ 1. _____ refers to change or growth.

_____ 2. Learning related to getting along with other people is called _____ development.

_____ 3. Improvement in ability to use the muscles is related to _____ development.

_____ 4. The ability to write is influenced by a child's fine _____ development.

_____ 5. The _____ processes used to gain knowledge are involved in cognitive developments

_____ 6. Ability to identify the colors red and yellow is part of _____ development.

_____ 7. _____ refers to a sequence of biological events occurring within a child.

_____ 8. Infants differ in _____, or the ways they react to their environment.

_____ 9. Looking, smiling, and crying are examples of _____ behaviors.

_____ 10. At birth the infant's physical abilities are limited to _____.

_____ 11. By four months of age, the infant will have _____ his or her weight.

_____ 12. The sucking, breathing, and rooting reflexes are necessary for _____.

_____ 13. The Moro reflex occurs when a baby is startled by a noise or sudden _____.

_____ 14. The _____ reflex occurs when the infant's palm is touched.

_____ 15. When an infant's feet touch a surface, the _____ reflex can be observed.

_____ 16. The fact that infants three to six months old try to locate noises indicates that these infants are starting to show _____.

Understanding Children from Birth to Age Two

Name _____

Date _____ Period _____ Score _____

Matching: Match the following terms and identifying phrases.

_____ 1. Occurs when the baby is startled by a noise or sudden movement.

_____ 2. After touching the infant's palm, his or her hands will grip tightly.

_____ 3. Infants turn their heads toward anything that brushes their faces.

_____ 4. The infant fans his or her toes upward when his or her feet are stroked.

_____ 5. When the infant is placed on his or her feet, his or her legs move in a walking motion.

_____ 6. Development proceeds from the head downward.

_____ 7. Development proceeds from the center of the body outward.

A. stepping reflex
B. grasping reflex
C. Babinski reflex
D. rooting reflex
E. Moro reflex
F. principle of proximodistal development
G. cephalocaudal principle

True/False: Circle *T* if the statement is true or *F* if the statement is false.

T   F   8. Development refers to change or growth in a child.

T   F   9. Studying and understanding child development is an important part of teaching young children.

T   F   10. The child's behavior remains the same throughout his or her preschool years.

T   F   11. Physical development includes changes in bone thickness and weight.

T   F   12. Cognitive development refers to the child's total scope of feelings.

T   F   13. Spinal cord development occurs after development in the child's outer body parts.

T   F   14. Maturation refers to a sequence of biological events occurring within the child.

T   F   15. Each child moves through development at his or her own rate.

T   F   16. Attachment refers to the quality and intensity of emotional reactions.

T   F   17. A child may not have normal language skills if his or her parents did not provide an opportunity to talk.

T   F   18. Growth is the slowest during the first two years of life.

T   F   19. Differences in infants' temperaments can be observed during the first few days of life.

T   F   20. Early attachment behaviors include smiling, crying, looking, and vocalizing.

T   F   21. Separation anxiety is strongest in the first three months after birth.

(continued)

Multiple Choice: Choose the best response. Write the letter in the space provided.

_____ 22. The average weight of a baby at birth is _____.
  A. six pounds
  B. seven and one-half pounds
  C. eight pounds
  D. eight and one-half pounds

_____ 23. The average newborn infant measures _____.
  A. nineteen inches
  B. twenty inches
  C. sixteen inches
  D. twenty-two inches

_____ 24. Most infants can first sit in a high chair at _____.
  A. three to five months of age
  B. four to six months of age
  C. six to eight months of age
  D. eight to ten months of age

_____ 25. Typically the child can roll over from stomach to back at about _____.
  A. one month of age
  B. two months of age
  C. three months of age
  D. four months of age

_____ 26. The concept of object permanence begins to develop at _____.
  A. birth to three months of age
  B. three to six months of age
  C. six to nine months of age
  D. nine to twelve months of age

_____ 27. Which of the following is not an attachment behavior?
  A. Crying
  B. Looking
  C. Eating
  D. Vocalizing

_____ 28. A social-emotional trait of a child at one month of age would be _____.
  A. showing general excitement and general distress
  B. smiling at familiar faces
  C. desiring constant attention
  D. showing fear of heights

_____ 29. A social-emotional trait of a child twelve to twenty-four months would be _____.
  A. playing next to, but not with, other children
  B. drawing simple shapes
  C. climbing stairs
  D. recognizing the colors red and blue

Essay Questions: Provide complete responses to the following questions or statements.

30. How can you test a child to see if he or she understands the concept of object permanence?

31. Explain the concept of deferred imitation.

32. As a caregiver, what would be your reaction to an occurrence of separation anxiety in a one-year-old?

Understanding Two- and Three-Year-Olds

5

Objectives

After studying this chapter, students will be able to
- describe the physical, cognitive, and social-emotional development of two-year-olds.
- explain how three-year-olds develop physically, cognitively, socially, and emotionally.
- relate how the development of two- and three-year-olds will affect the students' roles as teachers.

Teaching Materials

Text, pages 67–79
  Terms to Know
  Review and Reflect
  Apply and Explore
Student Activity Guide
  A. *Development of Two-Year-Olds*
  B. *Studying Two-Year-Olds*
  C. *Development of Three-Year-Olds*
  D. *Studying Three-Year-Olds*
  E. *Self-Help Skills*
  F. *Language Skills*
Teacher's Resource Guide/Binder
  Physical Skills of Two-Year-Olds,
    transparency master, 5-1
  Behavioral Traits of Two-Year-Olds,
    transparency master, 5-2
  Physical Skills of Three-Year-Olds,
    transparency master, 5-3
  Behavioral Traits of Three-Year-Olds,
    transparency master, 5-4
  Development Puzzle, reproducible master, 5-5
  Chapter Test
Teacher's Resource Binder
  Physical Skills of Three-Year-Olds,
    color transparency, CT-5
The Observation Guide
Mastering CDA Competencies

Introductory Activities

1. Have students list terms that they would use to describe two-year-olds and terms that they would

use to describe three-year-olds. Students should discuss their choices of descriptors. After studying the chapter, have students reevaluate their choices.
2. Prepare a videotape featuring two- and three-year-olds in typical activities at a child care center. Have students discuss their reactions to the video.

Instructional Concepts and Student Learning Experiences

Physical Development of Two-Year-Olds_____

3. Have each student find a photograph of himself or herself at two years of age. Each student should write a paragraph describing his or her physical appearance at that age.
4. *Development of Two-Year-Olds,* Activity A, SAG. Have students answer the questions related to the development of two-year-olds.
5. *Studying Two-Year-Olds,* Activity B. SAG. Have students interview the parents of a two-year-old and use the form to compare the child's actual development to usual development according to the text.
6. Have students observe two-year-olds and describe their physical, cognitive, and social-emotional traits.
7. *Physical Skills of Two-Year-Olds,* transparency master 5-1. Use the master as a basis for discussion of the motor skills of two-year-olds. Invite students to add skills that they have observed to the list.
8. Have students describe self-help skills. Students should discuss how a child's level of self-help skills affects the ways that a teacher interacts with the child.
9. Have students observe a two-year-old in a child care setting and record the types of activities in which the child needed assistance from an adult. Students should share their findings with the class.

Cognitive Development of Two-Year-Olds _____

10. Have students distinguish between language comprehension and expressive language skills.

11. Have students list routine questions that two-year-old children can answer.

Social-Emotional Development of Two-Year-Olds

12. Have students interview teachers to find out how the teacher would describe the relationship between two-year-old children and adults. Students should share their findings in class.

Teaching Two-Year-Olds

13. *Behavioral Traits of Two-Year-Olds,* transparency master 5-2. Use the master to review the traits listed with the class. For each trait, have students discuss how they as teachers may need to interact with, and react to, two-year-olds.
14. Have students list activities that two-year-olds might enjoy and explain their reasons for listing each activity.
15. Have students make a list of equipment that could be used to help promote motor development in two-year-olds.
16. Have students role-play ways of teaching self-help skills to two-year-olds.
17. Have students bring in articles on language activities that two-year-olds might enjoy. Students should share their articles with the class.

Physical Development of Three-Year-Olds

18. Have students prepare a bulletin board on the development of two- and three-year-old children. Students should use photographs or magazine pictures as illustrations.
19. *Development of Three-Year-Olds,* Activity C, SAG. Have students answer the questions related to the development of three-year-olds.
20. *Studying Three-Year-Olds,* Activity D, SAG. Have students interview the parents of a three-year-old and use the form to compare the child's actual development according to the text.
21. Have students observe three-year-olds and note characteristics of their physical, cognitive, and social-emotional development.
22. Have students weigh several two- and three-year-olds and compare the weights.
23. Have students use a developmental scale to evaluate the motor skills of a three-year-old.
24. *Physical Skills of Three-Year-Olds,* transparency master 5-3. Use the master as a basis for discussion of the motor skills of three-year-olds. Invite students to add skills to the list that they have observed.
25. *Physical Skills of Three-Year-Olds,* color transparency CT-5, TRB. Use this transparency to show some of the physical skills of a three-year-old child.

A. Have the students share their observations of the physical development of a three-year-old child.
B. Ask students to brainstorm a list of materials and equipment that would promote physical development.
C. Have the students describe the skills that are necessary to copy a cross or draw a face.

26. Have students observe a three-year-old in a child care setting and write a report on the child's self-help skills.
27. *Self-Help Skills,* Activity E, SAG. Have students indicate whether the self-help skills listed are typical of two-year-olds or of three-year-olds.

Cognitive Development of Three-Year-Olds

28. Have students describe the language comprehension skills of three-year-olds.
29. *Language Skills,* Activity F. SAG. Have students determine whether the skills described are language comprehension skills or expressive language skills.
30. Have students interview a teacher to find examples of a three-year-old's actions that show evidence of the child's thinking process. Students should share their findings in class.

Social-Emotional Development of Three-Year-Olds

31. Have students write a short description of the relationships between and among three-year-olds.

Teaching Three-Year-Olds

32. *Behavioral Traits of Three-Year-Olds,* transparency master, 5-4. Use this master to review the traits listed with the class. For each trait, have students discuss how they as teachers may need to interact with, and react to, three-year-olds.
33. Have students survey teachers to form a list of activities that three-year-olds tend to enjoy.
34. Have students review the list of equipment that promotes motor development in two-year-olds, developed in Activity 15. Students should evaluate whether or not the equipment would be appropriate for three-year-olds or if the equipment might be used differently for three-year-olds. Students should also add new equipment appropriate for three-year-olds to the list.
35. Have students demonstrate techniques for teaching three-year-olds self-help skills.
36. *Development Puzzle,* reproducible master, 5-5. Have students complete the puzzle by filling in the appropriate terms in the statements given.

Additional Resources

37. Panel discussion. Invite a panel of parents to discuss the behavior of two- and three-year-olds

with the class. Students should prepare questions in advance.

38. Guest speaker. Invite a teacher to share with students activities that two- and three-year-olds tend to enjoy. Encourage the teacher to bring examples of equipment that might be used in some of the activities.

Research Topic

39. Have the student research types of activities that have been successful with either a two-year-old or a three-year-old. The student should then develop an activity to try with a two- or three-year-old. The student should make arrangements to try the activity with three different children of the same age. Students should write a paper including a description of the activity, the interactions with the children, and an evaluation of the activity.

Answer Key

Text

Review and Reflect, page 79

1. (Student response. See pages 67–68 and the Appendix.)
2. false
3. more
4. Feeding-in is a strategy where you provide the child's language. Expansion is accomplished by reframing the child's utterance into a sentence.
5. B
6. Two-year-olds tend to express their anger physically through temper tantrums that may include screaming, crying, stamping, and kicking.
7. Two-year-olds have a tendency to dawdle, and they insist on doing things at their own pace.
8. true
9. (Student response. See pages 74–75.)
10. three
11. Three-year-olds have improved coordination, so they are less likely than two-year-olds to become frustrated due to lack of ability. Also, three-year-olds have improved language skills, so they can better understand reasons for what is happening around them.

Student Activity Guide

Development of Two-Year-Olds, Activity A

1. They are able to pick up balls by bending at the waist. They can kick large balls and can throw balls without falling. They can walk up and down stairs placing both feet on each stair. They are able

to stand with both feet on a balance beam. They can walk on their toes, and they can balance on one foot. They are able to jump.

2. They can insert keys into locks and turn pages in books one at a time. They can string large beads or spools and lace cards. They can hold scissors properly and open and close scissors. Hand preference is fairly developed. They will use writing tools and draw horizontal lines, vertical lines, and circles. They are skilled at building with blocks.
3. Language comprehension skills refer to a person's understanding of language. Expressive language is the ability to produce language forms. It is used to express a person's thoughts to others. Language comprehension develops first.
4. The child can give you "just one" of something and can understand size concepts such as *big* and *small.* Children become aware of shapes, forms, and colors.
5. Adult experiences, such as driving a car, making a bed, and talking on the phone.
6. Two-year-olds are usually possessive and do not want to share. They use body language to let people know how they feel. For example, they may push, hit, or shove a child who approaches their toys.
7. They are not always able to separate pretend from reality.
8. Let them know that people still care for them even if they get angry. Let them know they can depend on others. Give them regular routines.
9. (Student response.)

Development of Three-Year-Olds, Activity C

1. Their climbing skills are developed. They can catch balls with their arms.
2. Cutting skills become more refined. Drawing skills are improved. Children are able to copy and trace shapes and draw faces. They enjoy manipulating blocks and puzzles.
3. Two-year-olds are only able to think in terms of actions. Three-year-olds are also able to solve simple problems.
4. They do not think logically and are not able to see things from more than one perspective. They get confused about time concepts and about cause and effect.
5. They can give you two objects on request. They can remember and follow three-part instructions. They begin to understand the pronouns *you* and *they,* as well as the terms *who, whose, why,* and *how.* Space concepts become more clear.
6. They begin to understand the difference between past and present tense. They start to use question words.

7. They start to understand the concepts *full*, *more*, *less*, *smaller*, and *empty*. Counting skills begin. They can distinguish between *one* and *many*.

8. A three-year-old is less possessive than a two-year-old. Three-year-olds will share with others, but they do not like to share too much.

9. They have some control over their strong feelings because they realize adults do not approve of actions such as temper tantrums. They are eager to act in ways that please others. Many situations do not cause as much anger for three-year-olds as they do for two-year-olds. They begin to direct their anger at objects. They are less likely to be frightened by objects they know, but are quite fearful of imagined dangers. They are affectionate and seek affection in return.

10. They are likely to express their anger in words instead of actions.

11. (Student response.)

Self-Help Skills, Activity E

1. two	9. two
2. three	10. three
3. three	11. two
4. three	12. two
5. two	13. three
6. three	14. three
7. two	15. two
8. three	16. two

Language Skills, Activity F

1. E	9. C
2. C	10. C
3. E	11. E
4. C	12. C
5. C	13. C
6. E	14. C
7. E	15. E
8. E	

Teacher's Resource Guide/Binder

Development Puzzle, reproducible master 5-5

1. gender roles	7. expansion
2. self-concept	8. math
3. vocabulary	9. expressive
4. comprehension	10. egocentrism
5. self-help	11. tantrums
6. cognitive	

Chapter Test

1. D	15. T
2. E	16. T
3. E	17. T
4. B	18. T
5. A	19. T
6. B	20. F
7. D	21. D
8. D	22. B
9. A	23. A
10. B	24. C
11. T	25. C
12. T	26. D
13. F	27. C
14. F	28. D

29. (Student response.)

30. Two-year-olds are curious and they like to explore. These children delight in running and movement and are not afraid to try out new equipment. Therefore, several adults are needed to watch all the children and keep them safe.

31. (Student response.)

Physical Skills of Two-Year-Olds

◆ Run without falling

◆ Jump in place

◆ Stand with both feet on balance beam

◆ Attempt to balance on one foot

◆ Walk on toes

◆ Turn book pages one at a time

◆ Show hand preference

◆ String large beads

◆ Hold scissors properly

◆ Open and closes scissors

◆ Draw horizontal lines, vertical lines, and circles

◆ Build towers of six to seven blocks

Behavioral Traits of Two-Year-Olds

- ◆ Negative
- ◆ Possessive
- ◆ Often use baby language to express themselves
- ◆ May push, hit, or shove
- ◆ Curious
- ◆ Want their own way
- ◆ Have preference for certain part of the day
- ◆ Appetites vary
- ◆ Explorative
- ◆ Noisy
- ◆ Tend to dawdle
- ◆ Delight in movement
- ◆ Especially enjoy gross motor activity
- ◆ Affectionate
- ◆ Are demanding and dependent on relationships
- ◆ Like rituals

Physical Skills of Three-Year-Olds

- ◆ Walk up stairs with alternating feet

- ◆ Catch bouncing ball with hands

- ◆ Ride a tricycle

- ◆ Balance on one foot for eight seconds

- ◆ Hop on one foot up to three times

- ◆ Cut a five-inch square of paper in two

- ◆ Cut along a line to within one-half inch of line

- ◆ Copy the shape of a cross

- ◆ Trace a diamond

- ◆ Draw faces

- ◆ Build towers with nine to ten cubes

Behavioral Traits of Three-Year-Olds

- ◆ Happy

- ◆ Sociable

- ◆ Agreeable

- ◆ Eager to please

- ◆ Adjust easily to new adults, classmates, and situations

- ◆ Enjoy playing

- ◆ Often play in groups of two or three children

- ◆ Share with friends

- ◆ Use themes in dramatic play

- ◆ Are learning to take turns

- ◆ Are becoming increasingly independent

- ◆ Have strong visible emotions: anger, excitement, discouragement

- ◆ Explore by doing

- ◆ Are constantly moving, tasting, smelling, and touching

Development Puzzle

Name _____ Date _____ Period _____

Complete the puzzle by filling in the appropriate terms in the statements below.

1.						D								
2.						E								
3.						V								
4.						E								
5.						L								
6.						O								
7.						P								
8.						M								
9.						E								
10.						N								
11.						T								

1. Behaviors that are expected of girls or boys are called _____.

2. Your _____ is the way you see yourself.

3. The _____ of the average two-year-old is approximately 50 to 200 words.

4. The child's understanding of language is called language _____.

5. Dressing and feeding oneself are examples of _____ skills young children are ready to learn.

6. The child's _____ development includes his or her language skills, language comprehension skills, and math readiness skills.

7. Changing a child's utterance into a sentence is called _____.

8. An awareness of shape, form, and color are _____ skills.

9. _____ language is the ability to produce language forms.

10. Believing that everyone sees, thinks, and feels like you do is called _____.

11. Three-year-olds start to grow out of the temper _____ of the two-year-old stage.

Understanding Two- and Three-Year-Olds

Name _____

Date _____ **Period** _____ **Score** _____

Matching: Match the following terms and identifying skills. (Terms may be used more than once.)

_____ 1. Is cooperative in dressing.

_____ 2. Gives "just one" upon request.

_____ 3. Answers routine questions.

_____ 4. Does not like to share toys.

_____ 5. Runs without falling.

_____ 6. Likes to give affection to parents.

_____ 7. Sits on toilet without assistance.

_____ 8. Unsnaps a snap.

_____ 9. Kicks a large ball.

_____ 10. Displays jealousy.

A. physical development
B. social-emotional skills
C. math skills
D. self-help skills
E. language comprehension

Circle *T* if the statement is true or *F* if the statement is false.

T F 11 A two-year-old is usually able to throw a ball without falling.

T F 12. Two-year-olds are beginning to use one hand consistently for most activities.

T F 13. Two-year-olds develop the skill of dressing before undressing themselves.

T F 14. The child's understanding of language is called expressive language skills.

T F 15. Expressive language skills usually follow a sequence.

T F 16. The average two-year-old child has a vocabulary of approximately 50 to 200 words.

T F 17. Possessive is a word that describes the average two-year-old.

T F 18. The three-year-old can attend to routines such as washing and drying his or her hands.

T F 19. The three-year-old is able to solve simple problems.

T F 20. By the end of the third year, organized play with other children emerges.

Multiple Choice: Choose the best response. Write the letter in the space provided.

_____ 21. The gross motor skills of a two-year-old include _____.
A. catching a bounced ball with hands
B. riding tricycles
C. walking up steps with alternating feet
D. walking on toes

_____ 22. A two-year-old usually can _____.
- A. copy across
- B. scribble
- C. cut five-inch squares of paper in two
- D. built towers with 10 to 12 cubes

_____ 23. The two-year-old usually can _____.
- A. point to six body parts on a doll
- B. provide appropriate answers to "who" questions
- C. understand space concepts
- D. follow three-part instructions

_____ 24. A two-year-old is most likely to play _____.
- A. by sharing toys with other children
- B. by acting out experiences of other children
- C. next to, but not cooperatively with, other children
- D. organized games

_____ 25. Two-year-old children tend to be _____.
- A. sociable
- B. agreeable
- C. negative
- D. accepting

_____ 26. Physically, a three-year-old usually masters _____.
- A. jumping in place
- B. walking on toes
- C. throwing a ball without falling
- D. walking heel-to-toe for four steps

_____ 27. Typical self-help skills developed by a three-year-old include _____.
- A. cooperating with dressing
- B. removing shoes
- C. putting on shoes
- D. working small buttons and hooks

_____ 28. Three-year-old children are frequently _____.
- A. negative
- B. possessive
- C. pushing other children
- D. agreeable

Essay Questions: Provide complete responses to the following questions or statements.

29. Compare the emotional development of two-year-olds to the emotional development of three-year-olds.

30. Why is extra supervision needed when you take two-year-olds on field trips?

31. Give an example of how you would use expansion in teaching a two-year-old language skills.

Understanding Four- and Five-Year-Olds

6

Objectives

After studying this chapter, students will be able to

- describe the physical, cognitive, and social-emotional development of four- and five-year-olds.
- explain how they as teachers can plan programs and relate to four- and five-year-olds in developmentally appropriate ways.

Teaching Materials

Text, pages 81–92
  Terms to Know
  Review and Reflect
  Apply and Explore
Student Activity Guide
  A. *The Truth About Preschoolers*
  B. *Reading and Math Fun*
  C. *Handling Emotions*
  D. *Developing Activities*
Teacher's Resource Guide/Binder
  Patterns of Physical Development,
    reproducible master, 6-1
  Behavioral Traits of Four-Year-Olds,
    transparency master, 6-2
  Behavioral Traits of Five-Year-Olds,
    transparency master, 6-3
  Behavior Review, reproducible master, 6-4
  Chapter Test
Teacher's Resource Binder
  Development of Four-Year-Olds,
    color transparency, CT-6
The Observation Guide
Mastering CDA Competencies

Introductory Activities

1. Have students chart the physical, cognitive, and social-emotional changes that occur from birth to age three. Then have students predict how children might develop as four- and five-year-olds.
2. Have students discuss why the term *preschooler* is used to describe four- and five-year-olds.

3. *The Truth About Preschoolers,* Activity A, SAG. Before studying the chapter, have students determine whether the statements about four- and five-year-olds are true or false. Have students discuss their answers.

Instructional Concepts and Student Learning Experiences

Physical Development of Four- and Five-Year-Olds

4. Have students find photographs of themselves when they were four or five years old. Students should write paragraphs describing their physical appearance at that age.
5. Have students weigh several four- and five-year-olds and compare the weights.
6. *Patterns of Physical Development,* reproducible master 6-1. Have students determine whether the traits listed are typical of newborns, the first year, one-year-olds, two-year-olds, three-year-olds, four-year-olds, or five-year-olds. (Students may refer to Chapters 4, 5, and 6 and the Appendix to find the correct answers.)
7. Have students observe four- and five-year-olds and describe their motor skills.
8. Have students use a developmental scale to evaluate the motor skills of a four- or five-year-old.
9. Have students brainstorm a list of typical motor skills of four- and five-year-old children.
10. Have students observe a group of preschoolers in a child care or preschool setting. Students should note self-help skills of the children and share their observations in class.
11. Have students interview teachers to find ways of teaching self-help skills to four- and five-year-olds. As a class, have students compile these ideas into a helpful brochure for new teachers.

Cognitive Development of Preschoolers

12. Have a few students make audio or video recordings of four- and five-year-olds talking with them. The students should ask questions that would

reveal language comprehension as well as expressive language skills. Have the class listen or view the recordings and comment on the language skills of four- and five-year-olds.

13. Have students list routine questions that four- and five-year-old children can answer.

14. Have students observe four- or five-year-olds and record evidence of the children's thinking processes. Students should share their findings in class.

15. *Reading and Math Fun,* Activity B, SAG. Have students use the forms to plan a reading activity and a math activity.

Social-Emotional Development of Preschoolers

16. Have students describe how four- and five-year-olds relate to each other. Students should discuss how these relationships may affect their roles as teachers.

17. Have students describe the relationships between four- and five-year-olds and adults. Students should discuss how these relationships may affect their roles as teachers.

18. Have a group of students create a videotape that shows how four- and five-year-olds display their emotions. The students should show the tape in class and lead a class discussion on the subject.

19. *Handling Emotions,* Activity C, SAG. Have students read an article on helping preschoolers cope with emotions and use the form to report on the article.

20. *Development of Four-Year-Olds,* color transparency CT-6, TRB. Use this transparency to explore the development of four-year-olds.
    A. Stress how four- and five-year-olds can handle many self-help skills; however, they need new experiences and challenges to keep them growing.
    B. Ask students to compare the physical, social-emotional, and cognitive skills of four-year-old children with three-year-old children.
    C. Ask students to explain how they can plan programs that relate to four- and five-year-olds in developmentally appropriate ways.
    D. Have students discuss why teachers enjoy working with children of this age.

Teaching Four- and Five-Year-Olds

21. *Behavioral Traits of Four-Year-Olds,* transparency master 6-2. Use the master to review the traits listed with the class. For each trait, have students discuss how they as teachers may need to interact with and react to four-year-olds.

22. *Behavioral Traits of Five-Year-Olds,* transparency master 6-3. Use the master to review the traits listed with the class. For each trait, have students

discuss how they as teachers may need to interact with and react to five-year-olds.

23. *Behavior Review,* reproducible master 6-4. Have students review the traits listed and determine whether they are typical of children age two, three, four, or five.

24. Have students list activities to promote physical, cognitive, and social-emotional development that four- and five-year-olds would enjoy.

25. *Developing Activities,* Activity D, SAG. Have students suggest activities to promote areas of development using the forms provided.

Additional Resources

26. Panel discussion. Invite a panel of parents to discuss the behavior of four- and five-year-old children.

27. Guest speaker. Invite a pediatrician to discuss the physical development and abilities of four- and five-year-olds.

28. Guest speaker. Invite a teacher to discuss activities that four- and five-year-olds enjoy. Ask the teacher to bring some equipment that might be used with these activities.

Research Topic

29. Have the student research typical fears of four- and five-year-olds and ways of helping these children handle their fears. The student should also survey four- and five-year-olds, asking them what they are afraid of. Finally, the student should interview some teachers about ways of handling fears in four- and five-year-olds. The student should write a report or give an oral presentation on his or her findings.

Answer Key

Text

Review and Reflect, page 92

1. In these years, bones are becoming harder and permanent teeth are forming. Calcium and vitamin D are important to this growth.
2. false
3. Four- and five-year-olds' writing skills become more refined. Their drawings are more easily recognized. These children can copy a square and print a few letters. (The letters may be flawed, however.) By five years of age, children can copy triangles and trace diamonds. They also can stay within the lines fairly well when they color. Most five-year-olds can print their first names, copy most letters, and print some simple words.
4. D

5. four

6. Four- and five-year-olds can recognize and name many letters of the alphabet, and they can recognize their own names. As you read stories, these children may be able to pick out and say words that they recognize. They will also try to guess words that they do not recognize by focusing on the first letter of the word.

7. true

8. Four- and five-year-olds don't really understand how long an hour or a minute takes. They also get confused because time is described in many different ways.

9. false

10. (Student response. See page 89.)

11. The teacher does not function much as a playmate. The teacher does handle disputes and conflicts, and the teacher may add new ideas to play.

Student Activity Guide

The Truth About Preschoolers, Activity A

1. F	14. F
2. F	15. F
3. T	16. T
4. F	17. F
5. T	18. T
6. F	19. F
7. T	20. T
8. F	21. T
9. F	22. T
10. T	23. F
11. T	24. T
12. T	25. T
13. F	

Teacher's Resource Guide/Binder

Patterns of Physical Development,
eproducible master 6-1

Newborn (birth to three months): 1, 2, 9

First year (three to twelve months): 3, 5, 6, 14

One-year-old: 4

Two-year-old: 10, 13, 19, 21

Three-year-old: 16, 17, 20, 23

Four-year-old: 8, 12, 18, 22

Five-year-old: 7, 11, 15

Behavior Review, reproducible master 6-4

(Students may justify other answers.)

1. 2	10. 4 or 5
2. 4 or 5	11. 4 or 5
3. 3	12. 3
4. 2	13. 4 or 5
5. 2	14. 2
6. 4 or 5	15. 3
7. 4 or 5	16. 4 or 5
8. 3	17. 4 or 5
9. 2	

Chapter Test

1. C	13. T
2. A	14. T
3. B	15. F
4. E	16. T
5. D	17. T
6. F	18. A
7. T	19. C
8. T	20. B
9. F	21. D
10. T	22. A
11. T	23. C
12. F	

24. These children don't really understand how long an hour or a minute takes. Also, they get confused because time is described in many ways.

25. The child may regress to earlier behaviors, such as crying, following adults, or having toileting accidents. The child may also develop physical problems such as stomachaches or nightmares.

26. For most children, this action is simply a way of using the imagination and having fun. It does not usually indicate any social or emotional problem.

Patterns of Physical Development

Name _____ **Date** _____ **Period** _____

Although each child develops at his or her individual rate, certain traits are typical at certain ages. For each of the developmental traits listed below, write the number of each trait next to the age category to which it is most closely related.

Ages

Newborn (birth to three months) _____

First year (three to twelve months) _____

One-year-old _____

Two-year-old _____

Three-year-old _____

Four-year-old _____

Five-year-old _____

Developmental Traits

1. Twitches whole body when crying.
2. Needs support for head.
3. Grabs object with either hand.
4. Builds tower of two blocks.
5. Sits alone.
6. Crawls.
7. Copies a triangle.
8. Throws ball overhand.
9. May hold object, but drops it quickly.
10. Walks on toes.
11. Colors within lines.
12. Learns to skip.
13. Strings large beads.
14. Learns pincer grip, using thumb and forefinger in opposition.
15. Prints his or her first name.
16. Hops on one foot.
17. Rides a tricycle.
18. Copies a square.
19. Opens and closes scissors.
20. Wiggles thumb.
21. Turns pages in a book one at a time.
22. Completes a five-piece puzzle.
23. Builds a tower of nine to ten cubes.

Behavioral Traits of Four-Year-Olds

- ◆ Are Talkative

- ◆ Are Full of Questions

- ◆ Ask Many "Why" Questions

- ◆ Use When, What, and How to Form Questions

- ◆ Have Strong Need for Companionship

- ◆ Are More Talkative Than Physical

- ◆ Are Beginning to Understand

- ◆ Have Active Imaginations

- ◆ May Mix Fantasy and Truth

- ◆ May Have Imaginary Playmates

- ◆ Sleep 12 Hours per Day

- ◆ Remember Holidays

- ◆ Time Concepts

Behavioral Traits of Five-Year-Olds

- Are Friendly
- Like to Experience Independence
- Openly Tattle
- Seek the Advice of Adults
- Are Interested in Projects
- Enjoy Woodworking and Cooking
- Are Proud of and Interested in Their Own Possessions
- Like to Bring Favorite Toys to Center
- Call Attention to Their Own Clothing
- Know Difference Between Right and Left
- Use Lively and Interesting Language
- Carry on Lengthy Conversations
- Repeat Details of Story
- Are Eager to Please
- Like to Run Errands
- May Ask If There Is Something He or She Can Do to Help

Behavior Review

Name _____ **Date** _____ **Period** _____

Although each child develops at his or her own rate, certain behavioral traits are typical at specific ages. For each trait listed, place a check in the appropriate age column.

Behavioral Trait	Age		
	2	3	4 or 5
1. Is possessive.			
2. Is friendly.			
3. Likes to play with one or two main friends.			
4. Is affectionate.			
5. Is negative.			
6. Likes working on projects.			
7. Develops fear of being hurt.			
8. Has strong visible emotions.			
9. May push and hit.			
10. May appear reckless.			
11. Asks "why" questions.			
12. Is learning positive ways to get attention from others.			
13. Has strong need for companionship.			
14. Wants own way.			
15. Is willing to share with a few people.			
16. Likes to spend time talking.			
17. Is proud of his or her possessions.			

Understanding Four- and Five-Year-Olds

Name _____

Date _____ **Period** _____ **Score** _____

Matching: Match the following terms and identifying phrases.

_____ 1. Decides what he or she wants to draw and then draws it.

_____ 2. The ability to speak in clearly pronounced sounds.

_____ 3. Recognizes the numerals 1, 2, 3, and 4.

_____ 4. Repeating sounds or words and pausing for unusually long times when speaking.

_____ 5. Reciting numbers in their proper order.

A. articulatio
B. four-year-old
C. five-year-old
D. rote counting
E. stuttering

True/False: Circle *T* if the statement is true or *F* if the statement is false.

T   F   6. The five-year-old is awkward when marching to music.

T   F   7. The five-year-old can usually print his or her first name.

T   F   8. A four-year-old can carry a cup of liquid without spilling.

T   F   9. A four-year-old can complete a ten-piece puzzle.

T   F   10. Four-year-olds may still need supervision to dress and undress themselves.

T   F   11. A four-year-old is full of questions.

T   F   12. A four-year-old can understand five-step commands.

T   F   13. Concepts such as fat, short, tallest, and same size should be included in the curriculum for four-year-olds.

T   F   14. Five-year-olds can pick out and say words they recognize as someone reads them a story.

T   F   15. The five-year-old's vocabulary usually is about 100 words.

T   F   16. The five-year-old can usually dial his or her telephone number correctly.

T   F   17. Imaginary playmates are not uncommon for the four-year-old.

Multiple Choice: Choose the best response. Write the letter in the space provided.

_____ 18. The four-year-old can _____.
    A. throw a ball overhand
    B. march to music
    C. climb fences
    D. roller skate

_____ 19. A new skill for five-year-olds is _____.
   A. balancing on one foot for ten seconds
   B. throwing a ball overhand
   C. climbing fences
   D. walking down stairs with alternating feet

_____ 20. By four years of age, most children can complete _____.
   A. a three-piece puzzle
   B. a five-piece puzzle
   C. a ten-piece puzzle
   D. a twelve-piece puzzle

_____ 21. A four-year-old's self-help skills usually include _____.
   A. putting shoes on correct feet
   B. unbuttoning back buttons
   C. dressing and undressing without assistance
   D. distinguishing the front and back of clothing

_____ 22. The four-year-old usually _____.
   A. understands the passive voice
   B. uses the proper forms of pronouns in sentences
   C. understands the meanings of all words he or she uses
   D. tells original stories

_____ 23. The five-year-old usually can _____.
   A. recognize numerals 1 through 10
   B. rote count from 1 through 30
   C. recognize square and rectangle shapes
   D. write numerals 1 through 10

Essay Questions: Provide complete responses to the following questions or statements.

24. Why are time concepts difficult for four- and five-year-olds to understand?

25. Name five ways jealousy might surface in a child.

26. What does having an imaginary friend indicate about a child?

Middle Childhood  7

Objectives

After studying this chapter, students will be able to
- describe the physical, cognitive, and social-emotional development of school-age children.
- summarize potential health concerns of middle childhood.
- explain moral development during childhood.

Teaching Methods

Text, pages 93–106
Terms to Know
Review and Reflect
Apply and Explore
Student Activity Guide
A. *Understanding Middle Childhood Terms*
B. *Check Your Gender IQ*
C. *Health Dilemmas*
D. *Testing Mental Operations*
Teachers Resource Guide/Binder
Judgments of Self-Worth, reproducible master, 7-1
Friendships During the School-Age Years,
  reproducible master, 7-2
Handling Peer Rejection, reproducible master, 7-3
Team Sports, transparency master, 7-4
Chapter Test
Teacher's Resource Binder
Conservation Tasks, color transparency, CT-7
The Observation Guide
Mastering CDA Competencies

Introductory Activities

1. Ask the students to tell what they know about the differences in development between preschool children and children in middle childhood.
2. Prepare slides or photographs of children during the preschool years and middle childhood. Ask the students to describe the differences in physical development.
3. Ask the students to recall significant middle childhood experiences.

Instructional Concepts and Student Learning Experiences

Physical Development

4. *Understanding Middle Childhood Terms,* Activity A, SAG. Use this matching activity to help students review terms that will be introduced in this chapter.
5. Have students discuss the gender differences in physical development during middle childhood.
6. Have the students discuss why weight may double between age 6 and 12.
7. Have the students bring in photographs of themselves when they were between 6 and 12 years of age. Ask the students to write a paragraph describing how their appearance changed during this age span.
8. Obtain developmental checklists for the physical development of children during middle childhood. Have the students use the checklists as they observe children in a school-age program.
9. Have the students chart the weight and height of a group of school-age children. Ask them to compare the gender differences.
10. Have the students collect handwriting samples of school-age children. Ask them to describe the improvement of fine motor skills.

Health Concerns

11. Have the students interview a doctor or nurse to find out the health concerns of school-age children. Share the information with the class.
12. Discuss how permanent hearing loss can impact learning.
13. Have the students brainstorm signs of children who may have vision or hearing problems. How is this information important to a teacher?
14. Have the students bring in magazine pictures or photographs of children whose permanent teeth appear to be out of proportion to their faces.
15. Have the students list symptoms of asthma and review what happens during an asthma attack.

16. Have the students discuss how being obese can impact a child's emotional health.
17. *Health Dilemmas,* Activity C, SAG. Have the students divide into small groups and discuss possible approaches to each health dilemma. Write down their best ideas and share with the class.

Cognitive Development

18. Have the students define concrete operations.
19. *Conservation Tasks,* color transparency CT-7, TRB. Use this transparency in the following ways:
    A. Review the concept of conservation. Ask what *conservation* means.
    B. Ask the students how they would use each of these tests with children. What materials would they need to do these tests? What would they say to the children? What questions would they ask? What answers would they expect children to give if they understand the concept of conservation?
    C. Ask students at what age they would expect a child to be able to respond correctly to these tests.
    D. Ask students to describe other ways they could test for conservation. What materials could they use?
20. Have the students demonstrate the conservation of liquids, length, and mass.
21. Have the students brainstorm a list of objects that could be used for seriation activities.
22. Have the students design three classification activities.
23. *Testing Mental Operations,* Activity D, SAG. Students are to design their own activities to test the concepts of conservation, seriation, and classification. They are to test these concepts with a child between the ages of six and ten and record the child's responses.
24. Have the students brainstorm a list of jokes and riddles that school-age children tell.

Social-Emotional Development

25. Have the students describe the process of social comparison. Discuss how social comparisons may impact self-esteem.
26. *Judgments of Self-Worth,* reproducible master 7-1. Students are asked to identify ways that subtle messages by adults and peers can undermine a child's self-worth in five areas.
27. Have each student ask a school-age child to describe himself or herself. Compare the self-descriptions. How were they alike? How did they differ? Can any generalizations be made?
28. *Friendships During the School-Age Years,* reproducible master 7-2. Students are asked to complete sentences regarding friendship during the school-age years. Use these statements as a basis for class discussion. List all of the items students list under numbers 7 and 8 on the chalkboard. Compare the lists. Discuss the importance of friendships during the school-age years and how school-age caregivers can help children develop friendships.

29. Have the students brainstorm a list of ways to promote school-age children's self-esteem.
30. *Handling Peer Rejection,* reproducible master 7-3. Students are asked to read a case study about a school-age child who has few friends. They are to then describe ways the teacher can help the child develop social skills.
31. Invite some school-age children to class and ask them to describe their favorite persons. Have the children listen for personality descriptions and personality traits.
32. Have the students identify traits of school-age children who are well liked by other children. Ask them how teachers can help children develop these traits.
33. Have the students discuss what children learn from interacting with their peers.
34. *Check Your Gender IQ,* Activity B, SAG. Students are to indicate which statements generally describe girls and those that generally describe boys. They are then asked to observe school-age children and see how many of these characteristics they can see. Also discuss the importance of school-age teachers being aware of these differences, but not reinforcing sex-role stereotypes.
35. Have the students visit an elementary school to observe peer group activities. Ask them to describe the gender differences they observe.
36. Have the students list and describe the organized games they enjoyed during middle childhood.
37. *Team Sports,* transparency master 7-4. Review the benefits to children of participating in competitive sports. Then ask the students to identify drawbacks to participating in team sports. Add these to the transparency.

Moral Development

38. Ask students to define moral development and morality. Why is moral development important in our society?
39. Have the students discuss how children learn moral behavior.

Additional Resources

40. Invite a coach to class. Ask the coach to discuss how children can benefit from participating in competitive sports. Also have the coach present the drawbacks.
41. Panel Discussion. Invite a nurse or pediatrician, a school-age program director, and a school-age

teacher to discuss the rewards and challenges of working with school-age children.

Research Topic

42. Have the student research the impact of friendships. The student should write a research paper based on his or her findings and give a presentation to the class. The student should be encouraged to prepare and use visual aids in the presentation.

Answer Key

Text

Review and Reflect, page 106

1. true
2. Motor skills that require balance, coordination, flexibility, or rhythmic movement. Some examples include playing hopscotch, dancing, and skipping.
3. true
4. (List three:) overweight parents, environment, family stress, physical inactivity
5. Preschool children rely on what they see or perceive. During middle childhood, children begin to think mentally using logic and symbols. They begin to use logical thinking instead of perception.
6. (Student response.)
7. The child's vocabulary doubles between the ages of 6 and 12. Grammar skills improve. They learn to read. They learn sentence structure, using plurals, pronouns, and tense properly. They use both oral and written expression.
8. Self-concept is the view a person has of himself or herself. This affects self-esteem. Self-esteem is the belief that you are a worthwhile person.
9. Empathy is the ability to understand the feelings of others.
10. Boys tend to control large fixed spaces that are used for team sports. They control almost ten times more space than girls. Space occupied by girls is located closer to the school building.
11. They learn teamwork skills. They learn to get along with their peers. They benefit from exercise. Their activities bring enjoyment. A pattern for a healthy lifestyle begins to form.
12. true

Student Activity Guide

Understanding Middle Childhood Terms, Activity A

1. F	4. A	7. C	10. D	13. J
2. B	5. G	8. L	11. I	14. O
3. K	6. H	9. M	12. E	15. N

Check Your Gender IQ, Activity B

1. B	8. B
2. G	9. B
3. G	10. G
4. G	11. B
5. G	12. G
6. G	13. G
7. G	14. B

Health Dilemmas, Activity C

1. Antwann may have a visual problem. Ask the other staff to observe him. If they agree with your observation, contact Antwann's parents. Share your observations.
2. Toby may have a hearing problem. Encourage other staff to observe him during program hours. You may even want to hit two wooden building blocks together behind his back. If he does not act startled, he probably did not hear the noise. If available, ask the county nurse to screen Toby's hearing. Share your observations with his parents.
3. Rhonda's portions will need to be monitored and controlled at the center. The amount of food she puts on her plate will need to be restricted. Share your concerns with Rhonda's parents. Explain the impact obesity can have on her emotional and physical health.

Teacher's Resource Guide/Binder
Chapter Test

1. B	12. L	23. F
2. E	13. D	24. T
3. F	14. F	25. A
4. N	15. F	26. D
5. C	16. T	27. B
6. A	17. F	28. C
7. K	18. T	29. B
8. M	19. F	30. B
9. H	20. F	31. A
10. J	21. F	32. B
11. G	22. T	

31. (Describe three. Student response.)
32. (Name two benefits:) Children learn teamwork skills, learn to get along with their peers, benefit from exercise, activities bring enjoyment, a pattern for a healthy lifestyle begins to form. (Name two drawbacks:) Risk of injury, pressure to win at all costs, adults often control the game so children may not be developing decision-making and leadership skills.
33. Moral development is the process of acquiring the standards of behavior considered acceptable by a society. Standards of behavior become internalized during middle childhood.

Judgments of Self-Worth

Name _____ **Date** _____ **Period** _____

By continually evaluating themselves, some school-age children lose their confidence. Subtle messages echoed by adults and peers can undermine self-esteem. Children evaluate themselves in the areas listed below. For each area, give examples of messages children might receive that could undermine their self-esteem.

Academic competence: _____

_____

_____

_____

_____

_____

_____

Athletic competence: _____

_____

_____

_____

_____

_____

_____

Physical appearance: _____

_____

_____

_____

_____

_____

_____

_____

(continued)

Name_____

Behavior: _____

_____

_____

_____

_____

_____

_____

Social acceptance: _____

_____

_____

_____

_____

_____

_____

_____

If you worked with school-age children, what would you do to help them maintain their self-esteem? _____

_____

_____

_____

_____

_____

_____

_____

_____

Friendships During the School-Age Years

Name _____ **Date** _____ **Period** _____

During the school-age years, friendships take on greater importance. Complete the following sentences regarding friendships and the lack of friends during the school-age years.

1. A friend is _____

2. A friend offers _____

3. Choosing school-age friends is a more selective process than for younger children because _____
_____

4. Gender often influences the selection of a school-age friend because _____
_____

5. Children with common interests usually become friends because _____
_____

6. During middle childhood, appearance influences peer acceptance because _____
_____

7. Those children who are particularly well liked by other children usually have the following characteristics:

   _____   _____   _____

   _____   _____   _____

   _____   _____   _____

   _____   _____   _____

   _____   _____   _____

   _____   _____   _____

8. Those children who tend to be rejected and avoided by their peers often have the following characteristics:

   _____   _____   _____

   _____   _____   _____

   _____   _____   _____

   _____   _____   _____

   _____   _____   _____

   _____   _____   _____

(continued)

Name_____

9. Children who have few or no friends do not receive such important benefits as _____

_____

_____

_____

10. Children without friends are likely to _____

_____

_____

_____

Handling Peer Rejection

Name _____ **Date** _____ **Period** _____

Children who feel rejected by their peers often report low self-esteem and feelings of loneliness. They have difficulty developing social skills. Coaching is one technique to help these children. Coaching involves providing some form of direct instruction. Review the following case and answer the questions that follow.

Case

Melinda appeared to be rejected by her peers. She was either ignored or avoided in the classroom and on the playground. Melinda's teacher decided to observe Melinda's behavior with her peers to see if she had the social skills necessary for successful interaction with others.

The teacher noticed that Melinda was frequently disruptive in class. Melinda also had difficulty communicating her needs and desires to others. Instead of asking other children to share or pass materials, she grabbed them. At the water fountain, she refused to wait her turn, cutting in front of others who were waiting.

1. Would Melinda benefit from being coached with some form of direct instruction for acceptable interaction with peers? Explain your answer. _____

   _____

   _____

2. If you observed Melinda grabbing materials from other children, what could you say in the way of coaching that could help Melinda learn better social skills? _____

   _____

   _____

3. If you observed Melinda cutting in front of others who are waiting in line, what could you say in the way of coaching that could help Melinda learn better social skills? _____

   _____

   _____

4. If you were Melinda's teacher, would you speak to her parents? _____

   _____

   _____

5. Why should the teacher praise socially cooperative interactions? _____

   _____

   _____

Team Sports

Benefits to children:
- They learn teamwork skills
- They learn to get along with their peers
- They benefit from the exercise
- The activities bring enjoyment
- A pattern for a healthy lifestyle begins to form

Drawbacks for children:

-

-

-

-

-

Middle Childhood

Name _____

Date _____ Period _____ Score _____

Matching: Match the following terms and identifying phrases.

_____ 1. Ability to group by common attributes.

_____ 2. Ability to understand the feelings of others.

_____ 3. Technique children use to remember information.

_____ 4. Ability to see close objects more clearly than those at a distance.

_____ 5. Using accepted rules of conduct when interacting with others.

_____ 6. Respiratory disorder that causes labored breathing, gasping, wheezing, and coughing.

_____ 7. The use of logic based on what you have seen or experienced.

_____ 8. Belief that you are a worthwhile person

_____ 9. Ability to arrange items in increasing or decreasing order based on volume, size, or weight.

_____ 10. The concept that a change in position or shape of substances does not change the quantity.

_____ 11. The view a person has of himself or herself.

_____ 12. Manipulation of ideas based on logic rather than perception.

_____ 13. Being aware of others' distress and wanting to help them.

A. asthma
B. classification
C. morality
D. compassion
E. empathy
F. rehearsal
G. self-concept
H. seriation
I. farsighted
J. conservation
K. concrete operation
L. operation
M. self-esteem
N. nearsighted

True/False: Circle *T* if the statement is true or *F* if the statement is false.

T F 14. Developmental changes are more dramatic during middle childhood than they were during infancy and toddlerhood.

T F 15. Heredity accounts for most differences in physical growth.

T F 16. By the end of middle childhood, girls may reach 90 percent of their adult height and boys about 80 percent of their adult height.

T F 17. Middle childhood is often one of the unhealthiest periods for children.

T F 18. If left untreated, ear infections can cause permanent hearing loss.

T F 19. All of the 20 primary teeth are replaced with permanent teeth by eight years of age.

T F 20. A person is considered obese when he or she weighs 15 percent more than other people of the same sex, age, and build.

(continued)

T   F   21. During middle childhood, children have better control of their small muscles than their large muscles.

T   F   22. Language skills of school-age children can improve through the use of humor.

T   F   23. Preschool children usually have lower self-esteem than school-age children.

T   F   24. Games with rules encourage children to take another person's perspective.

Multiple choice: Choose the best response. Write the letter in the space provided.

_____ 25. To remember information, children repeat information after it is used. This technique is called
                 _____.
                 A. rehearsal
                 B. seriation
                 C. concrete operations
                 D. conservation

_____ 26. During middle childhood, children usually become more _____.
                 A. self-sufficient
                 B. independent
                 C. focused on friendships
                 D. All of the above.

_____ 27. At the beginning of middle childhood, boys are usually _____ than girls.
                 A. much taller
                 B. slightly taller
                 C. shorter
                 D. much shorter

_____ 28. The number of inches children usually grow per year during early childhood is _____.
                 A. under one inch
                 B. one to two inches
                 C. two to three inches
                 D. three to four inches

_____ 29. A factor that does *not* contribute to obesity is _____.
                 A. environment
                 B. controlling portion sizes
                 C. family stress
                 D. genetics

_____ 30. The child's vocabulary _____ between the ages of six and twelve.
                 A. remains the same
                 B. doubles
                 C. triples
                 D. increases fourfold

_____ 31. Seriation can involve _____.
                 A. sequencing story events
                 B. counting pennies
                 C. pouring liquids
                 D. None of the above.

(continued)

_____ 32. The process where people define themselves in terms of the qualities, skills, and attributes they see in others is called _____.
- A. empathy
- B. social comparison
- C. self-esteem
- D. compassion

Essay Questions: Provide complete responses to the following questions or statements.

33. Describe three gender differences in peer group activities during middle childhood.

34. Name two benefits of competitive sports for school-age children and two drawbacks of competitive sports.

35. Define moral development and explain what happens during middle childhood concerning social behavior.

Preparing the Environment  8

Objectives

After studying this chapter, students will be able to
- explain the value of planned indoor and outdoor space.
- name the basic activity areas in a center, along with the functions of each area.
- list criteria to consider when choosing playroom furniture and color schemes.
- summarize factors that affect the organization of space in a center.
- organize basic activity areas of the classroom and outdoor play yard.

Teaching Materials

Text, pages 109–130
  Terms to Know
  Review and Reflect
  Apply and Explore
Student Activity Guide
  A. *Meeting the Goals of a Well-Planned Space*
  B. *Responses to Color*
  C. *Activity Areas*
Teacher's Resource Guide/Binder
  Value of Activity Areas, reproducible master, 8-1
  Permanent Fixtures and Space,
    transparency master, 8-2
  Psychological Impact of Color,
    transparency master, 8-3
  Arranging Space Crossword,
    reproducible master, 8-4
  Arranging Basic Activity Areas,
    transparency master, 8-5
  Activity Area Responsibilities,
    reproducible master, 8-6
  Chapter Test
Teacher's Resource Binder
  *In Which Activity Area Would You Place the
    Computer?* color transparency, CT-8
The Observation Guide
Mastering CDA Competencies

Introductory Activities

1. Prepare some pictures or slides of different classroom arrangements to show to the class. Ask students which ones they like and why.
2. Ask the students to think about their homes. Ask which room is their favorite. Ask what it is about that room that makes it their favorite.
3. Have the class brainstorm a list of reasons why some early childhood classrooms are more appealing than others.

Instructional Concepts and Student Learning Experiences

Value of Planned Space _____

4. *Value of Activity Areas,* reproducible master 8-1. Have students review the values listed for each activity area. Students should discuss how arrangement of the areas would enhance the ability to achieve full value in each area.
5. Have students list the goals of planning space and give an example of how each goal can be met through space arrangement.
6. Have students discuss why safety is the most important concern in planning physical space.
7. Have students observe, draw, and describe the physical space of a child care center. As a class, students should discuss how the physical space observed meets the text goals for a well-planned space.
8. Have students observe an outdoor play yard and determine how the positioning of the outdoor equipment meets goals for a well-planned space.
9. Have students discuss how physical space arrangement affects the amount of time needed to maintain the space.
10. *Meeting the Goals of a Well-Planned Space,* Activity A, SAG. Students are asked to pretend that they have been hired as the director of a new child care center. They are asked to provide input into the design of the physical space. Under each of the goals listed in the activity, students are asked to give two examples of how they would meet each goal in designing the physical space.

Physical Space

11. Have students identify and describe the seven general areas included in a center's space.
12. Have students discuss the appearance of the entrance.
13. Have students explain the best location for the director's office.
14. Have students explain the importance of the isolation area.
15. Have students discuss ways to determine the appropriate size of a center kitchen.
16. Have students discuss the relationship between the staff room and the quality of teaching and care at a center.
17. Have students describe factors that must be considered when planning bathroom space.
18. Have students discuss the relationship between the quality of playroom space and children's development.
19. Have students describe an ideal playroom.
20. Have students make a chart denoting factors to consider related to walls, floors, windows, doors, acoustics, temperature, humidity, and electrical outlets.
21. Have students discuss the importance of acoustics in the playroom.
22. *Permanent Fixtures and Space,* transparency master 8-2. Have students discuss how the arrangement of the permanent fixtures listed may affect the arrangement of playroom space. Students should discuss when they might consider changing the permanent fixtures to improve space arrangement.

Furniture

23. Have students develop a brochure on factors to consider when selecting playroom or classroom furniture.
24. Have the class survey teachers to find out what types of surfaces they prefer on chairs and tables for young children. Students should summarize their findings as a class.
25. Have students visit a store that specializes in storage units and analyze a unit that would be appropriate for a child care center. Students should draw or take a picture of the unit and write a summary of its features, quality, and price. Students should display their pictures and summaries in class.
26. Have students work in groups to develop creative materials and designs for cubbies.

Color Choices for Child Care Centers

27. *Psychological Impact of Color,* transparency master 8-3. Discuss with the students the psychological effects listed for each color on the master.

Students should note whether they agree or disagree with the effects listed. Students also should be encouraged to add other possible effects of these colors.

28. Have the class survey children to find out their color preferences. Students should discuss the survey results as a class.
29. Have students plan color schemes for classrooms. Students should justify their color selections in writing.
30. *Responses to Color,* Activity B, SAG. Students are asked to match the given colors and psychological responses. Students should then answer the questions related to use of color in the classroom.

Factors That Affect Space Organization

31. Have students discuss the importance of having organized space.
32. Have students read the licensing requirements for their state and discuss how these requirements can be met in space arrangements.
33. Have students discuss the impact of licensing on the organization of space.
34. Obtain a list of program goals from a local child care center. Have students read these goals and determine how they would affect space arrangement.
35. Have students observe a classroom and record ways in which classroom arrangement supports classroom goals.
36. Have students create a design for a classroom based on the classroom goals given in the text.
37. Have students discuss how group size affects the organization of space.
38. Have students identify classroom furniture that should be scaled to the children's level. Students should discuss the importance of having these furniture pieces scaled for children.
39. *Arranging Space Crossword,* reproducible master 8-4. Have students complete the crossword by filling in the blanks in the statements related to space arrangement.

Organizing Basic Activity Areas

40. *In Which Area Would You Place the Computer?* color transparency CT-8, TRB. Use this transparency to stimulate discussion regarding the most appropriate classroom area for placing a personal computer. You may want to follow the following suggestions:
    A. Remind students that a classroom arranged according to activity areas allows children to make their own choices.
    B. Review the four basic activity areas.
    C. Have students identify the most appropriate activity area for placing a computer.

D. Discuss the best type of table on which to place a computer for use by children.

41. *Arranging Basic Activity Areas,* transparency master 8-5. Have students place various specific activity areas as they would fall along the continuum.

42. Have students draw a room arrangement in which activities are grouped according to whether they are dry, wet, active, or quiet.

43. Have students list three ways of introducing the environment.

44. Have students explain the purpose of using labels and signs in the classroom.

45. Have students discuss the placement of the block-building, art, dramatic play, sensory, woodworking, sleeping, small manipulative, library, music, private, science, and eating areas.

46. *Activity Area Responsibilities,* reproducible master 8-6. Have students read the master and discuss the teacher's responsibilities related to each area in the classroom.

Outdoor Play Area

47. Have students create a list of resources for fencing, surfaces, and landscaping used in child care centers.

48. Have students describe the proper location, purpose, and content of a storage shed.

49. Have students discuss the physical arrangement of stationary equipment, a sandbox, a water play area, and an animal shelter.

50. *Activity Areas,* Activity C, SAG. Students are asked to list 10 basic activity areas found in most classrooms. They are then asked to name their functions and describe where each area should be placed in the classroom.

Additional Resources

51. Guest speaker. Invite an interior decorator to discuss room arrangements, color schemes, and other factors involved in designing child care centers with the class.

52. Guest speaker. Invite an architect to discuss building designs for child care centers with the class.

53. Guest speaker. Invite a licensing agent to discuss physical requirements for a child care center.

54. Field trip. Arrange for students to visit a child care center and observe colors, space arrangements, and other factors related to the physical space.

Research Topic

55. Have the student research an aspect of room arrangement, such as space, color, or furniture, and its effects on children. The student should then devise and conduct an experiment to test the effects of this aspect on children. The student should give an oral report on his or her findings.

Answer Key

Text

Review and Reflect, page 130

1. D
2. true
3. (List four:) Providing a physically safe environment for children; providing children with areas for cognitive, emotional, social, and physical growth; providing adults with a space that is easy to watch; providing space that is pleasing to the eye for both adults and children; providing easy access to materials when needed so children are able to direct themselves; encouraging children to take part in activities.
4. An isolation area is a room or space for children who become ill or show signs of a communicable disease.
5. rectangular
6. D
7. B
8. height
9. cubbie
10. A
11. purple
12. limits
13. (Student response. See pages 117–118.)
14. Yes. Too much open space encourages children to run. This can be the cause of many problems.
15. traffic patterns
16. U, L
17. music, woodworking, blockbuilding, dramatic play
18. false
19. path
20. loose material, such as bark nuggets, shredded bark, or sand

Student Activity Guide

Responses to Color, Activity B

1. F   5. C
2. A   6. E
3. B   7. D
4. G
8. Cool colors, such as blue, green, and purple, make a room look larger.
9. Warm colors, such as red, yellow, and orange, make a room look smaller.
10. (List three:) available light in the room, room size, amount of time spent in the room

Activity Areas, Activity C

1.-10. (Student response for functions and descriptions of where to locate activity areas students list.)

11. (List three:) Equipment should be far enough apart so a child using one piece of equipment cannot touch a child using another piece of equipment. All equipment should be visible to the teacher from any spot in the yard or classroom. Children should not have to walk through one area to get to another. Between ⅓ and ½ of the yard should be used for play equipment, and the remainder should be open space.

12. fences, play yard surface, landscaping, storage, wheeled toy paths, stationary equipment, sandbox, water, animals, and their shelter

Teacher's Resource Guide/Binder

Arranging Space Puzzle, reproducible master 8-4

Across:

4.	intellectual	15.	easel
6.	tables	16.	safety
7.	playroom	17.	fixture
8.	space	18.	hook
10.	noise	19.	windows
12.	simpler		

Down:

1.	convenience	9.	entrance
2.	color	11.	sand
3.	materials	13.	licensing
5.	games	14.	teachers

Chapter Test

1.	C	16.	F
2.	A	17.	T
3.	E	18.	F
4.	F	19.	T
5.	B	20.	T
6.	D	21.	C
7.	T	22.	B
8.	F	23.	D
9.	T	24.	D
10.	F	25.	C
11.	T	26.	D
12.	F	27.	B
13.	T	28.	C
14.	F	29.	B
15.	T	30.	C

31. In centers with well-planned space, teachers tend to be more friendly, sensitive, and warm to the children. These teachers tend to teach their students to respect other's rights and feelings. In centers with poorly planned space, teachers tend to be more insensitive to their students.

32. This placement saves the parent's time. Classroom disruptions will be prevented. Also, additional cleanup time will be saved during unpleasant weather.

33. (Student response.)

Value of Activity Areas

The art area helps children:

Develop positive self-concept.

Experience creative process.

Learn to express ideas and feelings.

Learn names and use tools.

Develop visual perceptual skills.

Observe color, texture, and line composition.

Learn names of colors.

Learn to identify shapes.

Develop eye-hand coordination.

Promote language development.

The blockbuilding area helps children:

Develop problem-solving skills.

Learn mathematical and spatial relationships.

Develop language skills.

Learn classification of shape and size.

Develop large and small motor skills.

Develop size and shape classification skills.

Develop basic concepts of balance, proportion, shape, and weight.

Develop organization skills

The dramatic play area helps children:

Develop self-expression skills.

Develop sensitivity to peers.

Learn to interpret facial expressions, gestures, and tone of voice.

Develop an understanding of various roles.

Develop social relationships.

Improve self-image.

(continued)

The library helps children:

Increase vocabulary.

Increase appreciation of the printed word.

Develop listening skills.

Develop appreciation of ideas presented by others.

Learn care of books.

The science area helps children:

Develop observation skills.

Develop new vocabulary.

Practice classification skills.

Practice prediction skills.

Develop an understanding of the biological and physical environments.

The small manipulative area helps children:

Practice following directions.

Practice problem solving.

Increase visual perception skills.

Learn to take turns.

Observe likenesses and differences in objects.

Practice sorting and classification skills.

Practice matching colors, sizes, shapes, and similar objects.

The music area helps children:

Develop positive self-concepts.

Express feelings.

Learn names and sounds of instruments.

Develop language skills.

Practice listening skills by differentiating sounds.

Experience creative process.

Permanent Fixtures and Space

The location of all permanent fixtures must be studied before arranging space. These include:

- ◆ Doors
- ◆ Windows
- ◆ Electrical outlets
- ◆ Closet or storage space
- ◆ Sinks
- ◆ Shelf space
- ◆ Counters
- ◆ Carpeted and tiled areas

Psychological Impact of Color

Color	Psychological Impact
White	Clean Pure Frank Cool Youthful
Light Blue	Comfortable Soothing Secure Tender
Light Green	Calm Refreshing Peaceful Restful
Yellow	Happy Cheerful
Orange	Welcoming Forceful Energetic
Red	Welcoming Energetic Forceful Stimulating
Purple	Mournful

Arranging Space Crossword

Name _____ Date _____ Period _____

Across

4. A child's early years are critical for _____ development.

5. _____ should be light enough to be moved.

7. The _____ should be flexible and livable for children and adults.

8. Well-planned _____ is arranged based on children's developmental needs and interests, and on program goals.

10. The classroom _____ level can have a dramatic effect on children's behavior.

12. The lower the number of caregivers, the _____ the room arrangement should be.

15. To see if a(n) _____ is at the appropriate height, have the child stand next to it.

16. For _____ purposes, the water heater should be set on low heat.

17. The size of the toilet _____ will vary with the size and age of the children.

18. Each locker should have a _____ to hang the child's coat.

19. _____ should be placed so the children can view the outdoors.

Down

1. The arrangement of space should be designed for staff _____.

2. Draperies can add interest and _____.

3. An attractive, well arranged environment encourages children to use _____.

5. _____, art supplies, books, and blocks should be stored in storage units.

9. The center's _____ should be attractive and appealing to children and adults.

11. Carpeting, draperies, bulletin boards, and a _____ box can all be used to reduce noise.

13. Most state _____ rules require special space to isolate an ill child.

14. The _____ behavior is directly affected by the quality of space.

(continued)

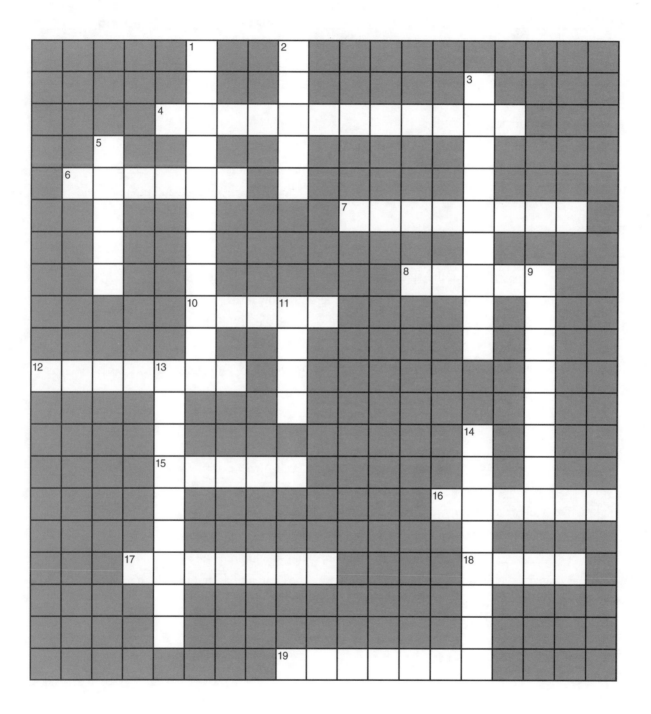

Small manipulative area

A. Clear all papers, toys, etc., from tops of shelves.
B. Sort small manipulative materials each day and place in their proper trays.
C. Place trays individually on gliders/shelves.
D. Check puzzles daily for missing pieces. If a piece is missing, report this to the director.

Book area

A. Remove and repair all damaged books.
B. Place books neatly, with covers forward, on the shelves.

Music area

A. Keep top of piano neat and free from clutter.
B. Stack or place musical instruments and equipment on shelves.
C. Place records in the proper record jackets, or CDs in proper boxes.
D. Double check at the end of program to make sure record or CD player is turned off.

Science area

A. Organize and dust science table(s) daily.
B. Clean aquarium or other animal cages as needed.

Eating area

A. Wash tables and chairs daily.
B. Sweep and wash floor daily.

Lockers or clothes cart

A. Place boots neatly in the children's lockers.
B. Return name tags to a shelf or a basket.
C. Clear tops of lockers except for lab teacher's materials in one corner.

Kitchen area and storage room

A. Straighten shelves daily.
B. Scour sinks daily.
C. Organize cupboards; dust once each week.
D. Notify the director or cook when supplies are needed.
E. Remove soiled dish towels and dishcloths on a daily basis.
F. Remove nonfood items from the refrigerator.

Care of carpeting

A. Clean spots of paint, milk, paste, etc., immediately.
B. Report all spots to the janitor or director.

Outdoor

A. Pick up all litter including paper, cans, and twigs daily.
B. Return all movable equipment to the classroom or storage shed after outdoor playtime.

Preparing the Environment

Name _____

Date _____ **Period** _____ **Score** _____

Matching: Match the following terms and identifying phrases.

_____ 1. Should be separated from the playroom and contain a cot and a few toys.

_____ 2. Includes carpets, draperies, and pillows.

_____ 3. Ways people move through the classroom area.

_____ 4. Contains the sensory table.

_____ 5. Contains the library.

_____ 6. Includes jungle gyms, slides, and tree houses.

A. acoustic materials
B. dry/quiet area
C. isolation area
D. stationary equipment
E. traffic patterns
F. wet/dry area

True/False: Circle *T* if the statement is true or *F* if the statement is false.

T   F   7. The organization of the classroom provides clues about expected behavior.

T   F   8. The organization of space does not influence the quality of learning.

T   F   9. The classroom should be planned with goals in mind.

T   F   10. For privacy, the director's office should be as far as possible from the entrance.

T   F   11. Most state licensing rules specify the number of fire extinguishers needed.

T   F   12. The recommended indoor space usually varies between 20 to 35 square feet of space per child.

T   F   13. In centers with high quality space, teachers tend to be more friendly.

T   F   14. To prevent injuries, classroom doors should always open to the inside.

T   F   15. Carpeting provides a sound cushion.

T   F   16. An easel is the appropriate height if the child can touch the top of the easel pad.

T   F   17. When sitting on a chair, the child should be able to place his or her feet flat on the floor.

T   F   18. Most preschool teachers prefer round tables.

T   F   19. In crowded spaces, children cry and fight more.

T   F   20. To promote independence, materials and equipment should be easily accessible to children.

Multiple Choice: Choose the best response. Write the letter in the space provided.

_____ 21. For two-year-old children, toilet fixtures generally are _____ high.
A. fifteen inches
B. twelve inches
C. ten inches
D. eight inches

(continued)

_____ 22. This color provides a happy and cheerful psychological response _____.
   A. red
   B. yellow
   C. green
   D. blue

_____ 23. The psychological response to purple is _____.
   A. pure
   B. youthful
   C. sterile
   D. mournful

_____ 24. Shades of colors children prefer up to age six include _____.
   A. blue and green
   B. purple and blue
   C. purple and green
   D. orange and red

_____ 25. The best play yard surface is made of _____.
   A. blacktop
   B. cement
   C. loose material
   D. bricks

_____ 26. The wheel toy path should be adjacent to the _____.
   A. classroom door
   B. outdoor fence
   C. utility entrance
   D. storage shed

_____ 27. Which of the following is not considered stationary equipment?
   A. Jungle gyms.
   B. Tricycles.
   C. Tree houses.
   D. Slides.

_____ 28. The sandbox is best placed near _____.
   A. the classroom door
   B. playground fence
   C. a water source
   D. None of the above.

_____ 29. The best shaped playground is _____.
   A. S-shaped
   B. a rectangle
   C. L-shaped
   D. U-shaped

_____ 30. The amount of play yard covered with equipment should not exceed _____.
   A. one-quarter
   B. three-quarters
   C. one-half
   D. one-eighth

Essay Questions: Provide complete responses to the following questions or statements.

31. How does the arrangement of space in a center affect the teacher's behavior?

32. Why should children's lockers be placed near the entrance of the child care center?

33. Choose an activity area and explain its optimum arrangement and location.

Selecting Toys, Equipment, and Educational Materials

9

Objectives

After studying this chapter, students will be able to
- explain guidelines for selecting developmentally appropriate toys, equipment, and educational toys.
- describe safety factors to consider when purchasing toys and play yard equipment.
- explain how to report unsafe toys and equipment to the appropriate agencies.
- list sources and methods for purchasing toys and equipment.

Teaching Materials

Text, pages 131–146
 Terms to Know
 Review and Reflect
 Apply and Explore
Student Activity Guide
 A. *Toys Meeting Goals*
 B. *Age Appropriate Equipment*
 C. *Actions to Take*
 D. *Comparing Prices*
Teacher's Resource Guide/Binder
 Equipment Construction: Advantages and Disadvantages, transparency master, 9-1
 Toy and Equipment Worksheet, reproducible master, 9-2
 Selecting Toys and Equipment, reproducible master, 9-3
 Criteria for Selecting Materials and Equipment, transparency master, 9-4
 Play Yard Equipment Dangers, transparency masters, 9-5A and B
 Chapter Test
Teacher's Resource Binder
 Selecting Computer Software, color transparency, CT-9
The Observation Guide
Mastering CDA Competencies

Introductory Activities

1. Ask students to identify toys that they liked and enjoyed when they were younger. Ask what appealed to them about the toys.
2. Have the class discuss what they think makes a toy interesting to a child.
3. Make a display of a variety of toys from toy catalogs. Ask students to determine whether each toy is safe for children age two, three, or four. Students should explain their reasoning.

Instructional Concepts and Student Learning Experiences

Selection Criteria

4. Have students identify and discuss criteria for selecting toys and equipment.
5. Have students discuss possible consequences of not planning toy and equipment purchases carefully.
6. Have students explain the relationship between program goals and classroom equipment and materials.
7. *Toys Meeting Goals,* Activity A, SAG. Have students complete the charts by listing toys that are appropriate for various classroom goals.
8. Have students explain the importance of considering space when purchasing equipment.
9. Have students define the term *supervision.*
10. Have students discuss how the selection of toys is related to supervision.
11. Have students discuss how considering maintenance before purchasing toys and equipment can save time later. Students should discuss how the time saved can be used for other program efforts. Point out to students that the time saved may, in some cases, justify buying equipment that is higher in price, but requires less maintenance.
12. Have students evaluate three pieces of equipment that are similar in function, but different in construction. The students should determine which item would require the least maintenance and explain why.

13. *Equipment Construction: Advantages and Disadvantages*, transparency master 9-1. Use this master to help students determine the advantages and disadvantages of various types of equipment construction. Ask students to describe examples of various types of equipment made of metal, plastic, or wood.

14. Have students explain the importance of choosing durable toys.

15. Have students differentiate between quantity and quality.

16. Have students visit a local child care center and make a list of toys available for children there.

17. Have students analyze Chart 9-4 and discuss whether they would add to or subtract from the specific items listed and why.

18. Have students give examples of toys that encourage children to explore, manipulate, and create.

19. Have students name five types of open-ended toys.

20. Have students discuss the benefits to children of playing with open-ended toys.

21. Have students compile a chart listing toys that are appropriate for children of different ages.

22. *Age Appropriate Equipment,* Activity B, SAG. Have students match the toys listed with the ages of the youngest children who should use them.

23. *Toy and Equipment Worksheet,* reproducible master 9-2. Have students complete the worksheet by listing equipment appropriate for various types of development.

24. Have students choose a toy and write a paragraph describing how it promotes various types of development.

25. Have students work in groups to develop skits on the teacher's role in conveying ideas related to violence and toys, and equality and toys. The groups should share their skits with the class.

26. Have students make a list of sources of safety information for teachers.

Selecting Safe Toys

27. Have students describe the best toys for children.

28. Have students evaluate toys according to the guidelines for selecting safe toys given in the text.

29. Have students make a display of safe and appropriate toys for children of various ages. (Catalog pictures can be used in place of actual toys.)

30. Have students develop a brochure for teachers on tips for selecting toys.

Selecting Play Yard Equipment

31. Have students observe a play yard and evaluate the safety of the equipment in it.

32. Have students list and describe the nine basic play yard equipment dangers.

33. Have students examine a swing set and identify its safety features.

34. *Actions to Take,* Activity C, SAG. Have students complete the chart by listing actions they can take to improve the toy or equipment features listed.

35. *Selecting Toys and Equipment,* reproducible master 9-3. Have students complete statements about selecting toys and equipment by filling in the blanks.

36. *Criteria for Selecting Materials and Equipment,* transparency master 9-4. Review the criteria listed with the class. Then have them use the checklist to evaluate a toy as a class, or have each student evaluate a toy or piece of equipment individually.

Reporting Unsafe Products

37. *Play Yard Equipment Dangers,* transparency master 9-5A and B. Review the play yard equipment dangers that can cause harm to children.

38. Have students describe the process of reporting unsafe products.

39. Bring actual examples of unsafe toys to class. Have students write a letter reporting the unsafe product(s).

Sources for Toys and Equipment

40. Have students look through equipment catalogs and note the variety of equipment available.

41. Have students compare prices of equipment from different sources. Discuss the reasons for cost differences among different vendors.

42. *Comparing Prices,* Activity D, SAG. Have students complete the charts by comparing prices of different items from three different sources.

43. Have students discuss different approaches for obtaining consumable supplies.

44. *Selecting Computer Software*, color transparency CT-9, TRB. Use this transparency to introduce criteria for selecting computer software for preschool children. You may want to:
   A. Remind students that preschool children lack the skills to read directions required for many computer programs.
   B. Ask students to share their personal observations of children using computer programs.
   C. Discuss the criteria for selecting appropriate computer software.
   D. Ask the students to identify computer software topics that would be developmentally appropriate for preschool children.

Additional Resources

45. Panel discussion. Invite a panel of parents of children ages two through five to discuss how they choose toys for their children.

46. Guest speaker. Invite a director or teacher from a child care center to discuss toy and equipment safety.
47. Field trip. Arrange for the class to visit a preschool supplier or toy store to assess toys for children.
48. Guest speaker. Invite an early childhood program director to discuss toy and equipment maintenance.

Research Topic

49. Have students research an aspect of toy safety or toy appeal. Students should then develop and conduct an experiment related to the aspect studied. Have students report the results of the study to the class.

Answer Key

Text

Review and Reflect, page 146

1. True.
2. (Student response. See page 132.)
3. program goals
4. Space must be available for the item purchased. If space is not available, the item may end up in an inconvenient location and seldom used.
5. false
6. D
7. If there is a shortage of play materials, undesirable behavior can result.
8. spectator
9. Physical age is determined by a birthdate. Developmental age refers to a child's skill and growth level compared to what is thought of as normal for that physical age.
10. Suitable toys help build self-esteem. Unsuitable toys can cause frustration.
11. B
12. Multicultural toys represent a variety of racial and ethnic groups.
13. false
14. (List three. Student response.)
15. a. Rings that are between five and ten inches in diameter can trap a child's head.
    b. Wooden swing seats can injure a child who might walk in the path of them.
    c. Screws and bolts can scratch and/or cut children.
    d. Unanchored equipment is in danger of overturning, tipping, sliding, or moving.

16. resilient tiles, wood mulch, fine sand, and fine gravel. (Also bark nuggets or shredded bark.)
17. A consumable supply is an item that, once used, cannot be used again.

Student Activity Guide

Toys Meeting Goals, Activity A

Goal A: Puppets, books, cassettes, CDs, alphabet cards, pictures, pencils, paper. (Other responses are possible.)

Goal B: Lacing cards, pegs and peg boards, small table blocks, dominoes, hammers and nails. (Other responses are possible.)

(Student response for second chart.)

Age Appropriate Equipment, Activity B

1. A
2. F
3. B
4. B
5. C
6. B
7. B
8. C
9. C
10. B
11. C
12. F
13. B
14. B
15. C
16. D
17. D
18. E
19. C
20. C

Actions to Take, Activity C

1. Provide a fresh coat of paint.
2. Sand and apply a fresh coat of varnish.
3. Tighten the nuts.
4. Sand and repaint the equipment.
5. Oil the wheels.
6. Discard the broken toy.
7. Cut off the cord and plug.
8. Remove from the classroom.
9. Remove from the classroom.
10. Remove from the classroom.
11. Pinch the "S" ring closed with pliers.
12. Remove the button eyes. Glue on pieces of black felt to represent eyes or stitch with black yarn.
13. Remove from the classroom immediately.
14. Replace with a lightweight material such as plastic or canvas.
15. Attach a plastic protective cap or tape.

Teacher's Resource Guide/Binder

Selecting Toys and Equipment,
reproducible master 9-3

1. goals
2. variety
3. balls
4. care
5. safe
6. durable
7. corners
8. metal
9. tension
10. two
11. music
12. glass
13. water
14. involve
15. limits
16. blocks
17. spectator
18. electrical
19. height
20. low

1. E   16. T
2. D   17. T
3. A   18. F
4. C   19. T
5. B   20. C
6. T   21. B
7. F   22. D
8. T   23. D
9. F   24. C
10. T   25. C
11. T   26. B
12. F   27. A
13. F   28. A
14. T   29. D
15. T

30. Children learn very little from toy guns. Also, aggressive behavior can result from having toy guns in the classroom.

31. Include a wide range of characteristic features and skin tones when choosing puppets, puzzles, and dolls. Also, pictures and books should represent different cultures.

32. (Student response. See pages 142–145.)

Equipment Construction: Advantages and Disadvantages

Type of Construction	Advantages	Disadvantages
Metal structures	◆ durable ◆ require less maintenance ◆ available in a variety of colors	◆ expensive ◆ subject to rust ◆ cold in winter, hot in summer, and slippery in damp weather
Plastic structures	◆ require minimal area ◆ less expensive ◆ colorful ◆ available in unique designs and shapes	◆ may lack structural integrity ◆ elements of weather may cause problem in durability
Wood structures	◆ less expensive ◆ aesthetically pleasing ◆ biodegradable	◆ require ongoing maintenance ◆ may present danger of splinters to children ◆ toxic chemicals are used in treating some wood

Toy and Equipment Worksheet

Name _____ **Date** _____ **Period** _____

List six pieces of equipment for large muscle development.

1. _____
2. _____
3. _____
4. _____
5. _____
6. _____

List eight pieces of equipment for language development.

1. _____
2. _____
3. _____
4. _____
5 _____
6. _____
7. _____
8. _____

List five pieces of equipment for small muscle development.

1. _____
2. _____
3. _____
4. _____
5. _____

List six pieces of equipment for social development.

1. _____
2. _____

(continued)

3. _____

4. _____

5. _____

6. _____

List four pieces of equipment for emotional development.

1. _____

2. _____

3. _____

4. _____

List six pieces of equipment for intellectual development.

1. _____

2. _____

3. _____

4. _____

5. _____

6. _____

Selecting Toys and Equipment

Name _____ **Date** _____ **Period** _____

Complete the statements about selecting toys and equipment by filling in the blanks.

_____   1. Classroom equipment should compliment program _____.

_____   2. Children need a balance and _____ of equipment.

_____   3. Choose large rubber _____ to help encourage large motor development.

_____   4. Aluminum outdoor equipment requires less _____ because it is weatherproof.

_____   5. Toys that break easily are not _____.

_____   6. Wood toys are generally more _____ than plastic toys.

_____   7. _____ should be rounded on all wooden toys.

_____   8. _____ toys should not be chosen for the sandbox as they may rust.

_____   9. Too few materials selected for the classroom can cause (sharing, tension) _____

_____   10. Generally teachers select _____ easels for the art area.

_____   11. An Autoharp® should be selected for the _____ area.

_____   12. A magnifying _____ should be selected for the science area.

_____   13. Funnels, strainers, and egg beaters should be selected for the _____ play area.

_____   14. Select toys that actively _____ the children.

_____   15. Too much detail (limits, expands) _____ the child's imagination.

_____   16. Playdough, paint, sand, and _____ are open-ended toys.

_____   17. _____ toys usually have brief appeal.

_____   18. _____ toys should never be purchased.

_____   19. When selecting outdoor equipment, consider the (height, weight) _____ of the children.

_____   20. (High, Low) _____ slides should be purchased.

Criteria for Selecting Materials and Equipment

	Yes	No
1. Does it complement the program?		
2. Does it add balance to existing materials and equipment?		
3. Is it suitable for available classroom space?		
4. Does it require a minimum of supervision?		
5. Is it easy to maintain?		
6. Is it durable?		
7. Is there a sufficient quantity?		
8. Does it involve the child?		
9. Is it developmentally appropriate?		
10. Is it nonviolent?		
11. Is it multicultural?		
12. Is it nonsexist?		
13. Is it safe?		

Play Yard Equipment Dangers

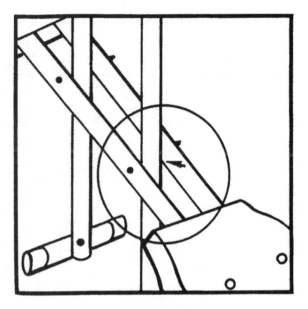

Pinch-Crush Parts

Moving parts particularly on gliders and seesaws can pinch or crush fingers.

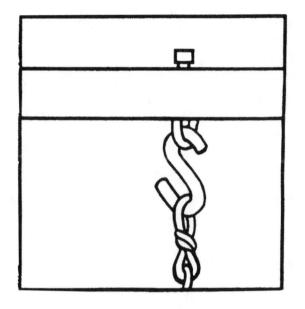

"S" Hooks

Open-ended hooks, especially the "S" hooks on swings which can catch skin or clothing, should be avoided. If a set has such hooks, pinch the ends in tightly with a pair of pliers.

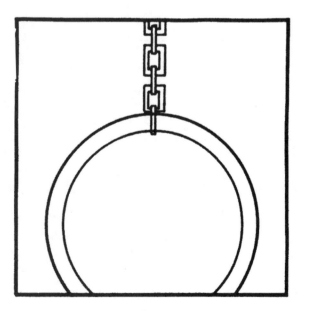

Rings

Swinging exercise rings with a diameter between five and ten inches can entrap a child's head. Remove such rings and discard them where children will not find and play with them.

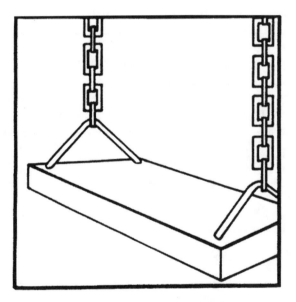

Hard, Heavy Swing Seats

Hard, heavy swing seats can strike a dangerous blow. Choose a set with lightweight seats or purchase such seats separately and replace the hard seats. Metal seats should have smooth, rolled edges.

Source: U.S. Consumer Product Safety Commission

Play Yard Equipment Dangers

Inadequate Spacing

Install the set a minimum of six feet away from fences, building walls, walkways, and other play areas such as sandboxes.

Hard Surfaces

Do not install the set over hard surfaces such as concrete, brick, blacktop, or cinders. Grass or sand is better.

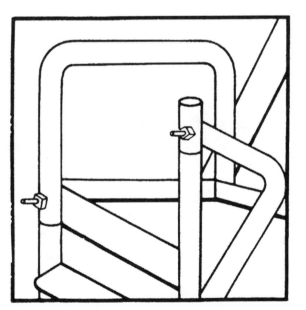

Exposed Screws and Bolts

Most sets include protective caps to cover screws and bolts. When protective caps are not included, tape over all exposed screws and bolts, even those which appear to be out of the child's reach.

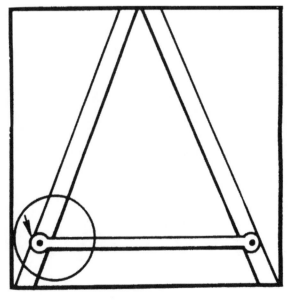

Sharp Edges

Some sets have sharp edges on points where the parts fit together. Tape over these areas with heavy tape and inspect the taped areas regularly for weather damage.

Source: U.S. Consumer Product Safety Commission

Selecting Toys, Equipment, and Educational Materials

Chapter **9** Test

Name _____

Date _____ Period _____ Score _____

Matching: Match the following terms and identifying phrases.

_____ 1. Tend to be costly and have brief appeal with children.

_____ 2. Free children to use their minds and express their creativity.

_____ 3. Determined by a birthdate.

_____ 4. Determined by a child's skill and growth level.

_____ 5. In most cases, can only be used once.

A. chronological age
B. consumable supplies
C. developmental age
D. open-ended toys
E. spectator toys

True/False: Circle *T* if the statement is true or *F* if the statement is false.

T F 6. Toys help children make choices.

T F 7. Toys should be selected on the basis of the child's chronological age.

T F 8. When planning the selection of toys, consideration must be given to storage space.

T F 9. Purchases should include toys that promote war and traditional roles.

T F 10. A toy that is safe for one child may be unsafe for another.

T F 11. Care requirements should be a consideration when choosing equipment.

T F 12. A broken toy is a safe toy.

T F 13. Toys constructed out of plastic are usually purchased for preschool programs.

T F 14. Too few materials can cause tension.

T F 15. Equipment and materials should be rotated on a regular basis to satisfy the child's demand for variety.

T F 16. Good toys stimulate the child's imagination.

T F 17. Research shows that violent behavior is increased by the mere sight of a gun.

T F 18. Only a few electrical toys should be included in an early childhood program.

T F 19. Equipment should not exceed twice the height of the children.

(continued)

Multiple Choice: Choose the best response. Write the letter in the space provided.

_____ 20. Good materials should be _____.
   A. sexist
   B. violent
   C. safe
   D. culturally biased

_____ 21. Toys for promoting sensory exploration include _____.
   A. balance boards
   B. drums
   C. bicycles
   D. boxes

_____ 22. Which toy would not promote language development?
   A. Puppet.
   B. Book.
   C. Picture.
   D. Walking beam.

_____ 23. Studies show that children who have been exposed to a wide variety of toys are _____.
   A. bored
   B. anxious
   C. unfulfilled
   D. creative

_____ 24. To encourage a child's creativity and imagination, a toy should _____.
   A. be elaborote
   B. have many details
   C. be simple
   D. be battery powered

_____ 25. For what age should unit wooden blocks be added to the class?
   A. Six months to one year of age.
   B. One year to two years.
   C. Two years to three years.
   D. Four years to five years.

_____ 26. A large proportion of accidents are caused by _____.
   A. puppets
   B. jungle gyms
   C. dolls
   D. blocks

_____ 27. Consumable supplies include _____.
   A. paint
   B. blocks
   C. puzzles
   D. lacing cards

_____ 28. At which age are children most vulnerable to playground equipment injuries?
   A. Five.
   B. Four.
   C. Three.
   D. Two.

(continued)

_____ 29. Choose outdoor equipment that has _____.
   A. open "S" rings
   B. exercise rings over seven inches in diameter
   C. sharp edges
   D. durable construction

Essay Questions: Provide complete responses to the following questions or statements.

30. Why should toy guns be avoided in the classroom?

31. How can racial and ethnic groups be represented in the classroom?

32. Give some general guidelines for selecting play yard equipment.

Promoting Children's Safety  10

Objectives

After studying this chapter, students will be able to
- list objectives for maintaining a safe environment for children.
- describe guidelines to follow for promoting children's safety.
- name the types of fires and the fire extinguishers used to fight them.
- outline the procedures for treating poisonings.
- recognize the signs of child abuse.
- teach children how to resist child abuse.
- explain types of liability as a child care provider.

Teaching Materials

Text, pages 147–160
  Terms to Know
  Review and Reflect
  Apply and Explore
Student Activity Guide
  A. *Safety Procedures*
  B. *Fire Safety Evaluation*
  C. *Understanding Child Abuse*
Teacher's Resource Guide/Binder
  Guiding Children's Safety Crossword,
   reproducible master 10-1
  You Are Liable, transparency master, 10-2
  Chapter Test
Teacher's Resource Binder
  Equipment Dangers, color transparency, CT-10
The Observation Guide
Mastering CDA Competencies

Introductory Activities

1. Have students discuss reasons why safety should be the highest priority in the classroom.
2. Have students think of preschool children they know. Students should discuss traits of these children that could make keeping them safe difficult.
3. *Safety Procedures,* Activity A, SAG. As a pretest, have students complete the safety statements using the terms listed.

Instructional Concepts and Student Learning Experiences

Safety Objectives

4. Have students discuss the importance of each of the safety objectives listed in the text.
5. Have students make posters illustrating one of the safety objectives listed in the text.
6. Have students discuss possible consequences of not following through on safety objectives.
7. *Equipment Dangers*, color transparency CT-10, TRB. Use this transparency to help students recognize equipment dangers associated with large, outdoor play equipment. You may want to do some or all of the following:
   A. Remind students that heavy, wooden swing seats can strike a dangerous blow to a child.
   B. Ask the students to identify how pinch-crush parts on gliders or seesaws can pinch fingers.
   C. Discuss why protective caps are needed to cover screws and bolts on outdoor play equipment.
   D. Stress the importance of using pliers to pinch closed the ends of open-end S-rings on play equipment to avoid catching children's skin or clothing.
8. Have students write clear, simple safety rules stated in a language children can understand.
9. Have each student make a poster designed to remind children of a safety rule.
10. Have students role-play situations in which they must enforce safety rules with reluctant children.
11. Have students create a brochure on toy safety in the classroom.
12. Have students create a checklist for checking play yard equipment. Students should use the form to check a local play yard.
13. Have students find out how to use fire extinguishers and give a demonstration to the class.
14. *Fire Safety Evaluation*, Activity B, SAG. Have students use the fire safety checklist to evaluate a center classroom for fire safety.
15. Have students design an evacuation chart for a classroom.

16. Have students list the five steps in evacuating a classroom.
17. Have students make a list of ways to prevent falls and cuts in the classroom.
18. Have students identify the treatments for various poisonous substances.
19. *Guiding Children's Safety Crossword,* reproducible master 10-1. Have students complete the crossword by filling in the blanks in the statements about guiding children's safety.

Child Abuse

20. Have students explain the role of the teacher in identifying and reporting child abuse.
21. Have students name and discuss the four types of abuse.
22. Have students describe signs of neglected children.
23. *Understanding Child Abuse,* Activity C, SAG. Have students use the text, other reference materials, and their own opinions to answer the questions related to child abuse.
24. Have students describe the teacher's role in teaching children about sexual assault.
25. Have students explain the importance of encouraging children to "yell and tell."
26. Have students prepare a puppet play using the "what if" game.

Liability

27. Have students discuss the primary role of the staff in a child care center.
28. Have students describe the types of liability to which a child care center is subject.
29. *You Are Liable,* transparency master 10-2. Use the master as a basis for discussion of child care personnel liability.
30. Obtain a copy of the licensing requirements for your state. Have the class review the requirements and list actions preschool personnel can be liable for failing to perform.
31. Have students explain the importance of constant supervision.
32. Have students role-play situations in which the "teacher" practices giving constant supervision and the "children" show lack of judgment.
33. Have students find out the maximum number of children allowed in a child care group and the minimum number of staff per children allowed in a child care group in your state.
34. Have students debate the necessity of staff/child ratio requirements.

Additional Resources

35. Guest speaker. Invite an automotive technician to discuss car, van, and bus safety with the class.

36. Guest speaker. Invite a local fire chief to discuss fire safety for the classroom with the class.
37. Field trip. Arrange for the class to visit the emergency room of a local hospital. Ask a doctor to discuss emergency procedures for poisonous substances.
38. Panel discussion. Invite a child psychologist, a social worker, and a state or local law enforcement agent to discuss the teacher's role in reporting and caring for child abuse victims.

Research Topic

39. Have students research methods used for testing the safety of toys. Students should then test five toys for safety and report their findings to the class.

Answer Key

Text

Review and Reflect, page 160

1. (Name four. See page 148.)
2. The primary role of the staff is to ensure the safety and health of the children in their care.
3. true
4. more
5. Keep fire extinguishers in the kitchen, in or just outside the classroom, and in the laundry area.
6. a. Class C. Use a purple K, standard, or multi purpose dry chemical extinguisher.
   b. Class A. Use a water type or multipurpose dry chemical extinguisher.
   c. Class B. Use a purple K, standard, or multi-purpose dry chemical extinguisher.
   d. Class B. (due to the paint) Use a multipurpose dry chemical extinguisher.
7. true
8. decals
9. true
10. An emetic is a substance that, when swallowed, will cause vomiting.
11. The four types of child abuse are nonaccidental physical injury, neglect, emotional abuse, and sexual abuse.
12. (List three. Student response.)
13. (List three. See pages 157–158.)
14. false

Student Activity Guide

Safety Procedures, Activity A

1. dangers
2. environment
3. rules
4. evacuation
5. child abuse
6. fire extinguishers
7. seat belts
8. protection education

9. food
10. physical
11. self-control
12. electrical
13. walk

14. spills
15. glass
16. fire drills
17. windows

Teacher's Resource Guide/Binder

Guiding Children's Safety,

reproducible master, 10-1

Across:

1. preventable
5. girls
6. emetic
8. liability
12. slippery
13. mistletoe
14. out

Down:

2. report
3. abuse
4. privacy
7. neglected
9. tickle
10. soft
11. five
13. mental

Chapter Test

1. A	16. F
2. F	17. T
3. C	18. T
4. B	19. F
5. E	20. F
6. D	21. T
7. F	22. F
8. T	23. C
9. F	24. B
10. T	25. D
11. T	26. C
12. T	27. B
13. T	28. B
14. T	29. D
15. T	30. D

31. (Student response. See page 148.)
32. (Student response. See page 153.)
33. (List three.) wearing clothing that is too small or dirty; wearing clothes that are inappropriate for the weather; being poorly groomed; being too thin or malnourished; being constantly fatigued or ill

Guiding Children's Safety Crossword

Name _____ Date_____ Period _____

Across

1. In a preschool, most accidents are _____.
5. _____ are sexually assaulted more often than boys.
6. A(n) _____ is a substance that provokes vomiting.
8. Teachers are provided immunity from _____ if abuse is reported in good faith.
12. Floors should not be _____.
13. _____ is poisonous.
14. When the fire truck arrives, report whether everyone is _____ of the building.

Down

2. Every center needs accident _____ forms.
3. Children do not lie about child _____.
4. The _____ law is designed to protect children.
7. A (n) _____ child has not been provided many of the basic necessities in life.
9. To induce vomiting, _____ the back of the child's throat with your finger.
10. Playground surfaces should be _____ whenever possible.
11. Children under _____ years of age account for almost two-thirds of poisonings.
13. Emotional abuse can cause _____ injury to the child.

You Are Liable

Preschool personnel can be liable for failing to:

♦ require a health form signed by a licensed physician for each child

♦ require a staff member to obtain an approved physical for working with children

♦ provide safe indoor and outdoor equipment

♦ operate a center with the required number of adults

♦ provide adequate supervision

♦ provide proper food storage

♦ maintain fence and door locks in proper condition

♦ provide staff with information on children's special needs including visual problems, hearing problems, allergies, epilepsy, emotional problems, or family problems

♦ refrain from corporal punishment

♦ provide a safe building

♦ remove a child who lacks self control and is dangerous to others as well as himself or herself

♦ cover electrical outlets

Guiding Children's Safety

Name _____

Date _____ Period _____ Score _____

Matching: Match the following terms and identifying phrases.

_____ 1. Substance that induces vomiting.

_____ 2. Formal document outlining the law.

_____ 3. Not giving children the basic needs of life.

_____ 4. Mental harm to a child's self-concept.

_____ 5. Includes fondling and indecent exposure.

_____ 6. Designed to protect children.

A. emetic
B. emotional abuse
C. neglect
D. privacy law
E. sexual abuse
F. statute

True/False: Circle *T* if the statement is true or *F* if the statement is false.

T   F   7. There are limited dangers in a child care center.

T   F   8. Most accidents are preventable in a child care center.

T   F   9. Children should only be left unattended for very short periods of time.

T   F   10. Education is a secondary function in an early childhood program.

T   F   11. Directors are always responsible for the acts of their employees.

T   F   12. Center personnel can be liable for improper food storage.

T   F   13. Center directors should constantly be supervising the environment to ensure that it is safe.

T   F   14. To properly supervise children, keep your back facing a wall.

T   F   15. If not reminded, children will ignore or forget rules.

T   F   16. Younger children should be organized in larger groups.

T   F   17. Balloons can cause suffocation.

T   F   18. Classroom lights should be left on during a fire.

T   F   19. A child is more likely to get cut from falling on grass than blacktop.

T   F   20. Two-thirds of poisonings occur in children under three years of age.

T   F   21. Preschool teachers may have to testify in court after making a child abuse report.

T   F   22. Parents should have limited access to all their child's records maintained by the center.

(continued)

Multiple Choice: Choose the best response. Write the letter in the space provided.

_____ 23. Electrical fires are classified as _____.
   A. class A fires
   B. class B fires
   C. class C fires
   D. class D fires

_____ 24. Class B fires involve _____.
   A. paper
   B. grease
   C. wood
   D. plastics

_____ 25. Class A fires do *not* include _____.
   A. fabrics
   B. paper
   C. plastics
   D. paints

_____ 26. Water-type extinguishers should be used in _____ fires.
   A. gases
   B. grease
   C. paper
   D. paints

_____ 27. Emotional abuse includes _____.
   A. burns
   B. insufficient love
   C. bruises
   D. lack of food

_____ 28. Neglect includes _____.
   A. refusing to talk
   B. inadequate medical care
   C. bruising
   D. burning

_____ 29. The percentage of strangers who are children's offenders range from _____.
   A. 90 to 95 percent
   B. 75 to 80 percent
   C. 40 to 50 percent
   D. 10 to 15 percent

_____ 30. The privacy law is designed to protect _____.
   A. teachers
   B. parents
   C. directors
   D. children

Essay Questions: Provide complete responses to the following questions or statements.

31. List four safety objectives.

32. Explain the six steps in evacuating a building.

33. Give three signs that a child is being neglected.

Planning Nutritious Meals and Snacks  11

Objectives

After studying this chapter, students will be able to
- list goals for a good nutrition program.
- explain the importance of a healthy diet.
- describe nutritional problems that can result from a poor diet.
- name the food groups in the Food Guide Pyramid and the main nutrients they supply.
- plan nutritious and appealing meals and snacks for children.

Teaching Materials

Text, pages 161–173
  Terms to Know
  Reflect and Review
  Apply and Explore
Student Activity Guide
  A. *Nutrients and Their Functions*
  B. *Nutrition Crossword*
  C. *Food Guide Pyramid*
Teacher's Resource Guide/Binder
  Nutrition Program Goals, transparency master, 11-1
  Fruit and Vegetable Sources of Vitamin A, Vitamin C, and Iron, reproducible master, 11-2
  The Food Guide Pyramid, transparency master, 11-3
  Breakfast, transparency master, 11-4
  Breakfast Foods Children Can Easily Make, reproducible master, 11-5
  Snacks, transparency master, 11-6
  Choosing Healthy Snacks, reproducible master, 11-7
  Lunch, transparency master, 11-8
  Chapter Test
Teacher's Resource Binder
  Food Guide Pyramid: A Guide to Daily Food Choices, color transparency, CT-11
The Observation Guide
Mastering CDA Competencies

Introductory Activities

1. Ask students to list all of the foods included in their favorite meals. Then ask students whether they think these meals meet guidelines for nutritious, appetizing meals.
2. Discuss with students what they think good nutrition means.
3. *Nutrition Program Goals,* transparency master 11-1. Without the master, have students discuss what goals they would set for a center nutrition program. Then use the master to discuss with students the nutrition program goals given in the text.

Instructional Concepts and Student Learning Experiences

Nutrition

4. Have students define the term nutrition in their own words.
5. Have students explain why proper nutrition is important to physical, cognitive, social, and motional development.
6. Have students describe nutrients and their functions.
7. Have students discuss the effects of undernutrition.
8. Have students discuss problems identified with overeating.
9. Have students read newspaper, magazine, or journal articles related to children's nutrition and share the articles with the class.
10. Have students make visual aids geared toward children to inform them of foods rich in various nutrients.
11. *Fruit and Vegetable Sources of Vitamin A, Vitamin C, and Iron,* reproducible master 11-2. Use the master to emphasize to students fruits and vegetables that can be served to children and are high in vitamin A, vitamin C, or iron.
12. *The Food Guide Pyramid,* transparency master 11-3. Use the master to discuss planning a well-balanced diet. Have students identify the food groups in the Pyramid, the nutritional value of the foods in each group, and foods typically included in each group.
13. Have students discuss factors that influence the planning of nutritious meals for young children. Students should then tell why each factor deserves consideration.

14. *Nutrients and Their Functions,* Activity A, SAG. Have students unscramble the letters to form the nutrients given. Students should then match the statements with the correct nutrients.

15. *Nutrition Crossword,* Activity B, SAG. Have students complete the puzzle by filling in the appropriate terms in the statements about planning nutritious meals for children.

16. *Food Guide Pyramid: A Guide to Daily Food Choices,* color transparency CT-11, TRB. Use this transparency to show students how the different food groups work together to form a balanced diet. You may want to:
    A. Have students list the six food groups included in the Pyramid.
    B. Ask students to list the number of recommended servings needed for each food group.
    C. Discuss why foods in the fats and sweets group should be limited.
    D. Have students brainstorm sources for each food group.

17. *Food Guide Pyramid,* Activity C, SAG. Have students place the food items given under the appropriate food groups.

Planning Meals and Snacks

18. Have students discuss the importance of using serving sizes that are appropriate for a child's age.

19. Give students food items and children's ages, and have the students determine the appropriate serving sizes for the food item and age given.

20. Have students observe meals or snacks in child care centers and describe the meals or snacks to the class. The class should evaluate the serving sizes and appeal of each meal or snack described.

21. Have students discuss what has influenced their own food preferences.

22. Have students discuss ways of planning meals to satisfy the food preferences of a variety of children.

Serving Meals

23. Have students describe factors that influence the planning of meals for young children.

24. Have students discuss the purpose of breakfast.

25. *Breakfast,* transparency master 11-4. Use the master to discuss the U.S.D.A. recommendations for an adequate breakfast. Then have students give menus that would meet these recommendations. (Menus may be written on the master.)

26. *Breakfast Foods Children Can Easily Make,* reproducible master, 11-5. Use this master as a source of nutritious breakfast ideas.

27. Have students plan an interesting breakfast that would be appropriate for a group of three-year-

olds. Students should follow the guidelines outlined in the text.

28. Have students prepare a recipe booklet containing recipes for breakfast foods that children can make.

29. Have students give guidelines for offering snacks in a child care center.

30. *Snacks,* transparency master 11-6. Use the master to discuss the types of foods recommended as snacks. Then have students list snacks that would fit these recommendations. (Snacks may be written next to the appropriate food types.)

31. *Choosing Healthy Snacks,* reproducible master 11-7. Have students check the snacks that would be acceptable according to U.S.D.A. guidelines.

32. *Lunch,* transparency master 11-8. Use the master to discuss the U.S.D.A. recommendations for an adequate lunch. Then have students give menus that would meet these recommendations. (Menus may be written on the master.)

33. Have students prepare a list of lunch foods appropriate for children, including desserts.

34. Have students plan a one-week breakfast, lunch, and snack menu for a group of three-year-olds.

Additional Resources

35. Guest speaker. Invite a dietitian to speak to the class on planning nutritious meals for children.

36. Guest speaker. Invite a cook from a child care center to discuss menu planning and children's food likes and dislikes.

Research Topic

37. Have students survey parents to find out considerations they make in planning their children's meals. Students should write a paper listing these considerations and summarizing how they may be used along with textbook recommendations to plan meals and snacks for children.

Answer Key

Text

Review and Reflect, page 173

1. true
2. (List four.) provide nutritious meals and snacks; introduce new foods that are nutritious; encourage good eating habits; involve children in meal activities; provide information to parents on nutrition.
3. Nutrition is the science of food and how the body uses the food taken in.
4. Nutrients are the chemical substances in food that help build and maintain the body.
5. proteins, carbohydrates, fats, vitamins, minerals, and water

6. calories
7. Undernutrition, a lack of proper nutrients in the diet, is caused by not eating enough food in an otherwise well-balanced diet. Malnutrition, a lack of nutrients, is caused by the inability of the body to use the nutrients in the food.
8. bread, cereal, rice, and pasta group; vegetable group; fruit group; milk, yogurt, and cheese group; meat, poultry, fish, dry beans, eggs, and nuts group; fats, oils, and sweets group
9. D
10. carbohydrates, iron, B-vitamins
11. A, C
12. fat
13. Children have poorly developed fine motor coordination skills. This makes handling forks and spoons difficult.
14. Fruit or juice, protein-rich food, with milk, bread, butter or margarine.
15. false
16. (Name four. See page 171.)

Student Activity Guide

Nutrients and Their Functions, Activity A

1. G
2. C
3. J
4. D
5. E
6. N
7. I
8. A
9. O
10. F
11. B
12. H
13. K
14. M
15. L

Nutrition Crossword, Activity B

Across
2. vitamin C
5. breads
7. fortified
9. nutrition
14. overeating
15. obesity
16. Food Guide Pyramid

Down
1. half
2. room temperature
3. calcium
4. undernutrition
6. malnutrition
8. protein
9. appetites
10. nutrients
11. iron
13. vitamin A

Food Guide Pyramid, Activity C

Breads, Cereals, Rice, and Pasta
   crackers
   waffles
   granola
   chow mein noodles

Vegetables
   broccoli
   pea pods

Fruits
   dates
   apples

Meats, Poultry, Fish, and Alternates
   kidney beans
   meatballs
   peanut butter
   beef chunks

Milk, Yogurt, and Cheese
   cottage cheese
   cheese
   yogurt
   cheese fondue

Teacher's Resource Guide/Binder

Choosing Healthy Snacks, reproducible master 11-7

The following snacks should be checked:

   milk and banana
   apple wedge and milk
   milk, peanut butter, and crackers
   milk and orange slices
   tomato juice and hard cooked egg

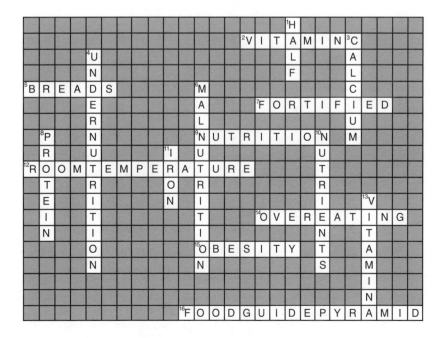

apple juice and celery stuffed with cheese spread

peanut butter balls and milk

vegetable dip, vegetables, and milk

fruit kabobs and milk

Chapter Test

1.	C	9.	T
2.	F	10.	F
3.	A	11.	F
4.	E	12.	T
5.	D	13.	T
6.	B	14.	T
7.	T	15.	T
8.	T	16.	F

17.	F	24.	D
18.	T	25.	A
19.	C	26.	B
20.	B	27.	A
21.	A	28.	C
22.	C	29.	B
23.	C	30.	C

31. Providing nutritious meals and snacks; introducing new foods that are nutritious; encouraging good eating habits; involving children in meal activities; providing nutrition information to parents.

32. Protein, carbohydrates, fats, vitamins, minerals, and water.

33. (Student response.)

Nutrition Program Goals

♦ To provide nutritious meals and snacks

♦ To introduce new foods that are nutritious

♦ To encourage healthy eating habits

♦ To involve children in mealtime activities

♦ To provide information to parents on nutrition

Fruit And Vegetable Sources of Vitamin A, Vitamin C, and Iron

Vitamin A		
Vegetables		**Fruits**
Asparagus	Spinach	Apricots
Broccoli	Squash—Winter	Cantaloupe
Carrots	Sweet potatoes	Cherries, red sour
Chili peppers (red)	Tomatoes	Peaches
Kale	Tomato juice, paste, or puree	Plums, purple
Mixed vegetables	Turnip greens	Prunes
Peas and carrots	Vegetable juices	
Pumpkin		

Vitamin C		
Vegetables		**Fruits**
Asparagus	Sweet peppers	Cantaloupe
Broccoli	White potatoes	Grapefruit
Brussel sprouts	Spinach	Grapefruit juice
Cabbage	Sweet potatoes	Oranges
Cauliflower	Tomatoes	Orange juice
Chili peppers	Tomato juice, paste, or puree	Raspberries
Collards	Turnip greens	Strawberries
Kale	Turnips	Tangerines
Okra		

Iron		
Vegetables		**Fruits**
Asparagus	Peas, green	Apples (canned)
Beans—green, wax, lima	Squash	Berries
Broccoli	Sweet potatoes	Dried fruits—dates, apricots
Brussel sprouts	Tomatoes, canned	Figs
Dark green leafy vegetables— beet greens, collards, kale, spinach, turnip greens	Tomato juice, paste or puree	Peaches
		Plums, purple
		Prunes
		Raisins
		Rhubarb

The Food Guide Pyramid

Name _____ Date_____ Period _____

A Guide to Daily Food Choices

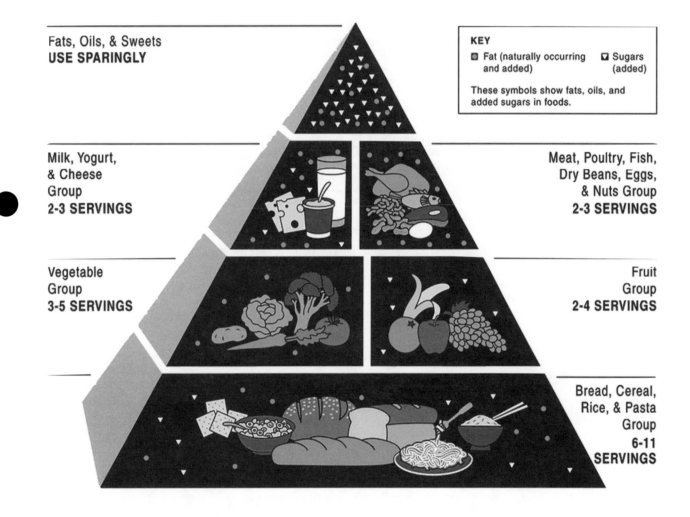

Fats, Oils, & Sweets
USE SPARINGLY

KEY
▨ Fat (naturally occurring   ▢ Sugars
   and added)   (added)

These symbols show fats, oils, and
added sugars in foods.

Milk, Yogurt,
& Cheese
Group
2-3 SERVINGS

Meat, Poultry, Fish,
Dry Beans, Eggs,
& Nuts Group
2-3 SERVINGS

Vegetable
Group
3-5 SERVINGS

Fruit
Group
2-4 SERVINGS

Bread, Cereal,
Rice, & Pasta
Group
**6-11
SERVINGS**

Breakfast

The United States Department of Agriculture
Child Care Food Program recommends:

- Fruit or juice
- Protein-rich food
- Milk
- Bread
- Butter or margarine

or

- Fruit or juice
- Cereal
- Milk

Breakfast Foods Children Can Easily Make

Fresh squeezed juices
Egg sandwich
Deviled eggs
Tomato stuffed with scrambled eggs
Eggs-in-a-basket of bread
Egg-foo-yung
Omelets with infinite fillings
Hashed brown potatoes with a
   poached egg on top
Cheesy mashed potatoes
Potato pancakes
Pizza or Breakfast Pizza
Tacos or burritos
Soups
Sandwiches:
   toasted cheese
   peanut butter and jelly waffles or French toast
   egg salad with lettuce and tomato
   hamburgers
   tuna salad with cheese
Fish sticks
Pigs in a blanket
Meatballs
Grits, mush, scrapple
Hot cereal topped with fruit, ice cream, or yogurt

Surprise muffins with different fillings
Salads:
   carrot raisin
   fruit salads
   vegetable salads
Baked apples with raisins and nuts
Stuffed fruits
Raisin-peanut mix
Yogurt with fruit and granola
Milk shakes, milk/fruit or juice blends
Bread, rice, pumpkin, egg noodle
   puddings/custards
Pancakes with fruit faces
Cottage cheese pancakes
A change from syrup for pancakes and waffles:
   applesauce
   fruit sauces (a thin cranberry sauce
      is especially good)
   sliced and slightly sugared fruits
   thin custard sauce or pudding
   scoop of ice cream
   chopped nuts
   peanut butter
   cheese spreads
   creamed, hard-cooked eggs
   creamed chicken, chipped beef, etc.

Adapted from: Smell, Touch, Listen, Look—Kids Cook, Project funded under U.S. Department of Agriculture, University of Wisconsin-Stout.

Snacks

Snacks should include one or more of the following:

♦ Milk

♦ Fruit

♦ Vegetable

♦ Juice

♦ Protein-rich food

♦ In addition, a snack may include
   a bread or cereal product.

Choosing Healthy Snacks

Name _____ **Date**_____ **Period** _____

Check the snacks that would be acceptable according to the U.S.D.A. guidelines.

_____ potato chips and pop

_____ milk and banana

_____ chocolate sandwich cookies and milk

_____ apple wedge and milk

_____ milk, peanut butter, and crackers

_____ milk and orange slices

_____ pretzels and milk

_____ tomato juice and hard-cooked egg

_____ apple juice and celery stuffed with cheese spreads

_____ caramels and orange juice

_____ corn chips and milk

_____ peanut butter balls and milk

_____ vegetable dip, vegetables, and milk

_____ fruit kabobs and milk

Lunch

The U.S.D.A. recommends the following pattern be used to insure that children receive the proper nutrients:

- ◆ Protein-rich food (main dish)
- ◆ Vegetable and/or fruit (two different kinds)
- ◆ Bread (whole grain or enriched rice or pasta)
- ◆ Butter or margarine as needed
- ◆ Milk
- ◆ Dessert (optional)

Planning Nutritious Meals and Snacks

Name _____

Date _____ Period _____ Score _____

Matching: Match the following terms and identifying phrases.

_____	1. The science of food and how the body uses it.	A. malnutrition
_____	2. Caused by not eating enough food.	B. nutrients
_____	3. Caused by the inability of the body to use the nutrients in food.	C. nutrition
_____	4. The intake of more food than the body needs to function properly.	D. obesity
_____	5. May lead to hypertension and diabetes.	E. overeating
_____	6. The chemical substances in food that provide for growth and maintenance of health.	F. undernutrition

True/False: Circle *T* if the statement is true or *F* if the statement is false.

T F 7. A child's ability to learn is connected to his or her diet.

T F 8. Lifelong good health may be a result of helping children learn healthy food choices.

T F 9. Without good nutrition, children may become lethargic.

T F 10. Only a child's age determines his or her activity level.

T F 11. Undernutrition can accelerate the child's growth and development.

T F 12. Children who are obese in childhood tend to be obese later in life.

T F 13. Obesity can be prevented easier than treated.

T F 14. Vitamin A helps to keep the skin clear and smooth.

T F 15. Vitamin C may be found in broccoli, cantaloupe, and strawberries.

T F 16. Each center can determine when and how much food must be provided for children.

T F 17. Whenever possible, avoid whole grain products.

T F 18. Dry foods and meat are hard for children to eat.

Multiple Choice: Choose the best response. Write the letter in the space provided.

_____ 19. Compared to other children, children who are undernourished may be _____.
  A. more intelligent
  B. heavier
  C. shorter
  D. more mature

(continued)

_____ 20. Which of the following is *not* a sign of malnutrition?
    A. Decaying teeth.
    B. High energy level.
    C. Sunken eyes.
    D. Irritability.

_____ 21. Obesity can lead to health problems such as _____.
    A. heart disease
    B. ear infections
    C. nearsightedness
    D. infected tonsils

_____ 22. The function of protein is to _____.
    A. protect vital organs
    B. add flavor to foods
    C. build and repair tissues
    D. help the body digest foods easily

_____ 23. One protein source is _____.
    A. sugar
    B. apples
    C. peanut butter
    D. jelly

_____ 24. The function of fat is to _____.
    A. promote growth
    B. prevent night blindness
    C. regulate fluid balance in the cells
    D. isolate the body from shock and temperature change

_____ 25. Sources of fat do *not* include _____.
    A. vegetables
    B. nuts
    C. olives
    D. chocolates

_____ 26. Carbohydrate sources include _____.
    A. egg yolks
    B. peas
    C. salad oils
    D. fish

_____ 27. From the milk, yogurt, and cheese group, children need _____.
    A. two to three servings
    B. three to five servings
    C. four to six servings
    D. five to seven servings

_____ 28. The most important nutrient in the milk group is _____.
    A. iron
    B. vitamin K
    C. calcium
    D. phosphorous

(continued)

_____ 29. A chief nutrient in the grain group is _____.
   A. calcium
   B. carbohydrates
   C. vitamin C
   D. phosphorous

_____ 30. A serving of milk for a child should be _____.
   A. ¼ cup
   B. ⅓ cup
   C. ½ cup
   D. ¾ cup

Essay Questions: Provide complete responses to the following questions or statements.

31. List the goals for a good nutrition program.

32. What are the six groups of nutrients needed for growth and maintenance of health?

33. Write a lunch menu appropriate for a four-year-old and explain why it is nutritionally adequate and appealing.

Guiding Children's Health  12

Objectives

After studying this chapter, students will be able to

- develop a workable health policy for a child care center.
- list steps for controlling the spread of food-borne illnesses.
- explain the importance of first aid training
- identify various injuries and outline procedures for treating them.
- explain how to care for children who become ill while in your care.
- describe your responsibility when caring for children with special illnesses.

Teaching Materials

Text, pages 175–192
Terms to Know
Review and Reflect
Apply and Explore

Student Activity Guide
A. *Health Match*
B. *Communicable Diseases*
C. *Burns*

Teacher's Resource Guide/Binder
Immunization for Preschoolers,
  transparency master, 12-1
Safety Rules for Avoiding Food Contamination,
  transparency master, 12-2
Emergency Medical Care, reproducible master, 12-3
Universal Precautions to Prevent Transmission of
  Blood-Borne Diseases, reproducible master, 12-4
Chapter Test

Teacher's Resource Binder
Six Steps for Handwashing, color transparencies,
  CT-12A and B

The Observation Guide
Mastering CDA Competencies

Introductory Activities

1. Ask students to list illnesses and diseases that they have had. Students should discuss the symptoms and treatments of these illnesses and diseases.

2. Have students give examples of ways to make the classroom environment more healthy.

3. Discuss with students signs of illness that they may notice in others or in themselves.

4. *Health Match,* Activity A, SAG. As a pretest of their health knowledge, have students match the given terms and definitions.

Instructional Concepts and Student Learning Experiences

Objectives for Guiding Health _____

5. Have students discuss the value of the text objectives needed to create a healthful classroom environment.

6. Have students interview parents of children in child care programs to find out how they feel about the center's role in keeping their children healthy. Students should share their findings in class and discuss how parent expectations relate to center objectives for guiding health.

Health Policies _____

7. Have students define the term *policy* in their own words.

8. Have students visit a local child care center and find out what health policies they have above and beyond state requirements. Students should list some of the policies and give reasons why they think the policies exist.

9. Have students explain the purpose of preadmission medical examinations.

10. *Immunization for Preschoolers,* transparency master 12-1. Use the master as a basis for discussion of immunizations required for children cared for in a center.

11. Have students discuss the possible consequences of not enforcing immunization policies.

12. Have students discuss the importance of having and enforcing attendance policies related to health. Students should discuss and possibly role-play responses to parents who want to leave a child at the center regardless of attendance policies.

13. Have students find out and discuss your state's licensing requirements related to medication.
14. Have students prepare a parent handout containing center health policies.
15. Have students describe a daily informal health inspection.
16. Have students list symptoms of various infections.
17. *Communicable Diseases,* Activity B, SAG. Have students complete the chart by listing the symptoms and incubation period for each disease given.
18. Have students discuss policies related to contacting parents when their children become ill.
19. Have students describe basic principles related to classroom cleanliness.
20. Have students discuss the importance of requiring employees to have a complete physical examination.
21. Six *Steps for Handwashing,* color transparencies, CT-12A and B, TRB. Use these transparencies to teach students effective handwashing techniques. You may want to:
   A. Stress that handwashing is the most effective method of preventing diseases in child care centers. Remind students that children also need to wash their hands after eating. Saliva containing bacteria are often transferred to children's hands when they eat finger foods.
   B. Remind students that handwashing is also important for staff. They should wash their hands:
      • whenever arriving at the center.
      • before preparing or serving food.
      • after changing diapers and using the bathroom.
      • before setting the table.
      • after handling classroom pets or other animals.
      • after handling any type of mucus, blood, or vomit.
   C. Ask students to identify ways that illness could be spread by the hands.
   D. Discuss why modeling proper handwashing techniques is important for teachers.

Controlling Diseases Transmitted by Foods

22. Have students research the symptoms and causes of various forms of food-borne illness and discuss their findings in class.
23. *Safety Rules for Avoiding Food Contamination,* transparency master, 12-2
24. Have students make posters or bulletin boards geared toward center employees on the importance of health habits that prevent food contamination.
25. Have students explain safe dishwashing procedures.
26. Have students list habits that children and staff should form to prevent the transmission of disease through food.

First Aid

27. Have students explain the importance of first aid training.
28. Have students investigate first aid course offerings in your area.
29. Have students create a first aid kit that would be appropriate for a classroom.
30. *Emergency Medical Care,* reproducible master 12-3. Have students describe how they would handle each of the medical emergencies listed.

Wounds and Their Treatment

31. Have students describe the types of wounds.
32. Have students explain the differences between closed and open wounds.
33. Have students research and demonstrate proper care for different types of open wounds.
34. Have students describe how rabies is transmitted.

Burns and Their Treatment

35. Have students explain the differences among first-degree, second-degree, and third-degree burns.
36. Have students discuss ways of preventing sunburn during class time.
37. *Burns,* Activity C, SAG. Have students match the descriptions with the types of burns.

Splinters

38. Have students explain how to remove a splinter.
39. Have students discuss why putting ointment or antiseptic on a splinter that cannot be removed is not recommended.

Insect Stings

40. Have students describe the symptoms of allergic reactions to insect stings.
41. Have students interview exterminators on ways of removing stinging insects and their nests from center areas. Students should write an article based on their findings.

Choking

42. Have students discuss why just watching the child is the best practice if a child who is choking can cry, talk, or cough.
43. Demonstrate the Heimlich maneuver (abdominal thrust) to the class.

Dental Emergencies

44. Have students explain procedures if a child has a toothache.
45. Have students explain emergency treatment for a knocked-out permanent tooth.

Head Lice

46. Have students discuss how to check for head lice in children.

47. Have students describe the most effective way to get rid of head lice.
48. Have students discuss the importance of notifying all parents if one child becomes infected with head lice.

Caring for Children Who Become Ill

49. Have students discuss the purpose of an isolation room.
50. Have students list the incubation periods for communicable diseases. Students should discuss the importance of isolation during these times.
51. Have students discuss why foods should not be given after vomiting.
52. Have students discuss the teacher's responsibilities when a child vomits.
53. Have students explain reasons for slight deviations in children's temperatures.
54. Have students discuss the teacher's responsibilities if a child has a fever.

Special Health Concerns

55. Have students list common allergies.
56. Have students explain how diabetes affects a child.
57. Have students describe the symptoms and treatment for an insulin reaction.
58. Have students discuss the importance of administering medication accurately if a child has epilepsy.
59. Have students describe the teacher's responsibilities if a child has a seizure.
60. *Universal Precautions to Prevent Transmission of Blood-Borne Diseases,* reproducible master 12-4. Use this master to give students information about precautions to follow when they come into contact with blood in various situations related to child care centers.

Additional Resources

61. Guest speaker. Invite a doctor or nurse to discuss common diseases and illnesses. The discussion should include symptoms, prevention, and treatment.
62. Guest speaker. Invite a first aid instructor to demonstrate first aid and CPR procedures.
63. Guest speaker. Invite a child care center director to describe their center's policies concerning accidents and illnesses.

Research Topic

64. Have students conduct a survey of centers in your area. Students should find out what their health policies are. Have students report their findings to the class in a written or oral report.

Answer Key

Text

Review and Reflect, page 192

1. A preadmission medical exam will help you learn if a child has any communicable diseases, has had all needed immunizations, has any allergies, and if the child has any special health problems that affect enrollment.
2. A. Measles, mumps, rubella, and HbCV.
   B. DTP (booster).
   C. Oral polio and DTP (booster).
3. true
4. (Name four:) rashes, sores, swelling or bruising, changes in eyes, runny noses, flushing of skin, coughing, sneezing, sweaty appearance
5. true
6. Food poisoning is an infection in the gastrointestinal tract caused by eating food containing harmful bacteria or other organisms.
7. 140, 40.
6. b. once a month
8. wound
9. bruise
10. abrasions
11. The animal may have rabies.
12. The most serious burn is the third-degree burn.
13. Apply cold water to the burn.
14. two hours
15. The best way for a child to get rid of blockage in the windpipe is for the child to cough up the object causing the blockage.
16. (List two.) Symptoms of head lice include a constant itch of the scalp, often including infected scratches or a rash; small, silvery eggs attached to individual hairs; swollen lymph glands in the neck or under the arms.
17. Insulin
18. Epilepsy is a condition in which a person suffers from periodic seizures.

Student Activity Guide

Health Match, Activity A

1. C	9. J
2. L	10. N
3. B	11. H
4. A	12. D
5. G	13. F
6. O	14. K
7. P	15. I
8. E	16. M

Burns, Activity C

1. A   6. C
2. C   7. A
3. C   8. B
4. A   9. A
5. B   10. A

11. Apply cold water to the burn.
12. See that the child receives medical treatment. Do not treat the burn by breaking blisters or placing an ointment on the burn.
13. Call an ambulance so the child can receive prompt medical attention.

Teacher's Resource Guide/Binder

Emergency Medical Care, reproducible master, 12-3

Situation 1:
> To control the pain, apply a cold application to the area.

Situation 2:
> Carefully wash the wound with soap and water. Medical attention should be obtained if the cut is deep and doesn't stop bleeding.

Situation 3:
> Check to see if any sand particles have entered the wound. Clean the wound if there is any evidence.

Situation 4:
> Check Rafia's leg. If the skin is broken, consult a doctor immediately.

Situation 5:
> Contact Benedict's parents immediately. Let the parents determine whether a doctor should be contacted.

Situation 6:
> Inform Josette's parents of your observation. Also, send notices home to all of the children's parents.

Chapter Test

1. B   19. T
2. F   20. F
3. C   21. T
4. I   22. F
5. A   23. B
6. D   24. B
7. G   25. A
8. E   26. A
9. H   27. D
10. F   28. C
11. F   29. D
12. T   30. D
13. T   31. D
14. T   32. C
15. T   33. B
16. T   34. D
17. T   35. D
18. F

36. The preadmission medical examination helps the teacher learn whether the child is free from communicable diseases, if the child has had all needed immunizations, whether the child has any known allergies, and if the child has any special health problems that would affect his or her enrollment.

37. As soon as each child arrives at school, observe for rashes, changes in appearance of eyes, runny nose, flushing of skin, coughing, sneezing, and/or a sweaty appearance.

Immunization for Preschoolers

Age	Immunization
2 Months	Oral Polio, DTP (Diphtheria, Tetanus, and Pertussis), and HbCV
4 Months	Oral Polio, DTP, and HbCV
6 Months	DTP, Measles, and HbCV
12-15 Months	Oral Polio, Mumps, Rubella, and HbCV
15-18 Months	DTP (Booster)
4 To 6 Years	Oral Polio and DTP (Booster)

Safety Rules for Avoiding Food Contamination

- Do not allow staff with infected sores or respiratory illnesses, such as colds and sore throats, to prepare or serve food.

- Never use home-canned foods.

- Quickly chill foods and keep refrigerated.

- Hold hot foods at above 150° F.

- Wash hands before preparing food and eating.

- Thoroughly wash equipment and hands after working with raw meat.

- Thoroughly cook pork and all other meats.

- Control flies, insects, and rodents.

- Cool foods in the refrigerator, instead of at room temperature.

- Discard cans with dents along side seams, swells, or off odors.

- Discard meats with off odors or slimy surfaces.

- Thaw foods in refrigerator.

- Prepare perishable foods just prior to serving.

- Keep lunches brought from home in the refrigerator.

- Discard leftover foods, with the exception of packaged foods such as crackers and bread.

- Wash raw fruits and vegetables before use.

- Pay attention to expiration dates.

- Discard foods that are moldy, soured, or beginning to liquefy.

- Store flours, cereals, and sugar in tightly covered containers to prevent rodent and insect infestations.

Emergency Medical Care

Name _____ **Date** _____ **Period** _____

Professionals working with young children need to develop skills in handling medical emergencies.
Describe how you would handle each of the situations listed below.

Situation 1:

Alycia is riding a tricycle on a cement path. She falls off the tricycle and begins to cry and hold her leg.
Immediately you approach her and check her leg. Although she is crying hard, there is not a break in the skin.
Alycia only appears to have tenderness and pain. What should you do?

_____

_____

_____

_____

_____

Situation 2:

Juan falls off the slide and starts to cry. Approaching him, you notice blood, which indicates that he has an
open wound. What should you do?

_____

_____

_____

_____

_____

Situation 3:

Kate is playing in the sandbox with sand accessories. She trips and falls on a sand toy. As a result, she obtains
an abrasion on her arm. What should you do?

_____

_____

_____

_____

_____

(continued)

Name_____

Situation 4:

Your class is having a pet day. Rafia is petting Swen's dog. All of a sudden, the dog bites him. What should you do?

_____

_____

_____

_____

_____

Situation 5:

While running across the play yard, Benedict falls and breaks his tooth. What should you do?

_____

_____

_____

_____

_____

Situation 6:

Josette is sitting in your lap. While looking down, you notice lice in her hair. What should you do?

_____

_____

_____

_____

_____

Universal Precautions to Prevent Transmission of Blood-Borne Diseases

(Adapted for child care settings)
Never delay emergency action because you can't apply universal precautions. The theoretical risk of transmission of a blood-borne disease is too small to postpone treatment.

Barrier Methods

♦ Wash your hands with soap and warm water for 30 seconds after contact with blood or body fluids containing blood. Rub all surfaces well, rinse thoroughly under running water, dry with a paper towel, and use the towel to turn off the faucet.

♦ Cover cuts or scratches with a bandage until they are healed.

♦ Use a barrier of absorbent material like paper towels or tissues to stop bleeding. Individually wrapped sanitary napkins are a good barrier to keep in a first aid kit.

♦ Wear disposable latex gloves when you encounter large amounts of blood or blood-stained body fluid, especially if you have open cuts or chapped hands.

♦ Wash you hands as soon as you remove your gloves. Never wash and reuse gloves.

♦ Use a clean mouthpiece for mouth-to-mouth resuscitation. However, because the risk of transmission of a blood-borne disease is so slight, the absence of a mouthpiece should not stop you from resuscitating a person in need.

Cleaning and Disinfecting

♦ Wear disposable latex gloves when you clean up blood-stained surfaces.

♦ Clean up blood spills immediately, using disposable, absorbent material.

♦ Wash the area with soapy water and disinfect with a solution of one part bleach (5.26 percent concentration) and nine parts water, made fresh daily. Leave it for 10 minutes before wiping.

♦ Place blood-stained clothing in a sealed plastic bag for parents to machine-wash separately in hot, soapy water. Care for center laundry the same way.

♦ Wipe the blood from toys, then spray them with (or put them into) a bleach solution and let them stand for at least 45 seconds. Rinse with fresh water before you give them back to the children. (Be sure to disinfect blood-splashed toys before you put them into the dishwasher.)

♦ Wash rugs with soap and hot water in a washing machine or roll them up and send them to the cleaners after the blood has dried. Clean wall-to-wall carpets or upholstery with soap and water and disinfectant, and rinse with water.

♦ Use a hose or scrape the blood from outdoor toys and equipment. Spray with a bleach solution. Then rinse thoroughly.

(continued)

- Remove blood-soaked sand or dirt from sandboxes, pike paths, and other ground surfaces, then discard it from the play area. Use soapy water or disinfectant soap, and hose down hard surfaces.

- Discard blood-stained disposable materials, including gloves, in a sealed plastic bag and place in a lined, covered garbage container. (If you have used a mop, discard and replace the mophead rather than disinfecting it.)

- Wash your hands thoroughly as soon as you remove and dispose of your gloves.

In Case of Exposure

- When there is exposure to blood (blood-to-blood contact, contact between blood and mucous membrane, contact between blood and non-intact skin, or a puncture with a sharp, blood-stained object):

- Bleed the wound gently.

- Wash with soap and water (rinse mucous membranes with clear water only).

- Record the details of the accident: what activity was involved, where, and when; the type of accident; the size of the wound; the quantity of blood; and the names of those involved.

- Inform the center director and the parents.

- Arrange for a rapid medical exam by calling the center's medical consultant, your local public health officer, or the children's hospital. A physician will decide if treatment and vaccinations are required.

Reprinted from "HIV/AIDS and Child Care: Fact Book" with permission from the Canadian Child Care Federation, Ottawa, Ontario (Canada).

Guiding Children's Health

Name _____

Date _____ **Period** _____ **Score** _____

Matching: Match the following terms and identifying phrases.

_____ 1. Microscopic organisms that can cause illness.

_____ 2. Infection of the gastrointestinal tract.

_____ 3. Injury to the tissue directly under the skin surface.

_____ 4. Break in the skin.

_____ 5. Scrape that damages a portion of the skin.

_____ 6. Disease in which the body cannot properly control the level of sugar in the blood.

_____ 7. Hormone needed to keep sugar in the blood at a proper level.

_____ 8. Condition in which a person has periodic seizures.

_____ 9. Virus that breaks down the body's immune system.

A. abrasion
B. bacteria
C. closed wound
D. diabetes
E. epilepsy
F. food poisoning
G. insulin
H. HIV
I. open wound

True/False: Circle *T* if the statement is true or *F* if the statement is false.

T F 10. State licensing rules and regulations give very detailed rules for protecting children's health.

T F 11. If a child appears sick, always wait until a temperature is evident before calling the parent.

T F 12. Children who may have an illness should be excluded from the group.

T F 13. All staff should have examinations before their first day of employment.

T F 14. The teacher is responsible for protecting, maintaining, and improving the children's health.

T F 15. Young children, the aged, and sick people are more likely to have a reaction to bacteria.

T F 16. Muscular pain is one symptom of food poisoning.

T F 17. If the temperature is below 40°F, bacteria will remain inactive.

T F 18. The safest temperature for storing foods is above 40°F and under 150°F.

T F 19. Rabies may be transmitted through the saliva of a rabid animal.

T F 20. When a child's skin has been broken by a human bite, just wash the wound.

T F 21. To control bleeding, compress the blood vessels against a bone or muscle.

T F 22. Exercise increases insulin requirements for the diabetic child.

(continued)

Multiple Choice: Choose the best response. Write the letter in the space provided.

_____ 23. The primary purpose of health policies is to _____.
  A. satisfy licensing requirements
  B. protect young children
  C. impress parents
  D. protect staff

_____ 24. Children should be kept at home when their temperature exceeds _____.
  A. 98°
  B. 100°
  C. 101°
  D. 103°

_____ 25. The daily health inspection is usually conducted by the _____.
  A. parent
  B. director
  C. teacher
  D. aide

_____ 25. Infection symptoms include _____.
  A. swollen lymph glands
  B. bright eyes
  C. red cheeks
  D. excitability

_____ 27. A communicable disease does not include _____.
  A. chicken pox
  B. influenza
  C. measles
  D. allergies

_____ 28. Serving temperature for food should be _____.
  A. below 60°F or above 100°F
  B. below 50°F or above 170°F
  C. below 40°F or above 140°F
  D. below 20°F or above 120°F

_____ 29. The least severe type of a burn is classified as a _____.
  A. fourth-degree burn
  B. third-degree burn
  C. second-degree burn
  D. first-degree burn

_____ 30. The time between exposure to the sun and development of a sunburn is usually _____.
  A. immediately
  B. within an hour
  C. two to four hours
  D. three to twelve hours

_____ 31. The best way for a child to get rid of a windpipe blockage is to _____.
  A. take it out
  B. have the teacher remove it
  C. try to swallow it
  D. cough it up

(continued)

_____ 32. To provide emergency treatment for a knocked-out tooth, first _____.
   A. call the parent
   B. contact a dentist
   C. find the tooth
   D. instruct the child to bite gauze

_____ 33. Head lice feed on _____.
   A. hair
   B. human blood
   C. skin of the scalp
   D. oils of the scalp

_____ 34. The best way to get rid of head lice is to _____.
   A. brush the hair
   B. shampoo daily
   C. wash the hair with vinegar
   D. seek medical help

_____ 35. With a severe diabetic reaction the child may _____.
   A. become confused
   B. cry
   C. perspire
   D. pass out

Essay Questions: Provide complete responses to the following questions or statements.

36. Explain the purpose of requiring all children to have a preadmission medical examination.

37. Describe an informal daily health inspection.

Developing Guidance Skills  13

Objectives

After studying this chapter, students will be able to
- identify goals of effective guidance.
- list personality traits of effective early childhood teachers.
- describe principles of direct and indirect guidance.
- explain various techniques for effective guidance.
- summarize ways to promote a positive self-concept in each child.

Teaching Materials

Text, pages 195–213
  Terms to Know
  Review and Reflect
  Apply and Explore
Student Activity Guide
  A. *Direct and Indirect Guidance*
  B. *Positive Guidance*
  C. *Putting Effective Guidance into Practice*
  D. *Guidance Techniques*
Teacher's Resource Guide/Binder
  Guidance on the Spot, reproducible master, 13-1
  A Teacher's Speech and Voice Should:,
    transparency master, 13-2
  Suggestions for Talking with a Child,
    reproducible master, 13-3
  Building Positive Skills, transparency master, 13-4
  Chapter Test
Teacher's Resource Binder
  Open-Ended Questions, color transparency, CT-13
The Observation Guide
Mastering CDA Competencies

Introductory Activities

1. Have students define the term *guidance* in their own words. Students should discuss how guidance is an ongoing process in the classroom.
2. Have students give examples of different types of guidance they have experienced throughout life.
3. *Guidance on the Spot,* reproducible master 13-1.

Cut a copy of the master apart on the dotted lines and place the pieces in a box or other open container. Have different students draw situations from the container. The student who draws should explain how he or she would handle the situation and discuss his or her choice with the class.

Instructional Concepts and Student Learning Experiences

Goals of Guidance

4. Have students describe the goals of guidance.
5. Have students give examples of prosocial behaviors.

Guidance and You

6. Have students find research articles on early childhood teacher behavior and share them with the class.
7. Have students discuss how teacher behavior affects children.
8. *Open-Ended Questions,* color transparency CT-13, TRB. Use this transparency to help students develop their skills in using open-ended questions. You may want to:
   A. Discuss the importance of using open-ended questions when interacting with children to develop a positive environment.
   B. Review the characteristics of open-ended questions: focus on problem solving and thinking, encourage multiword responses, promote reasoning, and allow for more than one answer.
   C. Have students explain the difference between closed-ended questions (questions that require one-word answers) and open-ended questions.
   D. Have students write three open-ended questions.
9. Have students divide into groups and prepare skits demonstrating the effects of various types of teacher behavior on children. Students should share their skits with the class.
10. Have students list 10 of their personality traits. Students should then write a few paragraphs on how those traits may affect children.

Preparing for Guidance

11. Have students discuss the content of observations.
12. Have students practice writing observations by having a group of two or three students role-play a classroom play situation while another student records his or her observations.
13. Have students interview teachers, asking them about situations in which discussing observations with other teachers has been helpful. Students should share their findings in class.

Direct Guidance

14. Have students define and give examples of direct guidance.
15. Have students list and explain eight guidance principles.
16. Have students discuss the importance of using simple language with children.
17. *A Teacher's Voice and Speech Should:,* transparency master 13-2. Use the master to review guidelines for speech techniques to use with children. Have students practice speaking using these guidelines.
18. Have students explain the importance of using a relaxed voice when speaking to children.
19. *Suggestions for Talking with a Child,* reproducible master 13-3. Have students review and discuss the suggestions listed.
20. Have students practice verbal guidance techniques by showing a child how to use a puzzle.
21. *Building Guidance Skills,* transparency master 13-4. Use the master to review with students guidelines for building positive guidance skills. Have students discuss situations in which each guideline might apply.
22. Have students role-play situations in which they use positive guidance skills.
23. *Positive Guidance,* Activity B, SAG. Have students rewrite the statements given in a positive manner so that children will know what behavior is expected of them.
24. Have students give examples of situations in which children should and should not be offered choices.
25. Have students write four examples of ways to encourage independence in children.

Indirect Guidance

26. Have students explain the influence of the physical set-up of the classroom on children's behavior.
27. Have students discuss the importance of the environment in relationship to the development of children.

28. *Direct and Indirect Guidance,* Activity A, SAG. Have students determine whether the statements listed describe indirect or direct guidance techniques.

Techniques for Effective Guidance

29. *Putting Effective Guidance into Practice,* Activity C, SAG. Students are asked to describe situations where various guidance techniques could be used. They are then asked to describe what they would do and say in each situation.
30. Have students brainstorm a list of ways to say, "Good for you."
31. Have students give examples of each of the following techniques: praising, suggesting, prompting, persuading, redirection, modeling, listening, ignoring, warning, and encouraging.
32. *Guidance Techniques,* Activity D, SAG. Have students match each statement to the guidance technique it describes.
33. Have students debate the value of using time out as a guidance technique.
34. Have students explain when and how to use time out in the classroom.

Promoting a Positive Self-Concept

35. Have students give examples of how they can promote a positive self-concept among children.
36. Have students role-play situations in which they, as teachers, promote the self-concept of a child.

Additional Resources

37. Panel discussion. Invite a panel of teachers to describe effective guidance techniques that they use in the classroom.
38. Panel discussion. Invite parents of children ages two, three, and four to describe methods they use in guiding their children.

Research Topic

39. Have students survey 10 to 20 teachers on guidance techniques they use in the classroom. Then have the students write a paper comparing and contrasting these techniques with those discussed in class.

Answer Key

Text

Review and Reflect, page 212

1. behaviors that include acts of kindness toward others, demonstrating cooperation and helpfulness
2. uncooperative
3. It is thought that failure of permissive teachers to become involved is seen by children as permission

to engage in aggressive and attention-seeking behavior.

4. (Describe one. See pages 197–198.)
5. (Student response. See pages 198–202.)
6. a. Talk quietly.
   b. Wear a smock.
   c. Pour the milk carefully.
   d. Walk.
7. a. Be consistent.
   b. Provide time for change.
   c. Intervene when necessary.
   d. Offer choices with care.
8. (Student response. See page 203.)
9. Children's behavior can be molded by rewarding positive behavior.
10. Natural consequences are those experiences that follow naturally as a result of a behavior. Artificial consequences are those that are set up by an adult to show what will happen if a rule is broken.
11. false
12. A prompt requires a response; a suggestion does not.
13. redirecting
14. Through active listening, you first listen to what the child is saying to you. Then you respond to the child by repeating what was just said.
15. false
16. (List three. Student response.)

Student Activity Guide

Direct and Indirect Guidance, Activity A

1. indirect
2. direct
3. direct
4. indirect
5. indirect
6. direct
7. direct
8. indirect
9. indirect
10. direct
11. direct
12. indirect
13. direct
14. indirect
15. indirect

Positive Guidance, Activity B

Other responses are possible in addition to responses listed below.

1. "Put the scissors on the table."
2. "Use your indoor voice."
3. "Place your milk above your plate."
4. "Walk around the slide."
5. "Put on an apron."
6. "Put the sand back in the sandbox."
7. "Pour the milk slowly."
8. "Wash your hands before you look at the book."
9. "Walk faster."
10. "Touch only the muffin you choose."
11. "Ride on the sidewalk."
12. "Gently hold the bunny."
13. "It's time to go inside."
14. "Use a fork."

Guidance Techniques, Activity D

1. J
2. H
3. F
4. E
5. A
6. I
7. C
8. G
9. B
10. D

(Student response for examples of each.)

Teacher's Resource Guide/Binder

Chapter Test

1. B
2. E
3. D
4. A
5. C
6. H
7. F
8. G
9. J
10. I
11. T
12. T
13. F
14. F
15. F
16. F
17. T
18. F
19. F
20. F
21. F
22. T
23. T
24. T
25. T
26. T
27. D
28. D
29. C
30. C
31. D
32. D
33. C
34. B
35. B
36. C
37. Direct guidance involves verbal and nonverbal behavior used to guide children's actions. Indirect guidance focuses on the selection of materials and the physical setup of the classroom.
38. (Student response. See pages 198–202.)
39. (Student response. See pages 203–209.)
40. (Describe three. Student response.)

Guidance on the Spot

Various guidance situations are described on the cards that follow. Cut the cards apart on the dotted lines. Have students draw a card and discuss how to handle the crisis selected.

"I-can-do-it" Attitude

Tom is a four-year-old child. He has attended child care for the past two years. Each day he enters the center, his mother removes his coat. After removing the coat, she hangs it up.

Problem: Tom's teacher is concerned. She feels that Tom needs to become independent. That is, he needs to remove and hang up his own coat. What should she do?

1. Schedule a parent conference with Tom's mother.
2. Tell the mother when she enters that Tom needs to remove his own coat.
3. When he enters, tell Tom to remove his coat.
4. Ignore the situation. Some day Tom will decide to remove his own coat.

Positive Consequences

Polly has begun to assist the teacher with arranging the cots at naptime. You want her to continue the behavior.

Problem: How can you encourage Polly to continue the behavior?

1. Ignore her.
2. Tell her parents how much you appreciate her help.
3. Tell Polly, "I like the way you help me with the cots."

Teacher Talk

During storytime, children should learn listening skills. Lately two of the classroom aides keep whispering. This is distracting.

Problem: What should you do?

1. Stop reading the story and remind the aides that everyone needs to listen.
2. Make a face to convey your feelings as you read.
3. Talk to the aides later.
4. Ignore the whispering and do nothing.

Attention-Seeking Behavior

Mark has been constantly pushing other children at group time. His teacher has been most permissive. Generally, she totally ignores this behavior.

Problem: How can Mark's behavior be changed?

1. The teacher should continue her permissive attitude.
2. Move Mark alongside a teacher or aide.
3. Threaten Mark.
4. Move Mark into the blockbuilding area to play during large group time.

(continued)

Overreacting

Toby broke a new toy. His teacher, who was tired, became angry and overreacted. He told him that he was clumsy. Then he yanked the toy from his hands. Toby immediately began sobbing.

Problem: How should the teacher have reacted?

1. Ignored the situation.
2. Said, "Sometimes toys break," and removed the toy.
3. Told the children of the dangers of broken toys.

Timing

Effective teachers develop a sense of timing. They intervene when necessary. Lucille, a new teacher, was not sure whether to intervene when she heard an aide tell the children that only girls should play with dolls.

Problem: What should Lucille do?

1. Tell the aide she wants to talk to her later.
2. Ignore the situation.
3. Say, "In our school girls and boys play with dolls."

Warnings

Leslie has been bumping into other children with his bike. This behavior has continued for several weeks. After each incident, you remind him that his behavior is impolite.

Problem: How can you get Leslie to change his behavior?

1. Ignore the behavior.
2. Make him move indoors during the outdoor play period.
3. Remind Leslie, "If you bump into someone, you'll lose your turn."
4. Say, "You bumped into Mack's bike. If you do that again, you'll lose your turn."

Natural Consequences

Hunter has been purposely spilling his milk. Each time his teacher wipes up the spilled milk and pours him another glass.

Problem: How can you get Hunter to change the behavior?

1. Ignore the behavior and give him more milk.
2. Tell him to leave the table.
3. Remind Hunter, "It is impolite to spill milk."
4. Warn Hunter by saying, "If you do this tomorrow, I will not give you more milk."

A Teacher's Speech and Voice Should:

- Be well-modulated with inflections appropriate to the message.

- Be pitched appropriately for his or her age and sex.

- Be distinct.

- Be correctly articulated.

- Be loud enough for the farthest child to hear.

- Be grammatically correct.

- Reflect words, phrases, and sentences appropriate for the children's age or developmental level.

- Have a rate that is neither too fast nor too slow.

- Be pleasant to hear.

- Be natural as opposed to affected.

- Be free of a condescending tone.

- Be mature rather than babyish sounding.

Suggestions for Talking with a Child

1. Get down at the child's level and as close to his or her ears as possible.

2. Maintain eye contact with the child throughout the conversation.

3. Let your face and voice tell the child that what you are saying or doing is important or interesting and fun.

4. Provide honest answers to the child's questions.

5. Use reminders rather than questions when children forget or refuse to follow directions.

6. Use short, simple sentences or directions.

7. Talk about the here and now.

8. Talk about what the child is seeing or doing or what the child is interested in.

9. Say the obvious.

10. Everything has a name. Use it.

11. Put the child's feelings into words.

12. Use new words over and over again.

13. Take a child's short response and put the response back into a whole sentence.

14. When a child uses incorrect language, say what he or she was attempting to say correctly.

15. Use a variety of sentence forms.

16. Expand a child's thoughts by adding more information.

17. Tell the child what you want him or her to do and not what you don't want him or her to do.

18. Make statements that will encourage the child to continue his or her desirable activity.

19. Praise children for efforts as well as accomplishments.

20. Provide simple explanations to a child's questions.

21. Explain the anticipated consequences of specific behaviors.

22. Speak distinctly and use correct grammar.

23. Never talk about a child when the child or other children are present.

24. Talk with the children and not other staff during program hours unless the conversation is related to immediate program activities.

25. Ask questions that will make a child respond with something other than yes or no.

26. Use phrases such as "Tell me . . ."

27. Provide clear directions and patience when handling transitions.

28. Address each child by name every day.

Building Positive Skills

Do	Don't
Help the child develop an "I-can-do-it" attitude.	Don't destroy the child's self-confidence by doing everything for him or her.
Use as few words as possible when giving verbal directions.	Don't use too many words and confuse the child.
Reinforce words with actions. Body gestures are another form of guidance.	Don't be inconsistent. Model the behavior you expect from the children.
Use simple words to communicate clearly.	Don't use a vocabulary that is beyond the children's level of understanding.
Speak in a calm, quiet, relaxed tone of voice.	Don't raise your voice. Save it for an emergency.
Encourage independence and cooperation.	Don't dress and feed children who are able to care for themselves.
Provide the children time to change activities.	Don't deprive the children of an adjustment time.
Accept children's sad or angry feelings.	Don't deprive the children of recognizing, understanding, and learning to express their feelings.

Developing Guidance Skills

Name _____

Date _____ Period _____ Score _____

Matching: Match the following terms and identifying phrases.

_____ 1. Actions used by an adult to help children develop socially acceptable behavior.

_____ 2. Turning children's attention in another direction.

_____ 3. Teaching children through all of your actions and words.

_____ 4. Listening to what a child is saying, then repeating what was just said.

_____ 5. Avoiding acknowledgment of negative behavior.

_____ 6. Experiences that follow as a result of behavior not requiring anyone's intervention.

_____ 7. Behaviors that demonstrate cooperation and helpfulness.

_____ 8. Experiences that are deliberately set up by an adult to show what will happen if a rule is broken.

_____ 9. A guidance technique that is used when a child's disruptive behavior cannot be ignored.

_____ 10. This should be used to tell a child how you feel about his or her behavior.

A. active listening
B. guidance
C. ignoring
D. modeling
E. redirection
F. prosocial behaviors
G. artificial (logical) consequences
H. natural consequences
I. I-message
J. time out

True/False: Circle *T* if the statement is true or *F* if the statement is false.

T F 11. A loud voice should be saved for emergencies.

T F 12. Understanding and guiding children's behavior requires knowledge of child growth and development.

T F 13. A teacher who does not follow through will find that the children will listen to him or her.

T F 14. Effective teachers use more commands than suggestions.

T F 15. Questions that only require a one-word yes or no answer are best for preschoolers.

T F 16. Indirect guidance involves nonverbal behaviors with children.

T F 17. Physically helping a child is a form of direct guidance.

T F 18. A good method of getting the children to listen is to speak in a loud tone.

T F 19. Always offer the child choices.

(continued)

T   F   20. If you ignore unpleasant behavior 100 percent of the time, it is likely to recur.

T   F   21. Self-control is the short-term goal of guidance.

T   F   22. Praise should be age appropriate.

T   F   23. Suggestions should always be positive.

T   F   24. A warning should be provided when children do not follow classroom rules.

T   F   25. Every time you speak or move around children, you are modeling.

T   F   26. Adults as well as children need personal recognition.

Multiple Choice: Choose the best response. Write the letter in the space provided.

_____ 27. According to research, teachers should ask _____.
A. close-ended questions
B. questions that require a one-word answer
C. complex questions
D. open-ended questions

_____ 28. Uncooperative teachers have children who are more _____.
A. calm
B. curious
C. cooperative
D. disruptive

_____ 29. Talkative teachers have children who are more _____.
A. outgoing
B. disruptive
C. shy
D. curious

_____ 30. A form of indirect guidance is _____.
A. patting
B. smiling
C. putting out new games
D. saying "It's time to eat lunch"

_____ 31. Which of the following is not a guidance principle?
A. Be positive.
B. Be consistent.
C. Consider feelings.
D. Intervene frequently.

_____ 32. Praise should not be _____.
A. age appropriate
B. provided verbally
C. given immediately, during, or following an action
D. used without establishing eye contact

(continued)

_____ 33. Negative suggestions usually produce _____.
   A. confidence
   B. self-esteem
   C. undesirable behavior
   D. compliance

_____ 34. Prompting should be _____.
   A. critical
   B. simple
   C. conveyed in an emotional manner
   D. complex

_____ 35. Warnings should be provided _____.
   A. four times
   B. once
   C. twice
   D. as often as necessary

_____ 36. A major goal of child guidance is to help children develop feelings of _____.
   A. authority
   B. justice
   C. self-control
   D. inferiority

Essay Questions: Provide complete responses to the following questions or statements.

37. What is the difference between direct and indirect guidance?

38. List and explain five direct guidance principles.

39. Choose three guidance techniques and describe and give examples of each one.

40. Describe three ways to promote a positive self-concept in children.

Guidance Problems  14

Objectives

After studying this chapter, students will be able to
- identify situations and feelings that cause tension in children.
- describe behavior problems that result from tension.
- guide children as they learn appropriate behavior.

Teaching Materials

Text, pages 215–226
Terms to Know
Review and Reflect
Apply and Explore

Student Activity Guide
A. *Guidance Match*
B. *Guidance Tips*
C. *Analyzing Behavior*
D. *Dialing for Answers*

Teacher's Resource Guide/Binder
Possible Signs of Stress in Children, transparency master, 14-1
Guidance Problems, reproducible master, 14-2
Chapter Test

Teacher's Resource Binder
Reactions to Tension, color transparency, CT-14
The Observation Guide
Mastering CDA Competencies

Introductory Activities

1. Have the class brainstorm a list of possible guidance problems in the classroom.
2. Have each student think about a child that he or she knows. Students should think about what causes these children to misbehave. Students should discuss these causes as a class.

Instructional Concepts and Student Learning Experiences

Causes of Tension _____

3. *Reactions to Tension,* color transparency CT-14,

TRB. Use this transparency to help students recognize how children's behavior changes in reaction to stress. You may want to:
A. Remind students that young children often behave in socially unacceptable ways when they are tense.
B. Ask students to share their personal observations of children's reactions to tension.
C. For each reaction listed on the transparency, discuss suggestions for guiding the unacceptable behavior.
4. Have students list ways of controlling overstimulation.
5. Have students prepare a checklist for teachers to use to avoid overstimulation in the classroom.
6. Have students discuss the importance of consistent routines as a way to control guidance problems.
7. Have students discuss how breaks in their own daily routines (lunch at a different time, cancellation of a class, etc.) can affect their attitudes and activities.
8. Have students discuss how noise level may be related to overstimulation.
9. As an experiment, tell the class that a student will give a presentation to the class. Arrange for the student to take five to ten minutes to prepare for the "presentation." When the student is "ready," have the class discuss how difficult it is to keep quiet and focused during long waiting periods. Students should then discuss how this might be even more difficult for young children.
10. Have students work in groups to determine methods of reducing waiting time in the classroom. Each group should share their methods with the class.
11. Have students list causes of frustration.
12. Have students discuss how they can set up the classroom environment to help prevent frustration in children.
13. Have students make a chart listing health problems in children and possible effects of these problems on behavior.
14. Have students list common causes of stress in children.

15. *Possible Signs of Stress in Young Children,* transparency master 14-1. Use the master to review and discuss the possible signs of stress in children. Students should discuss how careful observation is needed to determine whether or not the signs are stress-related.
16. *Analyzing Behavior,* Activity C, SAG. Have students complete each statement by filling in the factor to be considered in guiding children. Students should then write explanations of why each factor deserves consideration.

Reactions to Tension

17. Have students discuss how expressions of anger differ with children of different ages.
18. Have students discuss the need to react to exploration of the body carefully.
19. Have students discuss advantages of thumbsucking. Students should discuss adult habits that offer similar advantages.
20. Have students find articles or excerpts from books about thumbsucking. Students should share their findings in class.
21. Have students list typical fears of children.
22. Have students interview teachers to find out about ways of handling children's fears.
23. Have students work in teams to prepare skits demonstrating how to handle negativism, stealing, anger, biting, exploring the body, thumbsucking, and fear. The teams should present their skits to the class.
24. *Guidance Advice,* reproducible master 14-2. Have students write replies to questions about handling guidance problems.
25. *Guidance Match,* Activity A, SAG. Have students match the terms related to guidance problems with the given descriptions.
26. *Guidance Tips,* Activity B, SAG. Have students determine whether the guidance statements are true or false.
27. *Dialing for Answers,* Activity D, SAG. Have students use the given clues and numbers to complete the statements related to guidance problems.

Additional Resources

28. Guest speaker. Invite a child care teacher to discuss strategies to reduce overstimulation in the classroom.
29. Guest speaker. Invite a pediatrician to discuss how physical problems can affect children emotionally and socially.
30. Panel discussion. Invite a child care teacher, a child care director, and a child psychologist to discuss ways of handling guidance problems.

Research Topics

31. Have students research the effects of noise on classroom situations. Students should then devise and conduct an experiment to test the effects of various noise levels on children in a classroom. Have students give an oral report to the class regarding the results of the experiment.
32. Have students survey literature, parents, and teachers to find how children show symptoms of stress. Have students write a report based on their findings.

Answer Key
Text
Review and Reflect, page 226

1. Because they do not know how to handle tension.
2. (Name four. Student response.)
3. true
4. routines
5. false
6. Be prepared; manage time effectively.
7. feelings of discouragement, defeat, and lack of control (Student response for causes. See pages 217–218.)
8. B
9. (Name four:) dilated pupils, drowsiness, slurred speech, poor coordination, irritability
10. onlookers
11. The body's reaction to physical or emotional factors.
12. Accept the child's behavior; promote a positive environment.
13. The child will resist your requests even more strongly.
14. (Student response.)
15. true

Student Activity Guide
Guidance Match, Activity A

1. A		6. G	
2. B		7. F	
3. I		8. D	
4. C		9. H	
5. J		10. E	

(Student response for example.)

Guidance Tips, Activity B

1. T	6. F	11. T	16. T
2. F	7. F	12. T	17. T
3. T	8. T	13. T	18. F
4. T	9. F	14. F	
5. T	10. T	15. F	

Analyzing Behavior, Activity C

1. age
2. causes
3. overstimulation
4. materials
5. physical
6. stress

(Student response for explanations.)

Dialing for Answers, Activity D

1. disruptive
2. frustration
3. nutrition
4. stress
5. positive
6. negative
7. tantrums
8. hit
9. bite
10. thumbsucking

Teacher's Resource Guide/Binder

Chapter Test

1. B
2. C
3. A
4. D
5. E
6. T

7. T
8. T
9. F
10. T
11. T
12. T
13. F
14. T
15. F
16. T
17. T
18. F
19. T
20. F
21. T
22. B
23. C
24. B
25. D
26. C
27. C

28. (List five:) Accident proneness, anxiety, appetite loss, baby talk, bedwetting, biting, crying spells, detachment, excessive aggressiveness, excessive laziness, fingernail biting, grinding teeth, hitting, indigestion, insomnia, kicking, pounding heart, respiratory tract illness, stuttering, thumbsucking.

29. Anger calls attention to something that annoys the child. You can help that child learn to deal with anger.

30. (Student response. See pages 224–225.)

Possible Signs of Stress in a Child

- Accident proneness, anxiety, appetite loss, baby talk
- Bedwetting, biting, crying spells
- Detachment
- Excessive aggressiveness
- Excessive laziness
- Fingernail biting
- Grinding teeth, hitting, indigestion
- Insomnia
- Kicking
- Pounding heart
- Respiratory tract illness
- Stuttering
- Thumbsucking

Guidance Advice

Name _____ **Date** _____ **Period** _____

Pretend you are a columnist who writes a "Teacher Hotline" column for a professional journal. Answer the following letters from teachers about their concerns in handling problems.

Dear Teacher Hotline:

Two other teachers in my center and I have the children play outdoors at the same time. We have a problem. The children seem to be pushing, using loud voices, and snatching one another's toys. What can we do to stop these disruptive behaviors?

Dear Teacher:

_____

_____

_____

_____

_____

_____

_____

_____

_____

Dear Teacher Hotline:

Each year I have problems with my children before Christmas. I try to include a wide variety of interesting holiday activities each day, beginning right after Thanksgiving. These activities do not seem to hold the children's attention. There seems to be so much turmoil-running, loud voices, and pushing. What can I do to prevent this turmoil?

Dear Teacher:

_____

_____

_____

_____

_____

_____

_____

_____

_____

(continued)

Name_____

Dear Teacher Hotline:

This is my first year of teaching a group of preschool children. I seem to have a problem at 9 a.m. when the children arrive. From 9 to 9:15, I have scheduled a time to look at books. Some of the children are becoming restless. Others, the parents report, are not anxious to come into the room. This does not please their parents. Why are the children acting this way?

Dear Teacher:

_____

_____

_____

_____

_____

_____

_____

_____

_____

Dear Teacher Hotline:

Lucas is almost 3 years old, but he continues to have toileting accidents. Typically these occur after nap time or meals. My aide is losing his patience. Several times he has asked Lucas if he wants to use the bathroom. Lucas always replies by saying "no." What can we do to help Lucas?

Dear Teacher:

_____

_____

_____

_____

_____

_____

_____

_____

_____

Guidance Problems

Name _____

Date _____ **Period** _____ **Score** _____

Matching: Match the following terms and identifying phrases.

_____	1. Often is the cause of disruptive behavior.	A. frustration
_____	2. May result from having too many activities planned.	B. tension
		C. overstimulation
_____	3. May result from forcing children into activities they are not prepared to do.	D. stress
		E. onlooker
_____	4. The body's reaction to physical or emotional factors.	
_____	5. Watches other children, but does not get involved.	

True/False: Circle *T* if the statement is true or *F* if the statement is false.

T   F   6. Many guidance problems appear in the form of disruptive behavior.

T   F   7. The larger the group, the greater the likelihood that overstimulation can occur.

T   F   8. Holidays can be overstimulating.

T   F   9. To avoid overstimulation, plan a wide variety of activities.

T   F   10. Quiet activities should be followed by active activities.

T   F   11. Hitting and pushing may occur as a result of overstimulation.

T   F   12. Children may behave inappropriately when they have to wait for long periods of time.

T   F   13. To maintain interest, try to purchase only one of each one-of-a-kind toy.

T   F   14. If children sense you're upset, they will become even more upset.

T   F   15. Noise can help relieve aggression.

T   F   16. Medications can cause some children to act out.

T   F   17. Poor or inadequate nutrition can cause behavior problems.

T   F   18. The breakdown of the family is a minor stressor for young children.

T   F   19. Respiratory tract illnesses and accidents may be related to stress in young children.

T   F   20. Scolding children for thumbsucking usually helps the problem.

T   F   21. The harder you try to stop thumbsucking, the stronger it becomes.

(continued)

Multiple Choice: Choose the best response. Write the letter in the space provided.

_____ 22. Preschool children can be negative, particularly between the ages of _____.
    A. one and two
    B. two and three
    C. three and four
    D. four and five

_____ 23. Which is not a sign of stress in young children?
    A. Accident proneness.
    B. Grinding teeth.
    C. Smiling.
    D. Thumbsucking.

_____ 24. The highest number of tantrums usually occurs at about _____.
    A. one year of age
    B. eighteen months of age
    C. two years of age
    D. three years of age

_____ 25. To reduce a child's aggressive tendencies, the teacher should _____.
    A. ignore the child when he or she hits another child
    B. encourage the child to stay quiet and still
    C. wait until children react angrily to intervene
    D. encourage the child to fingerpaint or beat a drum

_____ 26. Thumbsucking will usually stop (except before bedtime) between _____.
    A. two and three years of age
    B. three and four years of age
    C. four and five years of age
    D. five and six years of age

_____ 27. Young children in early childhood settings commonly express fear of _____.
    A. the toys and equipment
    B. the teachers
    C. the dark
    D. other children

Essay Questions: Provide complete responses to the following questions or statements.

28. List five possible signs of stress in young children.

29. How does children's anger serve a useful purpose?

30. Describe how to guide young children's fears.

Establishing Classroom Rules  15

Objectives

After studying this chapter, students will be able to
- explain the reasons for having classroom rules.
- list guidelines for establishing classroom rules.
- describe methods for enforcing rules.
- list useful rules for various classroom areas and activities.

Teaching Materials

Text, pages 227–235
Terms to Know
Review and Reflect
Apply and Explore
Student Activity Guide
  A. *Stating the Positive*
  B. *Rule Pyramid*
  C. *Know the Rules*
  D. *Setting Rules*
Teacher's Resource Guide/Binder
  Classroom Rules, reproducible master, 15-1
  Setting Rules Throughout the Classroom,
    reproducible master, 15-2
  Chapter Test
Teacher's Resource Binder
  Communicating Classroom Rules,
    color transparency, CT-15
The Observation Guide
Mastering CDA Competencies

Introductory Activities

1. Ask students to describe the rules that their parents have set at home. Then ask the students to give reasons why they think these rules were set.
2. Have students explain why they think there should be rules in the classroom.
3. Have the class work together to brainstorm a list of class rules for use in an early childhood classroom.
4. *Classroom Rules,* reproducible master 15-1. Have students analyze the list of rules and discuss what

the results would be if one or more of these rules were not established. Students should also discuss ways that this list might be different for different classrooms.

Instructional Concepts and Student Learning Experiences

Establishing Rules

5. Have students discuss the three reasons given in the text for establishing classroom rules. Students should discuss other possible reasons for establishing rules.
6. Have students explain how limits protect a child's health and safety.
7. Have students explain why rules should be stated positively.
8. *Stating the Positive,* Activity A, SAG. Have students restate the rules given in a positive form.
9. Have students interview teachers to find examples of situations in which children violated classroom rules. Students should ask the teachers why the children may have acted in these ways. Students should share their findings in class.
10. Have students observe a classroom and identify ways that children violate classroom rules.
11. Have students discuss the importance of reviewing rules periodically.
12. *Rule Pyramid,* Activity B, SAG. Have students complete the pyramid by filling in the appropriate terms in the statements given.

Enforcing Rules

13. Have students discuss how establishing rules can be a form of rule enforcement in itself.
14. Have students discuss the importance of consistently maintaining classroom rules.
15. Have students observe a classroom and identify ways that teachers enforce rules in the classroom.
16. Have students role-play situations in which they enforce classroom rules.
17. *Know the Rules,* Activity C, SAG. Have students

determine whether the statements about rules listed are true or false.

Rules for Specific Areas and Activities___

18. Collect classroom rules from two centers for students to examine. Have students discuss the similarities and differences between these rules.
19. Have students discuss possible dangers and problems that could occur in the sensory area. Then have them list rules that prevent these problems.
20. Have students discuss the importance of keeping rules minimal in the dramatic play area.
21. Have students make posters stating rules for the small manipulative area that children would understand.
22. Have students list rules for cooking activities and explain the importance of each rule.
23. Have students develop a skit to demonstrate the importance of rules in the blockbuilding area.
24. Have students discuss the role of the teacher in ensuring that the book corner stays orderly and enjoyable for the children.
25. Have students give demonstrations appropriate for children on proper use of playground equipment.
26. Have students discuss how playground rules can change as children grow.
27. *Setting Rules Throughout the Classroom,* reproducible master 15-2. Have students complete the chart by writing rules for each of the classroom areas listed.
28. *Setting Rules,* Activity D, SAG. Have students use the form to set rules for various areas of the classroom. Then have students visit a center and list five of their most important rules and compare them with the rules studied in the text.

Communicating Rules ___

29. *Communicating Classroom Rules*, color transparency CT-15, TRB. Use this transparency to introduce methods of communicating rules to young children. You may want to:
    A. Stress the fact that effective rules are short and simple.
    B. Have students discuss the advantages of dividing rules into three categories.
    C. Ask students to brainstorm examples of rules under each category: "be safe," "be kind," and "be neat."
    D. Have students discuss why rules in one child care center may differ from those in another center.
30. Have students role-play situations of how to effectively communicate rules to young children.

Additional Resources

31. Panel discussion. Invite a panel of parents to describe how they establish rules at home.
32. Guest speaker. Invite a child care teacher to talk about establishing rules in the classroom.
33. Field trip. Arrange for students to visit a preschool to observe how classroom rules are enforced.

Research Topic

34. Have students research articles on establishing rules. Students should then collect classroom rules from two preschools and write a paper evaluating them, quoting resources throughout their evaluations.

Answer Key

Text

Review and Reflect, page 235

1. Rules are necessary for people to effectively work together in groups. Rules state the goals of the center. As such, the rules of the center stress actions and behaviors that reflect these goals.
2. To protect children's health and safety; to allow children freedom to explore, knowing their teacher will stop them if they go too far; to help children develop self-control.
3. (Name three. See page 228.)
4. (Student response for examples.)
5. Yes. Rules should change as the children grow and develop.
7. flexible
8. sequencing
9. Change books on a regular basis. Control the number of books available at any given time.
10. (Name one rule for each student response. See page 233.)

Student Activity Guide

Stating the Positive, Activity A

1. Sit when you slide.
2. Wipe up the spills.
3. Put the puzzle on the shelf.
4. Turn the pages carefully.
5. Walk.

Rule Pyramid, Activity B

1. all	6. language
2. sick	7. effective
3. rules	8. reasonable
4. change	9. responsible
5. explore	10. unacceptable

Know the Rules, Activity C

1. F	9. T
2. F	10. T
3. T	11. F
4. T	12. T
5. F	13. T
6. T	14. T
7. T	15. T
8. T	

Teacher's Resource Guide

Chapter Test

1. F	11. T
2. A,C,D	12. T
3. A,C,D	13. T
4. B	14. F
5. E	15. F
6. C	16. T
7. T	17. T
8. F	18. T
9. T	19. T
10. F	20. T

21. F	28. D
22. T	29. C
23. T	30. A
24. F	31. C
25. A	32. B
26. D	33. B
27. C	34. D

35. There are three main reasons for establishing classroom rules. First, the children's health and safety are protected. Second, the children feel freer to explore when they know the teacher will stop them from causing themselves harm. Finally, rules help the children develop self-control.

36. (List three:) Make rules short. Write the rules in language that the children can understand. State the rules in terms of positive behavior that you expect. Set rules that are reasonable and serve a useful purpose. Define both acceptable and unacceptable behavior.

37. When rules are enforced consistently, children know what is expected of them. Rules that are inconsistently enforced may confuse children as to what is acceptable behavior.

Classroom Rules

A center needs rules for the classroom and outdoor center areas. It is important that teachers, volunteers, aides, and the children understand the rules. The following rules should be included.

Classroom rules:

♦ Children and adults speak in conversationally quiet voices. No one shouts or yells in the classroom

♦ Children walk rather than run when inside the school building.

♦ Children are responsible for their own work. Each person takes out, works with, and puts away his or her own work and materials.

♦ Children may work independently or in small groups.

♦ Children may not disturb one another's work activities.

♦ Everyone is called and referred to by name.

♦ No one is allowed to harm or hurt another person or materials.

♦ Children who are unable to control themselves are asked to sit on a chair until they gain self-control. In extreme situations, the child may be removed from the classroom

♦ Some classroom areas may be limited to a certain number of people. Signs setting these limits are posted and to be respected due to ease of accommodating people. For example, the block area is limited to four people so that there will be ample room for construction projects.

♦ A set number, determined by the classroom teacher, may have a snack at one time. All children clean up their own place after eating the snack (throw away cup and napkin; wash place at table). Each child should record what he or she has eaten using the record keeping method provided. Children may have only one snack per day.

♦ Each child is assigned a cubby. These cubbies are for storage of all personal belongings. Anything brought from home by a child must be kept in his or her cubby during school hours.

♦ Children sit only on chairs or the floor.

♦ Aprons are worn during messy activities.

♦ Toilets are flushed and everyone washes their hands after toileting.

♦ Blocks can be built as high as the shoulders of the shortest child participating with the blocks.

Outdoor rules:

♦ Trikes stay on the sidewalk following the direction of the painted arrows.

♦ Children sit on the trike seat while riding.

♦ One child per trike.

♦ Trikes do not collide with one another.

♦ A teacher must supervise the trikes at all times.

♦ Sand stays in the sandbox.

♦ Children stay on the playground unless they need to go inside with an adult.

♦ Children are only allowed outside with adult supervision.

Setting Rules Throughout the Classroom

Name _____ **Date** _____ **Period** _____

Every area of the classroom needs rules. Write possible rules for the areas listed below. Refer to your text for help if needed.

Sensory Play	Dramatic Play
Cooking	**Music**
Art	**Book Corner**
Woodworking	**Science**
Playground	**Small Manipulative**

Establishing Classroom Rules

Name _____

Date _____ **Period** _____ **Score** _____

Matching: Match each rule to the area(s) to which it applies. (Some rules apply to more than one area. Areas may be used more than once.)

_____ 1. Handle pets with care.

_____ 2. Wipe up spills immediately.

_____ 3. Wear aprons or smocks for messy activities.

_____ 4. Return toys to the shelf after use.

_____ 5. Turn one page at a time.

_____ 6. Wash hands before beginning the activity.

A. sensory play
B. small manipulative
C. cooking
D. art
E. book corner
F. science

True/False: Circle *T* if the statement is true or *F* if the statement is false.

T F   7. Effective rules explain what is important and expected behavior at the center.

T F   8. Not all classrooms need rules.

T F   9. Adults working in the classroom need a copy of rules prior to participation.

T F 10. Rules should be lengthy.

T F 11. Rules should be written in a language the children can understand.

T F 12. On a regular basis, rules need to be re-examined by all of the staff.

T F 13. Undesirable behavior should be immediately stopped.

T F 14. Children best understand rules that are inconsistently maintained.

T F 15. It is unusual for children to test well-established rules.

T F 16. Children feel freer to explore when they know that their teacher will stop them if necessary.

T F 17. Rules help children develop self-control.

T F 18. Rules help protect the health and safety of the children.

T F 19. One of the center's goals should be to develop socially responsible behavior in young children.

T F 20. Rules should state the expected behavior, not the unacceptable behavior.

T F 21. If children do not follow rules, they should be able to remain in the area.

T F 22. After use, the children should return toys to the shelf.

T F 23. Swings require constant supervision.

T F 24. On the slide, the children should stay a hand's length behind the child in front of them.

(continued)

Multiple Choice: Choose the best response. Write the letter in the space provided.

_____ 25. Rules should focus on _____.
A. actions and behaviors that reflect center goals
B. the physical needs of the children
C. making work easier for the teacher
D. the most popular classroom areas

_____ 26. Effective rules are _____.
A. focused on undesirable behavior
B. long
C. written in a language for adults
D. stated in terms of expected behavior

_____ 27. Undesirable behavior should be _____.
A. observed
B. disregarded
C. stopped
D. ignored

_____ 28. A child's anger may be projected by _____.
A. positive behavior
B. compliance
C. cooperation
D. resisting limitations

_____ 29. For individual children, rules should be _____.
A. inflexible
B. rigid
C. adaptable
D. inconsistent

_____ 30. Depending upon the media used in sensory play, rules may _____.
A. change somewhat
B. be disregarded
C. be consistent
D. become unimportant

_____ 31. Rules in the small manipulative area are _____.
A. extensive
B. complex
C. minimal
D. ignored

_____ 32. During cooking experiences, the teacher should _____.
A. supervise the entire classroom
B. remain with the activity
C. call attention to negative behavior
D. memorize the recipe

_____ 33. Which should *not* be a rule of the art area?
A. Spills need to be wiped.
B. Children's artwork should be compared.
C. Tables need to be wiped.
D. Smocks must be worn.

(continued)

_____ 34. Rules for swings include _____.
   A. standing is allowed
   B. using one hand is allowed
   C. two children may swing at a time
   D. only teachers push children

Essay Questions: Provide complete responses to the following questions or statements.

35. Give three reasons for establishing classroom rules.

36. Give three guidelines to use when setting rules for children.

37. Why do rules need to be enforced consistently?

Handling Daily Routines  16

Objectives

After studying this chapter, students will be able to
- explain the importance of a daily schedule.
- guide children successfully through the daily routines of dressing and undressing, eating, napping, toileting, and cleanup.
- explain the use of transition techniques to move smoothly from one activity to another.

Teaching Materials

Text, pages 237–251
Terms to Know
Review and Reflect
Apply and Explore
Student Activity Guide
    A. *Your Style of Managing Daily Routines*
    B. *Planning a Daily Schedule*
    C. *Managing Conflicts*
Teacher's Resource Guide/Binder
    Daily Routine Puzzle, reproducible master, 16-1
    Not-So-Smooth Transitions, reproducible master, 16-2
    Chapter Test
Teacher's Resource Binder
    Tips for Oral Health, color transparency, CT-16
The Observation Guide
Mastering CDA Competencies
Observation Guide, Chapter 16

Introductory Activities

1. Brainstorm with students reasons for establishing routines in the classroom and in the home.
2. Ask students to describe their own daily routines. Then have students list benefits that these routines have for them.

Instructional Concepts and Student Learning Experiences

The Daily Schedule

3. Have students discuss factors that need to be considered when planning a daily schedule.

4. *Planning a Daily Schedule,* Activity B, SAG. Have students complete the given statements about planned daily routines using the terms provided.

Daily Routines

5. *Your Style of Managing Daily Routines,* Activity A, SAG. Have students indicate whether they agree or disagree with the given statements about daily routines. Students should explain their choices in the space provided. Then have students discuss their choices with the class.
6. Have students observe a child care center and record observations of various routines and how they are handled. Students should share their observations in class.
7. Have students observe a child care center and record observations of children's reactions to various routines. Students should share their findings in class.
8. *Managing Conflicts,* Activity C, SAG. Have students read each of the given situations related to conflicts during routines. Students should then discuss the situations in small groups and write suggestions for solving each of the conflicts in positive ways.
9. *Daily Routine Puzzle,* reproducible master 16-1. Have students complete the word puzzle by filling in the names of the daily routines described in the given statements.
10. Have students discuss the importance of explaining teacher expectations to children.
11. Have students discuss the importance of teaching children to hang up their coats.
12. Have students develop a letter or brochure designed for parents containing clothing suggestions for their children.
13. Have students prepare and give demonstrations for buttoning, zipping, pulling on boots, tying shoes, putting on coats, and putting fingers in gloves.
14. Have students practice putting on their coats or sweaters using the technique described in the text.
15. Have students discuss why flexibility is important in dealing with children during meals.

16. Have students make a chart identifying the food skills and interests of children at different ages.
17. Have students explain the reasons for the eating rules given in the text.
18. Have students role-play situations in which teachers must handle eating problems.
19. *Tips for Oral Health,* color transparency CT-16, TRB. Use this transparency to explain the importance of good oral hygiene in a child's daily routine. You may want to:
    A. Discuss the importance of having oral hygiene included in the child's daily routines. Then have students determine a schedule for daily toothbrushing.
    B. Demonstrate proper techniques for toothbrushing.
    C. Have students brainstorm ways the children's toothbrushes can be labeled.
    D. Discuss why fluoridated toothpaste is recommended.
    E. Ask students to explain why toothbrushes should be stored bristle end up and allowed to air-dry.
20. Have students interview teachers to find out successful nap time techniques. Students should share their findings in class.
21. Have students observe children at nap time. Students should record the techniques that were successfully used with the children. Students should discuss their observations in class.
22. Have students discuss ways to deal with problems at nap time.
23. Have students identify toileting needs of preschool children.
24. Have students discuss ways to guide children in toilet training.
25. Have students discuss why shaming and scolding is not recommended for toilet training.
26. Have students survey parents to find out what clues their preschoolers give when they need to use the bathroom. Students should share their findings in class.
27. Have students describe ways to help children maintain a positive attitude toward cleanup.

Transitions

28. Have students define the word transition. Students should discuss why transitions are an important part of routines for preschoolers.
29. Have students make a chart describing the four types of transition methods described in the text and giving three examples of each type.
30. Have each student demonstrate a transition method, including props if needed, to the class.
31. *Not-So-Smooth Transitions,* reproducible master

16-2. Have students write possible solutions to a teacher's problems with classroom transitions.

Additional Resources

32. Guest speaker. Invite a child psychologist or a pediatrician to discuss toilet training with the class. Have the guest speaker address how home efforts can be coordinated with center efforts.
33. Panel discussion. Invite parents of children ages two, three, and four to discuss the routines they have established with their children.
34. Panel discussion. Invite several teachers to discuss successful ways of handling routines in the classroom.

Research Topics

35. Have students research current literature and survey parents about successful ways of guiding children's eating. Then have students write a paper comparing and contrasting research and parent techniques.
36. Have students research successful nap time techniques through surveying literature and interviewing teachers. Students should then give a presentation on the topic. (Visual aids should be included in the presentation.)

Answer Key

Text

Review and Reflect, page 251
1. (Student response.)
2. Young children thrive on making choices. They enjoy selecting activities and deciding how long to play. Many children have short attention spans. Differences also exist in the speed at which they enjoy complete projects.
3. (Student response. See pages 238–239.)
4. A second set of clothes can be used in an emergency.
5. Illness, stage of development, amount of physical activity, body's chemical needs.
6. (List three:) taste all foods before asking for seconds of food or milk; remain at the table until everyone has finished; wipe up your own spills; eat food only from your own plate.
7. (List two. Student response.)
8. Pica is a craving for unnatural foods.
9. No. You must follow your state's child care licensing regulations.
10. after two years of age
11. (Student response.)
12. Concrete objects, visual signals, novelty, auditory signals. (Student response for examples. See pages 248–249.)

Student Activity Guide

Managing Conflicts, Activity C

1. Tell Shyrell she *must* take off her coat. Make your expectations clear.
2. Toby's behavior will become more dependent. Tell the teacher that Toby is capable of dressing and undressing himself. Therefore, she should let Toby try to do it by himself.
3. After Sally is given a reasonable amount of time, clear the table without comment. Sally needs to learn that if she wants food, she should eat it in a timely manner.
4. The other children may begin to imitate Christine. The teacher should remind Christine that she must remain at the table. If Christine attempts to leave, her teacher must insist she return.
5. Plan ahead and have the children get a drink before they lie down.

Teacher's Resource Guide/Binder

Daily Routines Puzzle, reproducible master 16-1

1. independence
2. eating
3. predictability
4. responsible
5. symbols
6. dressing
7. clothes
8. influenced
9. expectations
10. sufficient
11. tying
12. labeling
13. lockers

Chapter Test

1.	B	17.	T
2.	E	18.	T
3.	C	19.	F
4.	D	20.	F
5.	A	21.	T
6.	T	22.	F
7.	F	23.	T
8.	F	24.	T
9.	F	25.	T
10.	T	26.	D
11.	F	27.	C
12.	F	28.	C
13.	T	29.	B
14.	T	30.	A
15.	F	31.	B
16.	T		

32. (Student response.)
33. (Describe four:) Send an extra set of clothing. All children's clothes should be labeled. The clothing should have large buttons, zippers, snaps, etc., to make dressing easier. Boots and shoes should slide on and off easily. Slacks and shorts are easier for children to handle at toileting time if they have elastic waists. Shoe laces should not be too long.
34. (List four:) taste all foods before asking for seconds of food or milk; remain at the table until everyone has finished; wipe up your own spills; eat food only from your own plate.
35. (Student response. See pages 248–249.)

Daily Routines Puzzle

Name _____ **Date** _____ **Period** _____

Complete the puzzle by filling in the blanks in the sentences below.

1.								D								
2.								A								
3.								I								
4.								L								
5.								Y								
6.								R								
7.								O								
8.								U								
9.								T								
10.								I								
11.								N								
12.								E								
13.								S								

1. Daily routines should provide opportunities for the children to develop _____.

2. Routines such as dressing, undressing, _____, napping, and toileting are everyday experiences.

3. Routines provide the child with reassurance by providing _____ to the day.

4. Children should be _____ for hanging up their own coats.

5. Names and _____ are helpful for labeling the lockers of three-year-old children.

6. _____ can be time-consuming as well as frustrating.

7. Even two-year-olds can be taught to put on their own _____.

8. A child's appetite is _____ by a variety of factors.

9. Teacher _____ are important and need to be communicated to children.

10. It is important for young children to become self-_____.

11. _____ shoes is a skill that requires advanced coordination.

12. _____ the children's clothing will help prevent confusion.

13. _____ should be labeled so the child can identify his or her space.

Not-So-Smooth Transitions

Name _____ **Date**_____ **Period** _____

Read the story below and then write your ideas for a solution to the problem described.

Shavonne enjoys working with the four-year-olds in the center. They are generally active, curious, and fun. Consequently, it is easy to plan activities for them. They listen carefully to stories and use their imaginations in the art and dramatic play areas. These four-year-olds also work well together.

Beginning and introducing the curriculum has not been difficult. Rather, the problem is transitions—getting from one activity to another. During these periods, the children seem to be at their worst. They push and shove each other. Many times, the children do not clean up after one activity before starting a new one. The children's behavior has caused Shavonne to raise her voice in an attempt to improve the situation.

What advice would you give to Shavonne to help her solve this problem with transitions?

_____

_____

_____

_____

_____

_____

_____

_____

_____

_____

_____

_____

_____

_____

_____

_____

_____

_____

_____

_____

Handling Daily Routines

Name _____

Date _____ Period _____ Score _____

Matching: Match the following terms and identifying phrases.

_____ 1. Showing a picture of outdoor play.	A. concrete objects
_____ 2. Instructing the child to pretend to be any type of animal.	B. visual signal
	C. auditory signal
_____ 3. Playing a chord on an instrument.	D. individual transition
_____ 4. Telling one child to go to the snack table.	E. novelty
_____ 5. Having the child move an object from one place to another.	

True/False: Circle *T* if the statement is true or *F* if the statement is false.

T　F　6. Routines are everyday experiences.

T　F　7. Routines provide opportunities for children to develop dependence.

T　F　8. Children generally feel tremendous satisfaction in having others do things for them.

T　F　9. Experienced teachers provide the maximum amount of help.

T　F　10. Teachers should demonstrate dressing skills at a child's eye level.

T　F　11. Generally, preschool children can tie their own shoes.

T　F　12. Most centers provide formulas for infants.

T　F　13. Children's appetites change.

T　F　14. Emotions play an important part in appetite.

T　F　15. Infants do not care how food tastes.

T　F　16. Cup feedings can begin as early as six to seven months of age.

T　F　17. Between 15 and 18 months of age, children are interested in feeding themselves with spoons.

T　F　18. Food preferences may be based upon the color, shape, or consistency of food.

T　F　19. The older the children, the less likely there is to be verbal interaction at the table.

T　F　20. Pica is relatively common in preschool children.

T　F　21. Children are capable of inducing vomiting.

T　F　22. To make the children tired, active activities should be scheduled prior to nap time.

T　F　23. Most child care centers have a set napping time.

T　F　24. Shaming and scolding have no place in helping a child develop toileting control.

T　F　25. Hand motions can be used as a visual transition signal.

(continued)

Multiple Choice: Choose the best response. Write the letter in the space provided.

_____ 26. Routines include _____.
A. constructing materials
B. reading professional journals
C. designing games
D. dressing and undressing

_____ 27. Children are most likely to become interested in feeding themselves at _____.
A. two months
B. six months
C. fifteen months
D. twelve months

_____ 28. Which eating rule should be omitted?
A. Serve small portions.
B. Taste all foods.
C. All food must be eaten.
D. Wipe up spills.

_____ 29. The feeding problem associated with craving unnatural food is _____.
A. dawdling
B. pica
C. food refusal
D. vomiting

_____ 30. Naps are taken _____.
A. in accordance with state licensing requirements
B. to make up for lost sleep at home
C. to punish children
D. to allow teachers a break

_____ 31. The transition used when lights are blinked is called _____.
A. concrete object
B. visual signal
C. novelty
D. auditory signal

Essay Questions: Provide complete responses to the following questions or statements.

32. Explain the importance of a daily schedule.

33. Describe four clothing suggestions you might give to parents.

34. List four general rules that might be used when children eat.

35. Explain the use of transition techniques.

The Curriculum  17

Objectives

After studying this chapter, students will be able to

- develop program goals.
  indicate who is involved in curriculum development.
- cite the importance of assessment in curriculum planning.
- explain the content and process-centered approach to curriculum development.
- describe factors to consider in curriculum planning.
- illustrate the use of themes as a basis for planning curriculum.
- write a block plan and lesson plan for one week of a program.

Teaching Materials

Text, pages 255–274
  Terms to Know
  Review and Reflect
  Apply and Explore
Student Activity Guide
  A. *Dog Flowchart*
  B. *Learning Activities Related to a Theme on Dogs*
  C. *Behaviors*
  D. *Curriculum Building*
  E. *A Sample Lesson*
Teacher's Resource Guide/Binder
  Flowchart Example, transparency master, 17-1
  Apple Flowchart, reproducible master, 17-2
  Objectives for Apple Theme,
    transparency master, 17-3
  Apple Theme: Concepts for the Children to Learn,
    transparency master, 17-4
  Learning Activities Related to a Theme on Apples,
    reproducible master, 17-5
  Sample Block Plan, transparency master, 17-6
  Learning Objectives, transparency master, 17-7
  Writing a Lesson Plan, reproducible master, 17-8
  Assessing Curriculum, transparency master, 17-9
  Chapter Test

Teacher's Resource Binder
  Planning the Curriculum, color transparency, CT-17
The Observation Guide
Mastering CDA Competencies

Introductory Activities

1. Have a group of students present a skit based on what a classroom would be like if no lesson planning took place. Then have the class discuss the skit.
2. Have students discuss themes they think would be appropriate and fun for five-year-olds.

Instructional Concepts and Student Learning Experiences

Developing Program Goals _____

3. Have students define program goals.
4. Have students discuss the importance of meeting the program goals listed in the text.
5. Have students explain how program goals are met.
6. Have students discuss activities for meeting the following program goals: to develop independence; to develop language skills; to develop motor coordination; to develop problem-solving skills.

Who Plans the Curriculum? _____

7. Have students identify people responsible for curriculum decisions.
8. Have students conduct a poll in your community to find out how many centers use a preplanned curriculum.
9. Have students discuss the advantages and disadvantages of using a preplanned curriculum.

Assessment: An Important Step in Curriculum Planning _____

10. Have students discuss the assessment process.
11. Have students discuss the importance of assessment in planning curriculum.
12. Have students brainstorm examples of children's

work that could be collected for assessment purposes.

13. Have students identify observation forms from *The Observation Guide* that would be useful for assessment.

The Content and Process-Centered Curriculum

14. Have students describe the content and process-centered curriculum approach.

15. Have students describe the physical environment in a classroom that has a content and process-centered approach.

Factors to Consider in Curriculum Planning

16. Have students list and discuss three questions that must be answered when selecting learning activities.

17. *Planning the Curriculum*, color transparency CT-17, TRB. Use this transparency to introduce the framework or approach for planning curriculum. You may want to:
    A. Stress that quality early childhood programs assess the children's developmental needs and interests prior to planning curriculum goals.
    B. Have students discuss how child development knowledge and curriculum intersect.
    C. Ask students to brainstorm the benefits of using a theme to structure the curriculum.
    D. Have students select a theme and develop a flowchart.

18. Have students discuss the differences between structured and unstructured activities.

19. Have students explain the differences between field-sensitive and field-independent learning styles.

20. Have students describe auditory learners.

Themes

21. Have students brainstorm a list of themes appropriate for preschool children.

22. Have students discuss how children's interest in themes differs among children ages two, three, four, and five.

23. Have students explain the cautions that must be exercised in planning holiday themes.

24. Have students discuss the relationship between children's attention spans and theme length.

25. *Flowchart Example,* transparency master 17-1. Use this transparency as an example of how to construct a flowchart.

26. *Apple Flowchart,* reproducible master 17-2. Have students create a flowchart for an apple theme and write objectives based on the flowchart.

27. *Objectives for Apple Theme,* transparency master 17-3. Have students compare their objectives for an apple theme to the goals listed on the master.

28. *Apple Theme: Concepts for the Children to Learn,* transparency master 17-4. Use this master as a guide for students in developing a list of concepts they want children to grasp as a result of the theme.

29. *Learning Activities Related to a Theme on Apples,* reproducible master 17-5. Have students develop activities for each of the areas listed based on an apple theme.

30. *Dog Flowchart,* Activity A, SAG. Have students create a flowchart for a dog theme and write objectives based on the flowchart.

31. *Learning Activities Related to a Theme on Dogs,* Activity B, SAG. Have students develop activities for each of the areas listed based on a dog theme.

Written Plans

32. *Sample Block Plan,* transparency master 17-6. Use this sample block plan to introduce students to the preparation of a block plan.

33. Have students prepare a written block plan for a week.

34. Have students describe the difference between block plans and lesson plans.

35. Have students list the parts of a lesson plan.

36. Have students explain the purpose of developmental goals.

37. *Learning Objectives,* transparency master 17-7. Use the master to discuss the parts of learning objectives. Then have students complete the chart with appropriately written objectives.

38. *Behaviors,* Activity C, SAG. Have students check the behaviors that could be used in a lesson plan. Students should then use six of the checked behaviors to write learning objectives.

39. Have students write five learning objectives.

40. Have students identify learning objectives in textbooks and other teaching resources.

41. *Writing a Lesson Plan,* reproducible master 17-8. Have students write a lesson plan for an activity determined by you or the student using the form provided.

42. *Curriculum Building,* Activity D, SAG. Have students complete the puzzle by filling in the spaces with the correct terms.

43. *A Sample Lesson,* Activity E, SAG. Have students use the form to write a sample lesson plan.

44. *Assessing Curriculum,* transparency master 17-9. Use this transparency to help students evaluate the appropriateness of a curriculum.

Additional Resources

45. Panel discussion. Invite child care teachers and directors to discuss different methods of planning curriculum.

46. Guest speaker. Invite a preschool teacher to discuss how he or she plans lessons for children.

Research Topics

47. Have students research to find information on the effectiveness of preplanned curriculums. Then have students write a report based on their research.
48. Have the students review a teacher's lesson plan and then observe how he or she conducts the activities reviewed. Students should give an oral report to the class explaining how the lesson plan was carried out in the classroom.

Answer Key

Text

Review and Reflect, page 274

1. Program goals are broad statements of purpose that state the desired end result of what is to be achieved.
2. false
3. A preplanned curriculum is helpful to a staff with little training or experience and it saves teachers time and energy.
4. (Student response. See pages 257–258.)
5. Direct learning experiences are planned with a specific goal in mind. Indirect experiences occur on the spur of the moment.
6. Is the information gained worth knowing? Is the information testable by the children? Is the information developmentally appropriate for the children?
7. field-sensitive
8. field-independent
9. visual
10. auditory
11. Spiral curriculum is a concept that explains the growth of children's interests from the immediate surroundings to a wider variety of topics.
12. A flowchart outlines major concepts related to a theme.
13. A block plan is an overall view of the curriculum. It outlines the general plans. A lesson plan is more detailed than a block plan. It outlines specific actions and activities that will be used to meet goals and objectives.
14. Developmental goals state the expected outcome of a specific activity. Program goals state the expected outcome of an entire program.
15. The conditions of performance. The behavior. The level of performance. (Student response for explanations. See page 270.)
16. procedures

17. First, evaluate the learning experience. Then evaluate the children and their responses. Finally, evaluate your own teaching strategies.

Student Activity Guide

Dogs Flowchart, Activity A

Student responses may vary. One flowchart is:

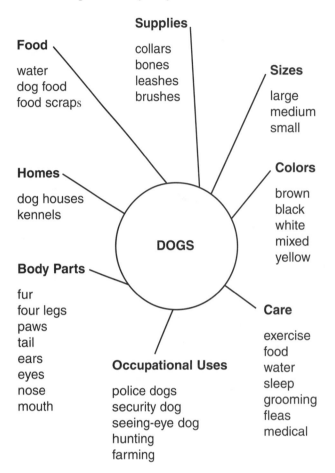

Behaviors, Activity C

The following behaviors should be checked: 1-5, 7-9, 11-13, 15-17, 19-22, 24, 25, 27, 28, 30-32, 34, 35, 37-39.

(Student response for objectives.)

Curriculum Building, Activity D

1. content and process-centered
2. auditory learners
3. conditions of performance
4. level of performance
5. learning objectives
6. block plan
7. spiral curriculum
8. lesson plan
9. visual learners

10. program goals
11. behaviors
12. closure
13. transition
14. field-independent
15. field-sensitive
16. motivation
17. direct learning experiences
18. indirect learning experiences

Teacher's Resource Guide/Binder

Apple Flowchart, transparency master 17-2

Student responses may vary. One flowchart is:

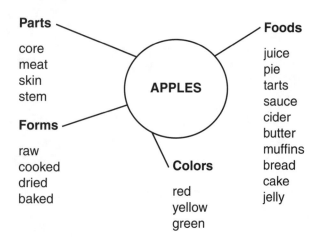

Parts

core
meat
skin
stem

Forms

raw
cooked
dried
baked

Colors

red
yellow
green

Foods

juice
pie
tarts
sauce
cider
butter
muffins
bread
cake
jelly

APPLES

Chapter Test

1. F	16. T
2. C	17. T
3. E	18. F
4. A	19. F
5. D	20. T
6. G	21. T
7. B	22. A
8. T	23. D
9. T	24. C
10. F	25. B
11. T	26. C
12. T	27. C
13. F	28. D
14. T	29. C
15. F	

30. (Student response. See page 256.)
31. Is the information worth knowing? Is the information testable by the child? Is the information developmentally appropriate?
32. (Student response. See pages 271–273.)

Flowchart Example

Flowchart of Hat Curriculum Theme

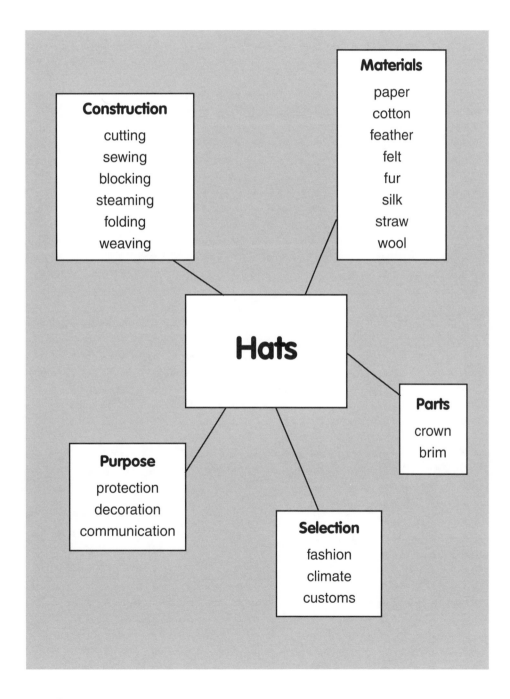

Materials

paper
cotton
feather
felt
fur
silk
straw
wool

Construction

cutting
sewing
blocking
steaming
folding
weaving

Hats

Parts

crown
brim

Purpose

protection
decoration
communication

Selection

fashion
climate
customs

Apple Flowchart

Name _____ **Date** _____ **Period** _____

Review the section on flowcharts in the text. Create a flowchart listing the possible concepts to be used in developing a theme on apples. Then write related objectives based on the concepts listed using a separate sheet of paper.

APPLES

Objectives for Apple Theme

Objectives to be used when planning a theme on apples could be for children to:

- Identify the parts of an apple.

- Wash apples for eating.

- Taste apples.

- Name the color of the apple.

- Tell which apple is the largest.

- Tell which apple is the smallest.

- Draw a picture of an apple.

- Color a picture of an apple.

Apple Theme: Concepts for the Children to Learn

♦ An apple is a fruit.

♦ Apples can be red, yellow, or green.

♦ An apple has five parts: seed, core, pulp, skin, and stem.

♦ Apples grow on trees.

♦ A group of apple trees is called an orchard.

♦ Apples can be large or small.

♦ Some apples are sweet and others are sour.

♦ Apples can be hard or soft.

♦ Seeds from an apple can grow into a tree.

♦ Pies, cakes, applesauce, butter, jelly, breads, juice, muffins, and breads can be made from apples.

Learning Activities Related to a Theme on Apples

Name _____ **Date**_____ **Period** _____

List below activities that you could use under each curriculum area for a theme focusing on apples.

Art:

Storytelling:

Sensory Table:

Dramatic Play:

Music:

Science:

Math:

Fingerplays:

Sample Block Plan

Afternoon Session—4 Year Olds Yvonne Libby

Week _____ Theme _____

	1:00-2:25 Free Play/ Centers Snack	2:25-2:40 Large Group	2:40-3:00 Snack	2:40-3:00 Small Groups — Rhonda	Cathy	Diana	3:00-3:30 Outdoors
Monday	*crayons, chunk crayons (Jaci) *soybeans on the sensory table *beauty shop (Sheila) *listening center— It's a small world	*Here are we together *Downright, Upright... song with puppet	Chex mix milk	Paper bag puppets *cutting & pasting	Parachute Fun!	We're Very Good Friends, My Brother and I - book	Game— "Grey Squirrel!"
Tuesday	*art rubbings (Sherry) *orange H2O and utensils in sensory table *driving wheel (Tammy) *cooking-making mini-pizza!	*Downright, Upright... *Cobbler, Cobbler, Mend My Shoe	mini-pizzas milk	We're Very Good Friends, My Brother and I - book	Paper bag puppets *cutting & pasting	Parachute Fun!	*Rakes! Jumping in piles of leaves
Wednesday	*colored glue and styrofoam pieces *leaves in the sensory table (Sheila) *toothpick structures (Jaci) *tumbling mat	The Clown's Smile story cards	fruit-flavored yogurt	Parachute Fun!	We're Very Good Friends, My Brother and I - book	Paper bag puppets *cutting & pasting	*trikes
Thursday	Fieldtrip to Connell's Apple Orchard						
Friday	*painting with roller paints (Mary) *Bubbles! in sensory table *Apple tasting! *Twister! *sharing center	*Discussion of apple orchard *Goodbyes to Rhonda and Cathy...	cheese & crackers milk	Show and Tell			*chalk on sidewalk

Learning Objectives

Conditions of Performance	Behavior	Level of Performance
Given a three-piece puzzle	The child will complete the puzzle	Within a five minute period
Given crayons	The child will draw	A four-inch line
Given a set of blocks	The child will stack	The blocks four high
Without the aid of a teacher	The child will climb	Four rungs on a ladder

Writing a Lesson Plan

Name _____ **Date**_____ **Period** _____

Write a lesson plan for the following subject: _____

Developmental Goals:

Learning Objectives:

Materials Needed:

Motivation/Introduction:

(continued)

 **Procedures:**

 **Closure/Transition:**

Assessing Curriculum

An appropriate curriculum...

♦ Promotes all developmental domains (physical, social, emotional and cognitive).

♦ Supports program goals.

♦ Involves assessment and reflects the children's needs, special abilities, and interests.

♦ Begins at children's developmental level and is sequenced step-by-step.

♦ Strengthens the children's sense of competence and identity.

♦ Supports linguistic and cultural diversity.

♦ Focuses on integration of subject matter around a concept or theme.

♦ Builds from simple to more complex levels of skills, knowledge, and interests.

♦ Provides opportunities for children to choose activities and pursue them in their own ways.

♦ Promotes interactive learning.

♦ Allows children to make meaningful choices.

♦ Encourages social interaction among children and adults.

♦ Achieves cognitive, physical, social, and emotional goals.

♦ Focuses on positive feelings.

Name _____

Date _____ **Period** _____ **Score** _____

Matching: Match the following terms and identifying phrases.

_____ 1. Broad statements of purpose, reflecting the consequences of education.

_____ 2. These children like to work with others.

_____ 3. A generalized idea or notion.

_____ 4. A variety of experiences designed to meet the children's developmental needs.

_____ 5. A simple method for listing possible concepts to be used in a theme.

_____ 6. Learning experiences are integrated by these in many child care programs.

_____ 7. These children prefer to work independently.

A. curriculum
B. field-independent
C. field-sensitive
D. flowchart
E. concept
F. program goals
G. themes

True/False: Circle *T* if the statement is true or *F* if the statement is false.

T F 8. Direct learning experiences are planned with a specific purpose.

T F 9. In some centers, a wide variety of people are involved in the curriculum process.

T F 10. A preplanned curriculum only has advantages.

T F 11. The emphasis in a content and process-centered curriculum stresses hands-on activities.

T F 12. Program goals outline the philosophy of the center.

T F 13. Two-year-old children are interested in themes related to community helpers.

T F 14. The children's interest can affect the length of a theme.

T F 15. A theme on circles would be appropriate for four-year-old children.

T F 16. Four- and five-year-old children may enjoy a theme on puppets.

T F 17. A good curriculum contains a balance of activities.

T F 18. Children move and learn at the same rate.

T F 19. Block plans are more detailed than lesson plans.

T F 20. The developmental goals tell the "why" of an activity.

T F 21. Successful learning experiences provide opportunities for the children to test their knowledge.

(continued)

Multiple Choice: Choose the best response. Write the letter in the space provided.

_____ 22. Indirect learning experiences _____.
A. occur on the spur of the moment
B. are planned with a specific goal in mind
C. are written in a curriculum
D. are lead by the teacher

_____ 23. An appropriate theme for two-year-olds is _____.
A. police officers
B. hair stylists
C. insects
D. my family

_____ 24. The outcomes of activities are _____.
A. developmental goals
B. procedures
C. learning objectives
D. motivations

_____ 25. The most detailed planning is contained in _____.
A. yearly goals
B. lesson plans
C. block plans
D. evaluations

_____ 26. Which is *not* a part of a learning objective?
A. The condition of performance.
B. The behavior.
C. The evaluation.
D. The level of performance.

_____ 27. An example of a condition of performance includes _____.
A. the child will jump
B. the child will sing
C. given a set of blocks
D. the child will stack

_____ 28. An example of level of performance includes _____.
A. the child will stack
B. given a three-piece puzzle
C. after listening to the story
D. within a five minute period

_____ 29. Which would be a behavior that is measurable?
A. Think.
B. Know.
C. Climb.
D. Realize.

Essay Questions: Provide complete responses to the following questions or statements.

30. List five examples of possible program goals for early childhood settings.

31. What are the three basic questions you need to ask when selecting activities?

32. Describe the evaluation of an activity.

238

Guiding Art, Blockbuilding, and Sensory Experiences

18

Objectives

After studying this chapter, students will be able to
- explain how art experiences promote physical, social, emotional, and cognitive growth.
- describe techniques for guiding art experiences.
- list the stages of art skill development.
- compile a list of art supplies needed for a well-stocked classroom.
- plan a variety of art, blockbuilding, sensory, and woodworking activities suitable for young children.

Teaching Materials

Text, pages 275–291
  Terms to Know
  Review and Reflect
  Apply and Explore
Student Activity Guide
  A. *Stages of Artwork*
  B. *Characteristics of Children's Art*
  C. *Sources of Free Art Materials*
  D. *Tips for Buying Art Supplies*
  E. *Rating Play Dough*
Teacher's Resource Guide/Binder
  Value of Art Experiences, transparency master, 18-1
  Paste Recipes, reproducible master, 18-2
  Painting Activities, reproducible master, 18-3
  Finger Paint Recipes, reproducible master, 18-4
  Chapter Test
Teacher's Resource Binder
  Art Stages, color transparency, CT-18
The Observation Guide
Mastering CDA Competencies

Introductory Activities

1. Ask students to list types of art activities, such as painting, drawing, etc. Then ask students which forms they enjoy doing and why.
2. Have students discuss the meaning of creativity and its relationship to art activities.

Instructional Concepts and Student Learning Experiences

The Importance of Art Experiences _____

3. *Value of Art Experiences,* transparency master 18-1. Before using the master, lead a discussion on what students feel is the value of art experiences for young children. Then share the values listed on the master.
4. Have students describe the value of art activities in relationship to physical, cognitive, social, and emotional development.

Techniques for Guiding Art Experiences _____

5. Have students discuss how teachers can take precautions to only help children with art activities when they need help.
6. Have students role-play situations in which positive techniques are used in guiding children's art experiences.

Stages of Art Skill Development _____

7. Have students describe the stages of art skill development.
8. *Art Stages,* color transparency CT-18, TRB. Use this transparency to introduce stages of children's art. You may want to:
   A. Stress that a teacher's knowledge of a child's development is the key to determining the appropriateness of an activity.
   B. Have students recall their earliest recollection of engaging with art materials. What did they do? What materials did they enjoy? How did their parents or teachers encourage or inhibit them?
   C. Discuss the art stages of one- to two-year-old, two- to three-year-olds, three- to four-year-olds, and four- to five-year-olds.
   D. Remind students that all children everywhere, at the same age, draw the same things in the same way.
9. Collect drawings done by children of different ages. Have the class determine the stage of art development represented in each drawing.

10. Have students duplicate the characteristics of children's artwork for the scribbles, basic forms, and first drawings stages.
11. Have students identify the color preferences of children.
12. Have students observe two children paint and write descriptions of their behavior.
13. *Stages of Artwork,* Activity A, SAG. Have students match the stages of artwork with the given descriptions.
14. *Characteristics of Children's Art,* Activity B, SAG. Have students complete the chart by reproducing children's artwork for each stage listed. Students should also indicate appropriate ages for each stage and describe characteristics of the artwork.

Art Supplies and Tools

15. Have students list sources of inexpensive art supplies.
16. *Sources of Free Art Materials,* Activity C, SAG. Have students complete the chart by listing free materials that might be available from each of the sources given.
17. Have students brainstorm a list of objects that could be used for printing activities.
18. *Tips for Buying Art Supplies,* Activity D, SAG. Have students complete the supply form by marking whether items would be purchased or donated and marking sources of donated items.
19. Have students explain how to purchase and mix tempera paint.
20. Have students explain how age relates to the types of brushes used by children for painting.
21. Have students demonstrate how to adjust an easel.
22. Have students brainstorm a list of types of paper that can be used for art activities.
23. Have students debate the merit (or lack of merit) of using coloring books in an art program.
24. *Paste Recipes,* reproducible master 18-2. Have students prepare the four paste recipes and compare their qualities, including ease of preparation.
25. Have students prepare a floor plan and design for the space and storage space in an art area.

Painting Activities

26. Have students describe the role of the teacher in guiding painting activities.
27. Have students brainstorm various methods for painting activities.
28. *Painting Activities,* reproducible master 18-3. Have students try the different painting activities given. Students should compare the types of senses used, enjoyment of the processes, and results of the activities.

29. Have students explain procedures for guiding children during easel painting.
30. Have students prepare the three finger paint recipes in the text and compare their qualities.
31. *Finger Paint Recipes,* reproducible master 18-4. Have students prepare the finger paint recipes given and compare their qualities, ease of preparation, and cost.
32. Have students make a chart of the various types of painting activities, materials needed, and processes used.

Molding

33. Have students observe children in molding activities and report their observations to the class.
34. *Rating Play Dough,* Activity E, SAG. Have students prepare the play dough recipes in the text and rate them using the form provided.
35. Have students list materials that could be added to play dough for variety.

Cutting

36. Have students describe the process by which children learn to cut.
37. Gather some samples of paper and scissors. Have students evaluate the appropriateness of each item for cutting activities for children.

Collages

38. Have students brainstorm a list of materials that can be used to make collages.
39. Have students collect a variety of collage materials and organize them in a storage container.
40. Have students experiment with using various collage materials and evaluate their appropriateness for children.

Blockbuilding

41. Demonstrate and identify the various stages of blockbuilding among children.
42. Set up a display of various types of blocks and accessories.

Sensory Experiences: Sand and Water Play

43. Explain why moist sand is preferable to dry sand.
44. Have students make a list of various utensils that would be fun for children to use at the water table.

Woodworking

45. Have students describe how tools should be selected for use in the woodworking area.

Additional Resources

46. Field trip. Arrange for students to visit a child care center and observe the types of art supplies available.

47. Panel discussion. Invite a variety of artists to discuss the various forms of art they produce.
48. Guest speaker. Invite a child care teacher to discuss the types of art activities that are made available to the children in his or her center. Ask the teacher to bring some samples of materials and finished artwork.

Research Topics

49. Have students research professional journals to find results of studies on the value of various types of art activities. Students should then write a report summarizing and commenting on the research findings.
50. Have students survey parents to find out what types of art projects their children do at home. Using the results of the survey and other resources, have students develop a brochure on tips for home art activities.

Answer Key

Text

Review and Reflect, page 291

1. Children learn responsibility. They learn to work and share with others. They learn to respect the property of others. They also learn to value the work and ideas of others.
2. They might just be experimenting with different tools and supplies and might not know what they are making. Some children lack the language skills needed to explain their artwork. Asking questions may make them uneasy.
3. Scribbles, basic forms, first drawings (Student response for one explanation. See pages 271–278 of the text.)
4. false
5. Add only a small amount of liquid to the tempera while stirring constantly. This will make a very thick paste. Then slowly add more liquid until you get the desired consistency.
6. true
7. These tools need to be pushed hard with small muscles that are not well-developed in small children. Paint, however, flows easily.
8. (Student response. See page 281 of the text.)
9. Finger
10. Two-year-old children pull, beat, push, and squeeze. By age five, children will often announce what they are going to make before they begin.
11. (Student response.)
12. (Name three: See 18-19 in the text.)
13. (Name three: claw hammers, hand drills, pliers, sandpaper blocks, vise, saws)

Student Activity Guide

Stages of Artwork, Activity A

1. A		9. C	
2. C		10. B	
3. B		11. B	
4. C		12. C	
5. A		13. A	
6. C		14. C	
7. B		15. B	
8. A			

Characteristics of Children's Art, Activity B

Scribbles: Between 15 months and three years of age. Children make zigzags, whirls, and circles. Children do not make connections between the marks on the paper and their own movements.

Basic forms: Between ages three and four. Children learn basic forms, such as ovals, rectangles, and circles. They have more control over their motor movements and better eye-hand coordination. They begin to see the relationship between their movements and the marks they make.

First drawings: During the fourth and fifth years of age. Children produce their first real drawings. They create objects and symbols of events they know.

Teacher's Resource Guide/Binder

Chapter Test

1. C		17. T	
2. D		18. F	
3. E		19. T	
4. F		20. T	
5. G		21. F	
6. B		22. T	
7. A		23. T	
8. T		24. C	
9. F		25. A	
10. T		26. B	
11. T		27. D	
12. F		28. D	
13. T		29. D	
14. T		30. A	
15. T		31. D	
16. F		32. C	

33. (Explain three:) Be creative in your approach; observe to find new ways to expand children's learning experiences; provide age-appropriate activities; allow children to express their ideas; provide time to experiment and explore; involve all five senses; help children carefully; tell chil-

dren what supplies are available; observe children without asking questions about what they are making; let children decide when their work is finished; praise children's work in ways that show respect for all children's work.

34. Studies show that these materials have a negative effect on creativity. Seeing the drawings and trying to color them also can undermine children's confidence in their art skills. These materials are not found to enhance art skills.

35. It promotes eye-hand coordination, small and large muscle development, and creative expression. In addition, it provides children with an emotional release.

Value of Art Experiences

Through art experiences children learn to:

♦ express feelings

♦ participate in self-chosen activities

♦ respect the property of others

♦ find new ways of using materials

♦ use a variety of equipment

♦ mix materials

♦ become aware of color, texture, line, and form

Paste Recipes

Colored Salt Paste

    1 part   flour
2 parts   salt
              powdered tempera paint
              water

Mix the flour and salt. Then add a small amount of powdered paint. Finally, slowly add water a small amount at a time. Mix well. Continue adding water and mixing the paste until a smooth heavy consistency is obtained.

Favorite Paste

          1 cup   cold water
          1 cup   flour
      2½ cups   boiling water
  1 tablespoon   powdered alum
¾ teaspoon   oil of wintergreen

Mix the cold water and flour together, stirring until smooth. Add the boiling water and mix well. Pour the mixture into the top of a double boiler. Cook until smooth over a low heat. Add the alum and stir. Remove from the heat. When the mixture is cool, add the oil of wintergreen.

Flour Paste

          1 cup   boiling water
1 tablespoon   powdered alum
      2 cups   flour
      2 cups   cold water
  1 teaspoon   oil of wintergreen (optional)

Boil 1 cup of water and add the alum. Add 2 cups of flour to the 2 cups of cold water. Stir until smooth. Add this mixture to the boiling alum water. Continue cooking, stirring constantly until the mixture develops a bluish cast. Remove from heat. If desired, add oil of wintergreen to give the paste a pleasing aroma. Cool. Store in airtight jars. If necessary, thin by adding a small amount of water.

Cornstarch Paste

      ¼ teaspoon   alum
   1 tablespoon   flour
2 tablespoons   cornstarch
      3 ounces   water

Mix the alum, flour, and cornstarch together. Slowly add the water, stirring to remove the lumps. Cook in a double boiler over low heat, stirring constantly. When paste begins to thicken remove from heat. The mixture will continue to thicken as it cools. If necessary, thin with water. Store in airtight jars.

Painting Activities

Blot Painting

Materials needed:
>
> paper
> thick tempera paint
> tongue depressors

Begin by demonstrating how to prefold the paper. Open the prefolded paper. Using a tongue depressor, drop thick tempera paint onto the paper. Refold the paper. Press the folded paper with your hands. Open the prefolded paper and discover the design. If desired, more than one color of tempera paint may be used.

Blow Painting

Materials needed:
>
> paper
> thin tempera paint
> straw

Place a small amount of tempera paint on the paper. To form a shape, blow the tempera with a straw.

Dry Powder Paint

Materials needed:
>
> cotton balls
> dry powdered tempera paint
> paper

In small dishes, place powdered tempera paint. Then slightly dampen the cotton balls. The children can use the cotton balls as tools to apply paint to the paper. If desired, a clip clothespin can be attached to the cotton ball and used as a handle.

Cotton Swab Painting

Materials needed:
>
> paper
> liquid tempera paint
> cotton swabs

Pour a small amount of liquid tempera paint into a shallow dish, pie pan, or tin. Using a cotton swab as a painting tool, the children can create designs.

(continued)

Salt Or Sand Painting

Materials needed:

> glue
> paper
> powdered tempera paint
> salt or sand
> salt shaker

Mix equal amounts of salt or sand and powdered tempera paint together. Pour the mixture into large salt shakers. To create a design, glue can be placed on a sheet of paper. Sprinkle the tempera mixture onto the paper. The mixture will adhere to the glued area only. Shake off excess tempera.

Soap Painting

Materials needed:

> brushes
> 2 cups powdered laundry soap
> powdered tempera paint
> water
> paper

Add a small amount of colored powdered tempera paint to the laundry soap. Then slowly add water until the mixture becomes the consistency of a thick pancake batter. Provide the children with paper, brushes, and the mixture. The brush can serve as a tool to apply the paint to the paper. Encourage the children to observe their art after the soap dries; the texture is interesting.

Spatter Painting

Materials needed:

> patterns to place under the screen
> tempera paint
> toothbrushes
> wire screens

Prepare pans of thin tempera paint. Place patterns such as leaves, cookie cutters, paper silhouettes, etc., under the screen. Demonstrate how to dip the toothbrush into the paint. Rub the brush over the wire. Remove the screen and encourage the children to observe the design and create some of their own.

Sponge Painting

Materials needed:

> paper sponges cut into shapes
> tempera paint in shallow pans

The sponge serves as a tool to apply the paint to paper. Dip it into the pan of paint, and press it onto the paper, repeating as desired.

(continued)

String Painting

Materials needed:

> large 12-by-18 inch pieces of construction paper
> tempera paint in pans
> thick yarn or string

Cut the string into approximately 1 6-inch pieces. Lay pieces of paper on a flat surface. Mix the tempera. Place the string in the tempera paint. Remove and pull it across the construction paper.

Texture Painting

Materials needed:

> brush
> construction paper
> glue
> sand, sawdust, or coffee grounds
> tempera paint

Begin by adding sand, sawdust, or coffee grounds to the tempera paint. Then add a small amount of glue. The mixture should be liquid to spread on paper.

Finger Paint Recipes

Whenever possible, let the children assist in preparing finger paint. Begin by premeasuring the ingredients to avoid costly mistakes.

Cooked Starch Finger Paint

Dissolve 1 cup of laundry starch in a small amount of cold water. To this mixture add 5 cups of boiling water. A tablespoon of glycerin, if desired, can also be added.

Cornstarch Finger Paint

Premeasure one cup of cornstarch. Add gradually two quarts water. Cook until clear, stirring constantly. Add ½ cup soap flakes. If desired, an extract such as almond, mint, or orange can be added for aroma.

Flour Finger Paint

Mix one cup of cold water and one cup of flour. Add the mixture to 3 cups of boiling water. Continue cooking, stirring constantly until the mixture thickens. Food coloring can be added for interest.

Flour And Salt Finger Paint

Combine one cup of flour with ½ cup salt. Add ¾ cup water. Thoroughly mix by stirring. This paint is very grainy, unlike other finger paints. As a result, the children will enjoy touching the artwork after it has dried.

Instant Flour Finger Paint

Pour 2 cups of water into a large mixing bowl. Add ½ cup of instant powdered flour (regular flour may be lumpy). Stir in the flour until a smooth texture is obtained. Add food coloring for appeal, if desired.

Liquid Starch Finger Paint

Pour liquid starch into empty squeeze detergent bottles. Also fill a salt shaker with colored tempera paint. The children can squeeze the starch onto paper or a washable surface. Then they can shake the tempera onto the starch, blending the paint mixture with their fingers.

Soap Flake Finger Paint

Pour soap flakes into a bowl. Add a small amount of water. Using an eggbeater, beat until stiff. Food coloring can be added for interest. If desired, the paint can be left white and used on dark paper.

Quick Finger Paint

Combine 2 cups of soap flakes, 1 cup cold water, and 1 cup of liquid laundry starch. Mix well.

Wheat Flour Finger Paint

Add three cups of water to one cup of wheat paste flour. (This flour can be purchased in a decorating store that sells wallpaper.) Stir until dissolved. Food coloring or tempera paint can be added to color the paint.

Guiding Art, Blockbuilding, and Sensory Experiences

Name _____

Date _____ Period _____ Score _____

Matching: Match the following materials and art activities.

_____ 1. Brushes and paint.

_____ 2. Pudding, partially-set gelatin, or shaving cream.

_____ 3. Trays of paint and yarn.

_____ 4. Paint and starch, sawdust, or coffee grounds.

_____ 5. Spools, clothespins, or pine cones.

_____ 6. Doilies, feathers, and tree bark.

_____ 7. A process of placing two blocks vertically a space apart, then adding a third block on top.

A. bridging
B. collages
C. easel painting
D. finger painting
E. string painting
F. texture painting
G. vegetable printing

True/False: Circle *T* if the statement is true or *F* if the statement is false.

T   F   8. Art should always be a creative process.

T   F   9. There are four stages through which a child progresses in developing art abilities.

T   F   10. Social learnings can be fostered through art activities.

T   F   11. The first stage of art is called scribbling.

T   F   12. The basic forms stage of art usually occurs in children between four and five years of age.

T   F   13. Art activities improve the control of arm muscles.

T   F   14. Children choose colors they like for art rather than those related to the usual world.

T   F   15. In the scribbling stage, the art product is merely a by-product of the experience.

T   F   16. Children produce their first real drawings during the basic forms stage.

T   F   17. Cotton swabs can be introduced as brushes to the older children.

T   F   18. Tempera paint comes only in a powdered form.

T   F   19. The least expensive kind of paper is tissue paper.

T   F   20. The best type of paper for easel painting is cream colored and slightly absorbent.

T   F   21. Easel brushes from three-fourths to one and one-half inches should be provided for the children.

T   F   22. The younger the child, the wider the easel brush should be.

T   F   23. Sand and water play are often referred to as sensory experiences.

(continued)

Multiple Choice: Choose the best response. Write the letter in the space provided.

_____ 24. Teachers should provide art activities because _____.
   A. parents demand them
   B. they take up time
   C. they allow children to express their feelings
   D. they are inexpensive

_____ 25. At what age does the scribbling stage of art occur?
   A. Fifteen months to three years.
   B. Two to four years.
   C. Three to five years.
   D. Four to six years.

_____ 26. Which is typical of the basic forms stage?
   A. Children do not make the connection between marks and their own movements.
   B. Children can control the size and shape of a line.
   C. Children attempt to mimic their own view of the world.
   D. Children draw crude human figures.

_____ 27. Drawings of animals appear at what age?
   A. Fifteen months to three years.
   B. Two to four years.
   C. Three to four years.
   D. Four to five years.

_____ 28. A beautiful color according to children is _____.
   A. brown
   B. white
   C. black
   D. green

_____ 29. To cut expenses, a thickening agent can be added to tempera called _____.
   A. superlax
   B. detergent
   C. duralax
   D. bentonite

_____ 30. Which of the following have been shown to have a negative effect on children's creativity?
   A. Coloring books.
   B. Finger paints.
   C. Play dough.
   D. Paste.

_____ 31. Which painting activity stimulates the sense of smell?
   A. Easel painting.
   B. String painting.
   C. Vegetable printing.
   D. Spice painting.

_____ 32. Children from three to six years of age prefer _____ blocks.
   A. cardboard
   B. plastic
   C. wooden
   D. foam

(continued)

Essay Questions: Provide complete responses to the following questions or statements.

33. Explain three general teaching techniques for guiding art experiences.

34. Why are worksheets and coloring books considered inappropriate for art activities?

35. Developmentally, how can woodworking be a valuable experience?

Guiding Storytelling Experiences

Objectives

After studying this chapter, students will be able to
- explain the advantages of storytelling.
- list the four types of children's books.
- discuss the process of choosing children's books.
- outline the steps to follow when reading aloud to children.
- explain a variety of storytelling methods.

Teaching Materials

Text, pages 293–305
Terms to Know
Review and Reflect
Apply and Explore
Student Activity Guide
  A. *Storytelling*
  B. *Choosing Books for Children*
  C. *Story Comparisons*
  D. *Evaluate Your Storytelling Technique*
Teacher's Resource Guide/Binder
  Why Use Stories and Books?
    transparency master, 19-1
  Age and Children's Books, transparency master, 19-2
  Book Evaluation Form, reproducible master, 19-3
  Types of Storytelling, transparency master, 19-4
  Chapter Test
Teacher's Resource Binder
  Language Arts, color transparency, CT-19A
  Effective Storytelling Techniques,
    color transparency, CT-19B
The Observation Guide
Mastering CDA Competencies

Introductory Activities

1. Ask students to recall the titles of storybooks they liked as young children. Have students discuss what they liked about those stories.
2. Discuss with students different ways in which stories can be told.

3. Have students discuss whether they think stories are important to children and why or why not.

Instructional Concepts and Student Learning Experiences

The Importance of Storytelling

4. *Why Use Stories and Books?* transparency master 19-1. Use the master as a basis for discussion of reasons for using stories and books in the classroom. Encourage students to add other reasons that may come to mind.
5. Have students give examples of stories that help children explore and wonder about their world.
6. *Language Arts,* color transparency CT-19A, TRB. Use this transparency to present the interrelationship of listening, speaking, reading, and writing. You may want to:
   A. Stress that as a result of research during the past decade, changes have occurred in approaches to teaching early literacy. It was once thought that during their early years, children learned how to speak and listen. Later, in kindergarten and primary school, they learned how to read and write. Now, studies show that they learn these skills simultaneously, beginning in infancy.
   B. Discuss the activities teachers can use to promote language arts: listening, speaking, reading, and writing.
   C. Ask students to provide examples of how children can learn concepts about book handling and print during storytelling.
   D. Discuss how teachers can attract children to the enjoyment of storytelling and, subsequently, books.
7. *Storytelling,* Activity A, SAG. Have students read the statements about storytelling and indicate whether they are true or false.

Books as Sources of Stories

8. Have students name and describe the types of books listed in the text.

9. Have students make a display of books that are labeled according to their types.
10. Have students discuss how age affects the types of books chosen for children.

Selecting Books for Children _____

11. Have students explain how book reviews can be used in the process of selecting books for children.
12. Have students discuss the importance of illustrations and children's reactions to them in selecting books for children.
13. *Age and Children's Books,* transparency master 19-2. Use the master as a basis for discussion of books that are appropriate for children of different ages.
14. Have students prepare a bibliography of children's books listed according to age groups for which they are appropriate.
15. *Choosing Books for Children,* Activity B, SAG. Have students use the form to list tips for parents on choosing books for children of various ages.
16. Have students define the terms sexism, racism, and ageism.
17. Have students give examples of stereotypes in stories.
18. Have students discuss why sexism should be avoided in children's books.
19. Have students create a brochure for teachers or parents listing tips for selecting children's books.
20. Have students select a book they would consider appropriate for reading to a group of children and explain to the class why they chose it.
21. *Book Evaluation Form,* reproducible master 19-3. Have students use the form to evaluate a book that they might select for reading to a group of children.
22. *Story Comparisons,* Activity C, SAG. Have students use the form to compare three books that a teacher might read to children.

Reading Stories to Children _____

23. *Effective Storytelling Techniques,* color transparency CT-19B, TRB. Use this transparency to introduce effective storytelling techniques. You may want to:
    A. Remind students that a combination of techniques contributes to effective storytelling.
    B. Ask students to brainstorm a list of ways that stories can be introduced.
    C. Discuss why eye contact is essential for effective storytelling.
    D. Have students identify ways that children can participate in storytelling.
24. Have students describe how they should prepare to read a story.
25. Have students discuss the value of becoming your own critic in preparing for storytelling.

26. Have students discuss methods for introducing a story.
27. Have students select a prop that could be used with a story and share the prop with the class.
28. Have students observe a teacher reading a story and share their observations with the class.
29. Have students discuss ways to handle story interruptions.
30. Have students describe methods of ending stories.
31. Have students make a chart outlining the steps in storytelling.
32. *Evaluate Your Storytelling Technique,* Activity D, SAG. Have students choose a partner and select a book to read to a small group of children. Have partners evaluate one another using the checklist provided.
33. Have students practice reading a story to the class.
34. Have students practice reading a story to a group of children in a child care center. The student should have the class teacher evaluate the reading.

Achieving Variety in Storytelling _____

35. Have students discuss the advantages and disadvantages of using a variety of methods to tell stories.
36. Have students list and describe the variations of storytelling.
37. *Types of Storytelling,* transparency master 19-4. Use the master as a basis for discussion of the various methods of storytelling.
38. Have students construct a flannel board.
39. Have students prepare a story using one of the methods given in the text and present the story to the class.

Displaying Books _____

40. Have students describe an ideal location for a reading area.
41. Have students discuss how books should be displayed.
42. Have students construct a book display for children.

Additional Resources

43. Guest speaker. Invite a librarian to discuss book selection for young children with the class.
44. Guest speaker or speakers. Invite a storyteller or group of dramatic readers to demonstrate and discuss storytelling with the class.
45. Panel discussion. Invite a panel of parents to discuss what they look for in choosing and reading books for their children.

Research Topic

46. Have students take a survey of children's libraries and child care centers to find out what books are

most popular with children. Students should then analyze some of the most popular books and give a presentation to the class on why they think these books are so popular.

Answer Key

Text

Review and Reflect, page 305

1. backgrounds
2. true
3. A
4. social understanding
5. fairy tales
6. false
7. to create interest and arouse children's imaginations
8. age
9. Sexism is any action, attitude, or outlook used to judge a person based only on the sex of that person.
10. true
11. ask a question, make a personal comment, use a prop
12. ending
13. Practice reading in front of a mirror; make a recording as you read.
14. (Student response. See pages 301–304.)

Student Activity Guide

Storytelling, Activity A

1.	F	5.	F
2.	T	6.	F
3.	F	7.	T
4.	T	8.	T
9.	F	15.	T

10.	T	16.	T
11.	F	17.	F
12.	T	18.	T
13.	T	19.	F
14.	T	20.	F

Teacher's Resource Guide

Chapter Test

1.	D	16.	T
2.	C	17.	T
3.	A	18.	F
4.	E	19.	T
5.	B	20.	T
6.	T	21.	F
7.	T	22.	A
8.	T	23.	A
9.	F	24.	C
10.	F	25.	D
11.	F	26.	A
12.	T	27.	C
13.	T	28.	B
14.	T	29.	D
15.	T		

30. Understanding other people; developing an enjoyment of books; building correct concepts of objects and ideas; forming new ideas; presenting information properly; developing an appreciation of beautiful things; increasing their vocabulary; desiring to read.
31. Student response. (See pages 297–298.)
32. Drawings for flipchart stories are predrawn and simply changed as the teacher tells the story. With draw and tell stories, the teacher makes drawings as the story is read or told.

Why Use Stories and Books?

- ◆ To add to and enrich children's first-hand ideas

- ◆ To foster social relationships

- ◆ To build concepts

- ◆ To develop an appreciation of books

- ◆ To present information

- ◆ To encourage verbal expression

- ◆ To call attention to the printed word

- ◆ To stimulate new ideas

- ◆ To provide a quiet activity or change of pace

- ◆ To help children learn that people read from left to right across a page

Age and Children's Books

Infant/Toddler
- Thick pages
- Pictures of simple objects
- Large, clearly outlined pictures

Two-Year-Old
- Imitate familiar sounds
- Repeat their own experiences
- Contain large pages with big pictures
- Include the familiar

Three-Year-Old
- Include things and people outside of home
- Explain the who's and why's
- Interpret the child's own experiences
- Contain words like surprise and secret

Four-Year-Old
- Include humor in reality
- Contain new words
- Explain the how's and why's
- Include exaggeration

Five-Year-Old
- Add something to their knowledge
- Take them beyond the here and now
- Contain new information and relationships between familiar facts

Book Evaluation Form

Name _____ **Date** _____ **Period** _____

Name of book: _____

Date of publication: _____

Publisher: _____

Number of pages: _____

Intended age: _____

	Yes	No
I. Pictures		
A. Brightly colored		
B. Action is familiar		
C. Correlated with text		
D. Objects are clearly recognized		
E. People not in stereotype roles		
F. Free from sexism		
G. Free from racism		
II. Words		
A. Familiar words		
B. Rhythmic sound and repetition		
C. Clear and simple		
D. Number of words are appropriate for development of child		
E. Colorful language		
F. Simple, well-developed plot		
G. Free from sexism		
H. Free from racism		

Should this book be used with young children? Explain why or why not. _____

_____

_____

_____

Types of Storytelling

♦ Draw and Tell

♦ Tapes

♦ Puppets

♦ Individual or Group Stories

♦ Flip Charts

♦ Slide Stories

♦ Flannel Boards

Guiding Storytelling Experiences

Name _____

Date _____ **Period** _____ **Score** _____

Matching: Match the following age groups and identifying phrases.

_____ 1. Enjoy stories that explain how and why.

_____ 2. Enjoy stories that explain what people do and why.

_____ 3. Enjoy books with pictures of simple objects.

_____ 4. Enjoy stories that take them beyond here and now.

_____ 5. Enjoy stories that repeat their own experiences.

A. infants/toddlers
B. two-year-olds
C. three-year-olds
D. four-year-olds
E. five-year-olds

True/False: Circle *T* if the statement is true or *F* if the statement is false.

T F 6. Exposure to books is a means of developing reading readiness.

T F 7. Books help children better understand themselves.

T F 8. Storytelling helps children understand other people.

T F 9. In family life books, the main character must confront witches and giants.

T F 10. Fairy tales are usually the first type of book shared with children.

T F 11. The best illustrations contain a lot of detail and shading.

T F 12. Illustrations in children's books should represent the written word.

T F 13. The book's binding should allow it to lie flat when opened.

T F 14. Stories should match the child's developmental level and experience.

T F 15. Two-year-olds like books about things they do, enjoy, or know.

T F 16. Sexism refers to any actions or attitudes that make women or men appear inferior in status.

T F 17. Four-year-olds are interested in understanding how and why things work.

T F 18. Two-year-olds will remain interested in a book for eight to twelve minutes.

T F 19. Five-year-olds like stories that add something to their knowledge.

T F 20. Three-year-olds are interested in people outside the home.

T F 21. Until they are about six years old, children are usually not ready for fantasy.

(continued)

Multiple Choice: Choose the best response. Write the letter in the space provided.

_____ 22. The book *Cinderella* is _____.
   A. a fairy tale
   B. a picture book
   C. a family life story
   D. an animal story

_____ 23. *Three Little Pigs* is _____.
   A. a fairy tale
   B. a picture book
   C. a family life story
   D. an animal story

_____ 24. *Timid Timothy* is an example of _____.
   A. a fairy tale
   B. a picture book
   C. a family life story
   D. an animal story

_____ 25. *Angus and the Cat* is an example of _____.
   A. a fairy tale
   B. a picture book
   C. a family life story
   D. an animal story

_____ 26. Books for two-year-olds should _____.
   A. imitate familiar sounds
   B. contain many words
   C. include exaggeration
   D. explain the who's and why's

_____ 27. Children enjoy books that include humor at age _____.
   A. two
   B. three
   C. four
   D. five

_____ 28. Children who like books about familiar subjects and community helpers are age _____.
   A. two
   B. three
   C. four
   D. five

_____ 29. Children enjoy books that add something to their knowledge at age _____.
   A. two
   B. three
   C. four
   D. five

Essay Questions: Provide complete responses to the following questions or statements.

30. What skills do children learn from storytelling experiences?

31. How can a teacher avoid stereotypes in stories?

32. Describe the difference between flip charts and draw and tell stories.

Guiding Play and Puppetry Experiences  20

Objectives

After studying this chapter, students will be able to
- describe the stages of play.
- explain the stages of material use in play.
- summarize the benefits of socio-dramatic play.
- prepare the classroom environment and guide socio-dramatic play activities.
- summarize the benefits of puppetry experiences.
- make and use three types of puppets.
- write and tell a puppet story.

Teaching Materials

Text, pages 307–320
Terms to Know
Review and Reflect
Apply and Explore
Student Activity Guide
 A. *Playtime Match*
 B. *Encouraging Socio-Dramatic Play*
 C. *Design a Puppet*
 D. *Writing Puppet Stories*
Teacher's Resource Guide/Binder
Dramatic Play Themes and Props,
  transparency master, 20-1
Value of Puppets, reproducible master, 20-2
Materials to Make Puppets, reproducible master, 20-3
Chapter Test
Teacher's Resource Binder
Dramatic Play, color transparency, CT-20
The Observation Guide
Mastering CDA Competencies

Introductory Activities

1. Have students describe the types of fantasy play they engaged in as young children.
2. Have students discuss with the class the value of fantasy play.
3. Ask students if any of them have ever seen a puppet show. If so, ask them to describe the show and its value for young children.

4. *Playtime Match,* Activity A, SAG. As a pretest, have students match the given terms and definitions.

Instructional Concepts and Student Learning Experiences

Stages of Play

5. Have students describe and give examples of solitary play, parallel play, and cooperative play.

Stages of Material Use in Play

6. Have students describe the three stages children move through in using play materials.
7. Have students discuss how the stage of material use affects the types of props the teacher should provide for play.
8. Have students visit a local child care center and observe the children's use of play materials. Students should record their observations and share them with the class.

Socio-Dramatic Play

9. Have students explain the value of socio-dramatic play.
10. *Dramatic Play,* color transparency CT-20, TRB. Use this transparency to introduce questions that stimulate children's thinking during socio-dramatic play. You may want to:
 A. Remind students that effective teachers ask more questions rather than just make statements. Questioning helps children focus, examine, and make corrections.
 B. Discuss the importance of the teacher's role in "orchestrating" the learning environment by asking questions to promote learning.
 C. Ask students to share examples of effective questions.
 D. Discuss how questions engage children's minds and encourage them to think.
11. Have students discuss the relationship of age to the themes children choose for play.

12. *Dramatic Play Themes and Props,* transparency master 20-1. For each theme listed, have students list ideas for props that could be used with the theme. Students should also discuss resources for the various props listed.
13. Have students describe the teacher's role in encouraging socio-dramatic play.
14. Have students discuss the importance of adult modeling.
15. Have students identify the difference between coaching and reinforcing.
16. Have students discuss the best time for scheduling dramatic play.
17. *Encouraging Socio-Dramatic Play,* Activity B, SAG. Have students use the form to develop prop boxes for various themes. The students should then describe actions the teacher could take to encourage children to participate in socio-dramatic play.
18. Have students explain the purpose of a prop box.
19. Have students brainstorm a list of prop box materials for a secretary, painter, baker, and carpenter.
20. Have students state the purpose of a costume corner.
21. Have students describe the physical appearance of a housekeeping area.
22. Have students make a plan for the arrangement and appearance of a housekeeping area.
23. Have students plan a dramatic play activity and introduce it to a small group of children. Students should write a summary of their activity.

Puppetry

24. Have students discuss the value of using puppets in the child care program.
25. *Value of Puppets,* reproducible master 20-2. Use the master as a basis for discussion of how puppets can be used in all areas of the curriculum.
26. Have students describe the different types of puppets.
27. Have students explain how puppets can be created.
28. *Materials to Make Puppets,* reproducible master 20-3. Use the list to assign materials to students to acquire. The materials should be available to students for designing their own puppets.
29. *Design a Puppet,* Activity C, SAG. Students are asked to design a puppet for use with preschool children. They are then to answer the questions provided.
30. Have students practice making "me" puppets.
31. Have students discuss the steps in writing puppet stories.
32. *Writing Puppet Stories,* Activity D, SAG. Have students use the form to develop and write a puppet story.

33. Have students practice making various movements, such as running and falling, with a puppet.
34. Have students describe how to prepare children for a puppet story.
35. Have students create a portable stage that is lightweight and easy to store.
36. Have students prepare a puppet play and present it to a group of children at a child care center.

Additional Resources

37. Guest speaker. Invite a child care teacher to discuss the purpose of dramatic play with the class. Have the teacher describe items typically found in a dramatic play area.
38. Field trip. Arrange for students to visit a child care center and observe the dramatic play area. Students should make a list of the equipment and materials available to the children.
39. Guest speakers. Invite a group to present a puppet show to the class. Ask the group members to discuss the use and care of puppets.

Research Topics

40. Have students research articles on materials for socio-dramatic play. Students should also survey area teachers about materials they use for socio-dramatic play. Students should then create an informational pamphlet listing materials and their uses.
41. Have students research the history and evolution of puppets. Students should give a presentation to the class, including visual aides, on the subject.

Answer Key

Text

Review and Reflect, page 320

1. Socio-dramatic play involves several children imitating others and acting out situations together.
2. C
3. false
4. manipulative
5. false
6. a. four-year-old children
   b. three-year-old children
   c. five-year-old children
   d. toddlers
7. modeling
8. coaching
9. (State two:) Schedule during self-selected play periods. These must be long enough for the children to carry out their ideas. The first hour of the morning is good. Avoid scheduling too many activities. This affects the number of children who

take part in and remain in socio-dramatic play. Schedule only activities that complement each other.

10. Materials and equipment that encourage children to explore various roles.
11. (Student response.)
12. "Me"
13. Conflict adds interest. It should be resolved in the end.
14. (Student response.)

Student Activity Guide

Playtime Match, Activity A

1. F
2. A
3. Q
4. H
5. D
6. K
7. J
8. E
9. L
10. C
11. B
12. O
13. G
14. R
15. M
16. P
17. I
18. N

Teacher's Resource Guide/Binder

Chapter Test

1. F
2. E
3. B
4. D
5. A
6. C
7. F
8. F
9. F
10. T
11. T
12. T
13. T
14. T
15. F
16. F
17. T
18. T
19. T
20. T
21. B
22. D
23. C
24. B
25. A
26. A
27. Manipulative, functional, imaginative. (Student response for descriptions.)
28. Schedule dramatic play during the play period; allow enough time for children to carry out their ideas; avoid scheduling too many other activities during the play period

Dramatic Play Themes and Props

- Hair stylist
- Farmer
- Grocer
- Circus
- Store
- Baker
- Fire fighter
- Hospital
- Builder
- Florist
- Pilot
- Fast-food restaurant
- Zoo
- Dentist
- Camping
- Post office

Value of Puppets

Art	◆ Offers emotional release ◆ Provides sensory stimulation ◆ Promotes large and small muscle development ◆ Encourages problem solving and decision making ◆ Provides for the exploration of materials
Math	◆ Encourages thinking through problems ◆ Introduces concepts ◆ Develops classification skills ◆ Encourages measuring, ordering, and counting skills
Social Studies	◆ Promotes communication skills ◆ Models sharing and cooperation with others ◆ Models critical thinking skills ◆ Demonstrates concepts, such as friendship and self-esteem
Language Arts	◆ Encourages development of language skills ◆ Encourages listening and speaking skills ◆ Promotes the development of abstract concepts such as *above, below, under, in front of,* and *behind*
Dramatic Play	◆ Offers emotional release ◆ Promotes listening skills ◆ Encourages problem-solving skills ◆ Promotes decision-making skills ◆ Promotes self-expression and creativity ◆ Provides opportunities to gain self-confidence as group members ◆ Provides opportunities to express feelings
Science	◆ Classifies foods into food groups ◆ Discovers the value of the five senses ◆ Observes changes in texture, shape, and sizes ◆ Evaluates ideas ◆ Identifies food groups through the five senses

Materials to Make Puppets

Accessories

- aluminum foil
- terry cloth
- velvet
- velour
- suede cloth
- felt
- fur scraps
- socks
- hats
- brooms
- buttons
- paper bags
- mittens and gloves
- fly swatters
- dish mops
- wooden spoons
- plastic foam packing shapes
- construction paper
- coat hanger frames covered with hosiery
- paper plates, cups, and drinking straws
- pictures
- plastic bottles
- cardboard cylinders
- plastic bubbles from packaged items
- pliers
- paper envelopes
- food boxes such as gelatin, cake mix, and spaghetti
- egg cartons
- yarn
- boxes

- beads
- buttons
- foil
- fur
- glitter
- jewelry
- paper
- clips
- pipe cleaners
- ribbons
- sequins
- shoe laces
- yarn

Guiding Play and Puppetry Experiences

Name _____

Date _____ **Period** _____ **Score** _____

Matching: Match the following terms and identifying phrases.

_____ 1. Placing feelings and emotions onto an object such as a puppet.

_____ 2. Giving human traits to nonliving objects.

_____ 3. Providing children with ideas for different play situations.

_____ 4. Showing correct behavior for children during socio-dramatic play.

_____ 5. Children play at being a wife, husband, doctor, etc.

_____ 6. Method used to add interest to puppet stories.

A. role-playing
B. coaching
C. conflict
D. modeling
E. personification
F. projection

True/False: Circle *T* if the statement is true or *F* if the statement is false.

T   F   7. Socio-dramatic play is a form of play in which one child imitates others.

T   F   8. By age two, socio-dramatic play is usually observed.

T   F   9. There are two stages children move through in using materials in their play.

T   F   10. Without realistic props, some children have a difficult time getting involved in socio-dramatic play.

T   F   11. Socio-dramatic play is the most complex form of play observed in child care settings.

T   F   12. Play themes usually focus on everyday situations.

T   F   13. Socio-dramatic play involves all four areas of development.

T   F   14. The play of three-year-olds involves personification.

T   F   15. Teachers should always avoid comments and suggestions during play.

T   F   16. Most programs allow one-half hour in the morning for socio-dramatic play.

T   F   17. Every dramatic play corner should have a costume corner.

T   F   18. Outdoors, jungle gyms, plants, sawhorses, and transportation toys can all facilitate dramatic play.

T   F   19. Problem-solving skills are developed as children make decisions and choices during socio-dramatic play.

T   F   20. Play themes change with age.

(continued)

Multiple Choice: Choose the best response. Write the letter in the space provided.

_____ 21. In their play, two-year-olds _____.
    A. are outgoing
    B. use play materials on their own
    C. are tolerant
    D. are interactive

_____ 22. Infants' play can be classified as _____.
    A. cooperative
    B. parallel
    C. interactive
    D. solitary

_____ 23. A term used to describe two or more children playing together is _____.
    A. interdependent
    B. parallel
    C. cooperative
    D. dependent

_____ 24. The play in which children play alone, but near other children, is called _____.
    A. aloof
    B. parallel
    C. dependent
    D. interdependent

_____ 25. The easiest type of puppet to construct is a _____.
    A. hand puppet
    B. marionette
    C. mascot puppet
    D. arm puppet

_____ 26. The first step in writing a puppet story is _____.
    A. choosing a theme
    B. developing a plot
    C. creating conflict
    D. planning the ending

Essay Questions: Provide complete responses to the following questions or statements.

27. Name and describe the three stages children move through using materials in their play. Provide an example of each stage.

28. Give considerations for scheduling of socio-dramatic play.

Guiding Manuscript Writing  21

Objectives

After studying this chapter, students will be able to
- define manuscript writing.
- list reasons for encouraging the development of writing skills in preschool settings.
- explain activities that help children develop writing skills.
- make letters following the Zaner-Bloser system.
- outline the sequence children follow in learning alphabet letters.
- discuss guidelines to use to help children develop writing skills.

Teaching Materials

Text, pages 321–330
Terms to Know
Review and Reflect
Apply and Explore
Student Activity Guide
    A. *Practice Your Writing*
    B. *Manuscript Writing*
Teacher's Resource Guide/Binder
    Practicing the Zaner-Bloser Writing System,
      reproducible master, 21-1
    Chapter Test
Teacher's Resource Binder
    Zaner-Bloser's Six Simple Strokes,
      color transparency, CT-21
The Observation Guide
Mastering CDA Competencies

Introductory Activities

1. Ask students to recall how and when they learned to write. Students may share some early experiences involving writing with the class.
2. Prepare a display of different types of writing to share with the class. Have students discuss the different styles.
3. Instruct the class to remove their shoes and stockings. (You may want to prepare the students to dress accordingly a day in advance.) Give each student a pencil and paper and have them write their names with their toes. Then have the students discuss the difficulties a child might have in learning to write.

Instructional Concepts and Student Learning Experiences

Objectives for Writing

4. Have students explain why visual discrimination skills are important for writing.
5. Have students discuss the teacher's role in calling attention to the printed word.
6. Have students describe the four elements needed for children to achieve the objectives for writing.

Prewriting Skills

7. Have students identify the two prewriting skills.
8. Have students discuss the teacher's role in developing prewriting skills.
9. Have students brainstorm a list of small muscle activities.
10. Have students divide into groups and develop a list of hand-eye coordination activities.
11. Have students observe children involved in small muscle and hand-eye coordination activities and observe the range of skills at various ages.

Manuscript Writing Systems

12. *Zaner-Bloser's Six Simple Strokes,* color transparency CT-21, TRB. Use this transparency to introduce the six simple strokes included in the Zaner-Bloser writing system. You may want to:
    A. Stress that children learn that written marks have meaning. Their interests in producing writings usually increases as they notice adults communicating by using writing tools. They will also note print on signs and in books. Then they will usually recognize the marks used to make their name. Gradually they will learn to identify and to write the letters in their names.
    B. Discuss the prewriting skills needed to begin writing.

C. Have students brainstorm a list of activities that will promote skills needed to produce writing.

D. Have students brainstorm a list of writing tools and materials.

13. *Practicing the Zaner-Bloser Writing System,* reproducible master 21-1. Have students practice writing by tracing over the given letters. Students should then practice writing the letters without tracing.

14. *Practice Your Writing,* Activity A, SAG. Have students use the form to practice their writing skills.

15. Have students make a classroom poster using well-formed letters.

16. Have students discuss the types of materials that children should use as they learn writing skills.

17. Have students discuss reasons why the Zaner-Bloser sequence should be used when teaching children to write letters.

Building Writing Skills

18. Have students explain the relationship between coordination and letter size.

19. Write a sentence on the board without allowing extra space between words or allowing space at the wrong points in the sentence. Have students try to read the sentence and discuss the importance of teaching proper spacing to children.

20. Gather some samples of children's writing. Have students classify the samples as having sufficient or insufficient line quality.

21. Have students identify the letters that children frequently reverse and explain how to guide children and correct the reversals.

22. Have students role-play guiding a child through practice with writing tools.

23. Have students describe techniques to identify children's hand preferences.

Early Experiences in Writing

24. Have students discuss techniques for encouraging writing.

25. Have students make a set of sandpaper letter blocks or another tool to encourage writing skills.

26. Have students prepare a list of materials and tools that could be used in a writing center.

27. Have students explain the value of a chalkboard.

28. Have students make labels for equipment and fixtures in the classroom.

29. Have students plan a handwriting activity to try with children.

30. Have students observe a teacher conducting a handwriting activity and record children's actions throughout the activity.

31. *Manuscript Writing,* Activity B, SAG. Have students unscramble the letters to find the terms that are described.

Additional Resources

32. Guest speaker. Invite a child care teacher to discuss how writing can be encouraged in the classroom.

Research Topics

33. Have students visit five classrooms to see how writing readiness is encouraged. Students should discuss their observations in a paper.

34. Have students research books and journals to find activities that have been used successfully to encourage writing readiness. Students should present their findings to the class in a speech.

Answer Key

Text

Review and Reflect, page 330

1. C
2. false
3. (List three:) Note differences in the formation of letters; learn to write the alphabet letters and numerals; learn that words are made up of letters; learn that letters represent sounds; learn that letters in the English language go from left to right, and top to bottom.
4. interest, enthusiasm, clear instructions, support
5. small muscle, eye-hand coordination
6. true
7. Young children lack the muscle control and eye-hand coordination needed to use lined paper.
8. C, B, A, D
9. false
10. capitals
11. reversal
12. (Accept all appropriate responses. They may include alphabet molds, sandpaper letters, and sandboxes.)

Student Activity Guide

Manuscript Writing, Activity B

1. print script
2. small muscle
3. cursive
4. hand-eye
5. spacing
6. wavering
7. illegible
8. reversals

9. ten
10. skywriting
11. alphabet models, sandpaper letters, sandbox, chalkboard
12. (Student response.)
13. (Student response.)

Teacher's Resource Guide/Binder

Chapter Test

1. D   3. B
2. A   4. C

5. F   13. T
6. F   14. T
7. T   15. C
8. T   16. C
9. T   17. D
10. T   18. D
11. F   19. B
12. F   20. D
21. Interest, enthusiasm, clear instructions, and support.
22. Small-muscle activities and hand-eye coordination activities.
23. (Student response.)

Practicing the Zaner-Bloser Writing System

Name _____ **Date**_____ **Period** _____

Using a felt-tip marker, trace over each of the letters and numerals below, noting the directions of the strokes. Then practice making the letters without tracing on the next page.

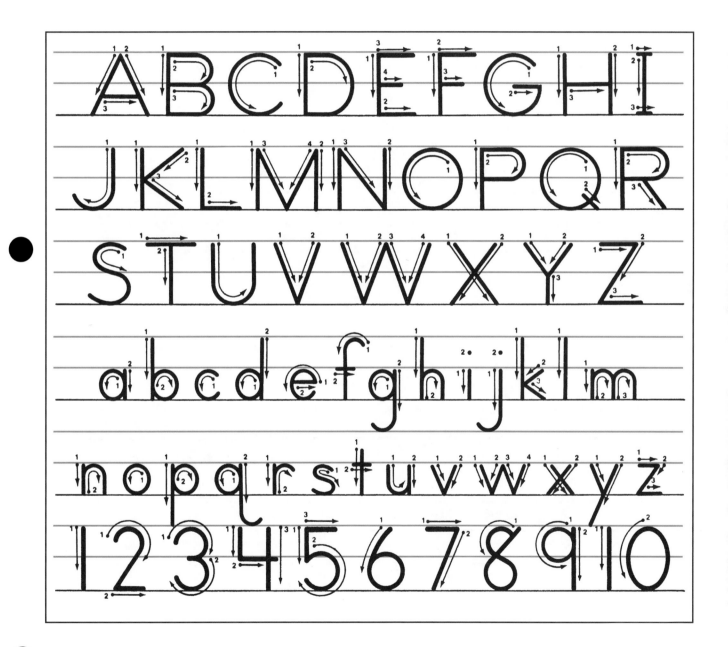

(continued)

Name

Guiding Manuscript Writing

Name _____

Date _____ Period _____ Score _____

Matching: Match the following terms and identifying phrases.

_____ 1. Contains unconnected letters made of simple, separate strokes.

_____ 2. Muscle control needed before children can perform manuscript writing.

_____ 3. A common problem in the early stages of writing.

_____ 4. Teaching technique used when children are having trouble with a particular letter.

A. hand-eye coordination
B. reversals
C. skywriting
D. manuscript writing

True/False: Circle *T* if the statement is true or *F* if the statement is false.

T F 5. Manuscript writing should be formally taught in a preschool setting.

T F 6. When teaching writing skills to young children, form and style should be given primary attention.

T F 7. Teacher-made materials should use proper manuscript writing.

T F 8. Manuscript writing is a simple form of calligraphy.

T F 9. Cursive writing is a faster process than manuscript writing.

T F 10. Weaving and typing are good activities for hand-eye coordination.

T F 11. There is only one approved manuscript writing system.

T F 12. Spacing is the easiest writing skill for children to achieve.

T F 13. Drills that require rewriting of letters are not recommended for practicing writing skills.

T F 14. Children who are ready should be encouraged to print their names on their artwork.

Multiple Choice: Choose the best response. Write the letter in the space provided.

_____ 15. Another word for manuscript writing is _____.
  A. printing
  B. calligraphy
  C. print script
  D. cursive

_____ 16. To learn how to write children must have _____.
  A. a high level of intelligence
  B. a chronological age of five years
  C. interest and enthusiasm
  D. prior experience

(continued)

_____ 17. Small-muscle activities include _____.
    A. playing ball
    B. jumping rope
    C. climbing a jungle gym
    D. finger painting

_____ 18. Activities that promote hand-eye coordination include _____.
    A. sliding
    B. running
    C. skipping
    D. stringing beads

_____ 19. If you were to compare manuscript writing systems, you would find _____.
    A. no difference
    B. minimal differences
    C. great differences
    D. moderate differences

_____ 20. The size of the child's writing varies according to _____.
    A. age
    B. instruction
    C. interest
    D. muscle development

Essay Questions: Provide complete responses to the following questions or statements.

21. What are the four elements that are necessary to learn print script?

22. Name the two types of prewriting activities.

23. List five small-muscle activities.

Guiding Math Experiences  22

Objectives

After studying this chapter, students will be able to
- list objectives of early math experiences.
- use two basic assessments to determine math skills of children.
- recognize a variety of items that can be used to promote math experiences.
- identify math experiences that promote the development of key math concepts.
- design math experiences that stress specific math concepts.

Teaching Materials

Text, pages 331–344
Terms to Know
Review and Reflect
Apply and Explore
Student Activity Guide
  A. *Math Match*
  B. *Discussing Colors*
  C. *Teaching Space, Size, Volume, and Time*
  D. *Using Recipes to Teach Math Concepts*
Teacher's Resource Guide/Binder
Mathematical Classroom Materials,
  reproducible master, 22-1
Math Terms and Techniques,
  reproducible master, 22-2
Chapter Test
Teacher's Resource Binder
Graphing, color transparency, CT-22
The Observation Guide
Mastering CDA Competencies

Introductory Activities

1. Ask students to give examples of math concepts used in everyday life, such as size, space, and time.
2. Ask students what math concepts they find hardest to understand. Students should then discuss what math concepts children might find difficult to understand.
3. Ask students to explain how they would teach the math concept of volume to young children.
4. *Math Match,* Activity A, SAG. As a chapter pretest, have students match the terms with their definitions.

Instructional Concepts and Student Learning Experiences

Goals of Early Math Experiences

5. Have students list the math concepts to be included in the preschool curriculum.
6. Have students identify the types of math experiences that should be included in the curriculum.
7. Have students ask early childhood teachers what math concepts they include in their curriculum and share their findings with the class.

Assessing Math Ability

8. Have students describe the two forms used for assessing math ability.
9. Have students provide examples of specific task assessment.
10. Have students visit an early childhood program and assess the math ability of one of the children using one of the methods described in the text. Students should discuss their assessments with the classroom teacher to determine whether their assessment reflects the teacher's assessment of that child.

Math Equipment

11. Have students try to explain a math concept without using any materials. The students should then try explaining the same math concept using some form of equipment. Students should discuss how materials make math concepts more relevant and easier to understand.
12. Have students look through early childhood equipment catalogs to find examples of math equipment that can be purchased.
13. Have students prepare a list of equipment that can be used to teach space concepts.

14. *Mathematical Classroom Materials,* reproducible master 22-1. For each material listed, have students write how it might be used to help teach math concepts.

Mathematical Activities

15. Have students list the skills children should develop from participating in mathematical activities.
16. Have students observe a teacher conducting a math activity in the classroom and record their observations.
17. Have students discuss the development of color concepts.
18. Have students describe and give examples of the ways color concepts can be taught.
19. Have students prepare an "eye colors" chart or a similar type of chart that can be used to teach children color concepts.
20. *Discussing Colors,* Activity B, SAG. Have students write their own responses and a child's responses to the feelings created by the colors listed. Then have students answer the questions to evaluate the responses.
21. Have students explain how children develop shape concepts.
22. Have students brainstorm a list of activities that could be used to teach the identification of shapes.
23. Have students explain the process by which children develop classification skills.
24. Have students explain the difference between matching and sorting.
25. Have students create a set of materials that could be used to help teach classification skills.
26. Have students define the term sets as it is used mathematically with young children.
27. Have students develop a list of common items that are in sets of two, three, four, etc.
28. Have students plan three activities to teach children the concept of an empty set at snack time.
29. Have students explain why counting concepts should be included in the curriculum.
30. Have students describe and provide examples of the two counting stages.
31. Have students create a brochure designed to give parents ideas for teaching counting to their children.
32. Have students discuss methods of helping children understand space, size, and volume concepts.
33. Have students discuss ways of making time concepts easier for children to understand.
34. *Teaching Space, Size, Volume, and Time,* Activity C, SAG. Have students write original ways each of the concepts listed could be taught to children.
35. *Using Recipes to Teach Math Concepts,* Activity D, SAG. Have students find two recipes that could be used to teach children math concepts. Students should record the recipes in the space provided and then answer the questions related to them.
36. Have students plan an activity to teach one of the math concepts listed in the text. Students should make or acquire any materials needed to conduct the activity and then try the activity with a small group of children. Students should write a short evaluation of the activity.
37. *Graphing,* color transparency CT-22, TRB. Use this transparency to introduce graphing as a method of visually communicating information. You may want to:
   A. Stress that graphing is a way to display information. These experiences provide children with an opportunity to classify, measure, count, and compare.
   B. Have students brainstorm other information that can be graphed. Examples may include favorite colors, foods, toys, holidays, or people.
   C. Remind students that concept words can be used as graphs are described and discussed: higher or taller, less than, more than, some, most, none, all.
   D. Ask students to recall examples of graphs they have observed in classroom settings.
38. *Math Terms and Techniques,* reproducible master 22-2. Students are asked to complete statements by writing terms related to math in the blanks.

Integrating Computers in Child Care Centers

39. Have students discuss the two characteristics that are vital in selecting computer software programs.
40. Have students discuss where a computer should be placed in the child care center classroom.
41. Have students evaluate a children's software program.

Additional Resources

42. Guest speaker. Invite a child care teacher to discuss with the class how math concepts are integrated into the curriculum.
43. Field trip. Arrange for the class to visit a center with a large observation room. Have the class observe how math concepts are included in a variety of activities.

Research Topics

44. Have students research journals to find out what types of materials have been used to successfully teach math concepts. Students should then make a display of some of these materials with cards explaining how the materials were used.

45. Have students conduct a survey of parents and early childhood teachers to find out how they teach math concepts to children. Have students write a paper comparing the different methods used.

Answer Key

Text

Review and Reflect, page 344

1. (List four:) observing and describing concrete objects; recognizing colors and shapes; comparing objects and using terms that describe quantity; classifying objects; copying patterns; recognizing and writing numerals; counting; using logical words
2. Observation, specific task assessment. (Student response for explanations. See page 333.)
3. false
4. because color helps children learn to discriminate between objects
5. shape
6. No, because children may confuse color names with shape names.
7. classification
8. Matching involves putting objects together that are the same. Sorting is the process of separating objects into categories based on a unique feature.
9. set
10. time
11. Answers will vary but may include thermometer, hot, cold, warm, cool.
12. age appropriate; easy to operate
13. six

Student Activity Guide

Math Match, Activity A

1. J	6. G	11. E
2. K	7. H	12. D
3. B	8. C	
4. L	9 I	
5. A	10. F	

Teacher's Resource Guide/Binder

Math Terms and Techniques, reproducible master, 22-2

1. Cooking	12. Classification
2. Transitions	13. Sorting
3. Task	14. Sets
4. Mathematical	15. Counting
5. Color	16. Rote
6. Red	17. Group
7. Primary	18. Space
8. Charts	19. Size
9. Circles	20. Volume
10. Parquetry	21. Time
11. Masking	22. Temperature

Chapter Test

1. A	13. T
2. D	14. T
3. B	15. T
4. F	16. F
5. E	17. D
6. C	18. B
7. T	19. C
8. F	20. A
9. F	21. A
10. F	22. B
11. F	23. C
12. F	24. B

25. Mathematical skill can be determined through assessment by observation. In this method, the teacher informally views a child during self-selected activities and watches for behaviors that indicate math skill. Specific task assessment is a second method that can be used to determine mathematical skill. In this method, the teacher gives a child a set activity to determine a specific skill or need.
26. Color helps children discriminate among objects. It is used to classify, pattern, and sequence.
27. Rote counting: children recite numbers in order, but do not understand the quantity attached to the numbers. Rational counting: children are able to attach a number to a series of grouped objects.

Mathematical Classroom Materials

Name _____ **Date** _____ **Period** _____

For each of the objects listed below, write at least one way they can be used in math activities.

Flannel boards, felt-covered numerals:

Felt cutouts of various sizes, colors, numbers, and shapes:

Scraps of cloth:

Pegboards:

Magnetic shapes:

Calendars:

Lines numbered 0 through 20:

Rulers, yardsticks, and tape measures:

Thermometers—indoor, outdoor, play:

(continued)

Alarm clock:

Egg timer:

Giant wooden dominoes:

Giant counting rods:

Scales—bathroom and balance:

Light and heavy objects—rocks, pennies, corks:

Measuring containers of various sizes and types:

Buttons:

Empty spools:

Puzzles and geometric inserts:

Jigsaw puzzles:

Math Terms and Techniques

Name _____ **Date** _____ **Period** _____

Complete the statements below using the words from the list. Write the words in the space provided.

Charts	Counting	Primary	Size	Temperature
Circles	Group	Red	Sorting	Time
Classification	Masking	Rote	Space	Transitions
Color	Mathematical	Sets	Task	Volume
Cooking	Parquetry			

_____ 1. _____ activities teach how quantities are related and sequenced.

_____ 2. _____, those periods of time between scheduled activities, are a good opportunity to teach new math concepts.

_____ 3. _____ assessments are a method of collecting data on the children's math abilities.

_____ 4. _____ ideas are learned from interacting with a variety of materials that promote physical and mental activity.

_____ 5. _____ identification comes before shape identification.

_____ 6. _____, yellow, and blue are sometimes referred to as the primary colors.

_____ 7. _____ colors are recognized more readily by children than secondary colors.

_____ 8. _____ can be used to teach children the usefulness of graphing.

_____ 9. _____ are the first shape a child can reproduce.

_____ 10. _____ blocks can be used to formally and informally teach shape concepts.

_____ 11. _____ tape can be used to make shapes on the floor.

_____ 12. _____ is the process of grouping objects into categories or classes.

_____ 13. _____ is the process of separating objects into categories according to unique characteristics.

_____ 14. _____ are collections of objects that are alike in some way and consequently belong together.

_____ 15. _____ is a basic math skill that is important for problem solving.

_____ 16. _____ counting is mastered before rational counting.

_____ 17. _____ time is an excellent time to reinforce numbers by keeping daily attendance records.

_____ 18. _____ concepts include far, near, above, inside, and outside.

_____ 19. _____ concepts include big, little, wide, and thin.

_____ 20. _____ concepts include much, empty, full, little, and some.

_____ 21. _____ is a difficult concept for children to develop because the word needs to represent the future, present, and past.

_____ 22. _____ concepts include vocabulary such as warm, hot, cold, and cool.

Guiding Math Experiences

Name _____

Date _____ Period _____ Score _____

Matching: Match the following terms and identifying phrases.

_____ 1. First mathematical behavior exhibited by young children.

_____ 2. Allows a child to integrate a new experience into the same category as an earlier one.

_____ 3. Form of discrimination that involves putting objects together that are the same.

_____ 4. Collection of objects that are alike in some way.

_____ 5. Recitation of numerals in order.

_____ 6. Attaching a number to a series of grouped objects.

A. classification
B. matching
C. rational counting
D. recognizing
E. rote counting
F. sets

True/False: Circle *T* if the statement is true or *F* if the statement is false.

T   F   7. A well structured environment should provide play experience for children to develop mathematical concepts.

T   F   8. Only mental activities need to be provided to develop a child's mathematical ability.

T   F   9. Color is not a mathematical concept.

T   F   10. Children cannot match a color to a sample by age two.

T   F   11. Identifying and drawing shapes occur at the same time.

T   F   12. Shape identification comes before color identification.

T   F   13. Most children cannot reproduce shape forms other than a circle until age five.

T   F   14. Classification is one of the first math behaviors exhibited.

T   F   15. Typically, most children can count up to their ages.

T   F   16. Time is an easy concept for children to understand.

Multiple Choice: Choose the best response. Write the letter in the space provided.

_____ 17. Presenting a child with circle, triangle, diamond, square, and rectangle shapes and having the child point to the square is an example of _____.
A. conducting a color activity
B. teaching rote counting
C. assessment by observation
D. specific task assessment

(continued)

_____ 18. Math equipment should not encourage _____.
   A. sorting
   B. tasting
   C. ordering
   D. developing patterns

_____ 19. Primary colors are _____.
   A. red, green, and blue
   B. red, yellow, and orange
   C. red, yellow, and blue
   D. green, blue, and yellow

_____ 20. The first shape that can be copied by most children is _____.
   A. circles
   B. triangles
   C. squares
   D. rectangles

_____ 21. Children begin to learn classification skills _____.
   A. in the first few weeks after birth
   B. at two months of age
   C. at six months of age
   D. at one year of age

_____ 22. The process of sorting or grouping objects into categories or classes is called _____.
   A. counting
   B. classification
   C. recognizing
   D. numbering

_____ 23. An example of an empty set would be a set of _____.
   A. cards in a deck
   B. puzzle pieces
   C. corners on a circle
   D. wheels on a car

_____ 24. Which terms express space concepts?
   A. Big, little.
   B. Above, below.
   C. Early, late.
   D. Wide, thin.

Essay Questions: Provide complete responses to the following questions or statements.

25. Describe two ways you can determine a child's level of mathematical skill.

26. Why is color considered a mathematical concept?

27. Describe the two stages of counting.

Guiding Science Experiences  23

Objectives

After studying this chapter, students will be able to
- explain what is meant by the term science.
- discuss reasons for studying science.
- outline the procedure for planning science activities.
- list a variety of science supplies and sources for supplies.
- explain the role of the teacher in guiding science experiences.
- identify methods for developing children's understanding of their senses.
- name and explain various ways to teach science concepts.

Teaching Materials

Text, pages 345–363
  Terms to Know
  Review and Reflect
  Apply and Explore
Student Activity Guide
  A. *Science Overview*
  B. *Methods of Teaching Science*
  C. *Planning Field Trips*
  D. *Pet Care*
Teacher's Resource Guide/Binder
  Science Activities, transparency master, 23-1
  Sources of Science Supplies and Equipment,
    reproducible master, 23-2
  Learning Science Through Cooking Experiences,
    reproducible master, 23-3
  Science, reproducible master, 23-4
  Chapter Test
Teacher's Resource Binder
  Science Processing Skills, color transparency, CT-23
The Observation Guide
Mastering CDA Competencies

Introductory Activities

1. Have students discuss what kinds of topics and

experiments they enjoy related to science. Students should discuss what makes them enjoyable.
2. Have students discuss what kinds of science topics and activities they think young children might enjoy.
3. Have students discuss science concepts that are evident in everyday life. Students should discuss how these concepts can become a part of classroom experiences with children.

Instructional Concepts and Student Learning Experiences

What is Science? _____

4. Have students define the terms science, observing, measuring, comparing, classifying, predicting, and discovering using a dictionary as a reference.
5. Have students explain why observation is important to an effective science program.
6. Have students discuss the benefits to children of studying science.
7. *Science Processing Skills,* color transparency CT-23, TRB. Use this transparency to introduce the thinking skills needed to learn science concepts. You may want to:
  A. Stress that by applying science process skills to concrete experiences, children can learn the content of science. For preschool children, these skills include observing, classifying, measuring, and communicating. As children progress into kindergarten and primary grades, these skills will help them develop higher level skills for interfering, predicting, and hypothesizing.
  B. Remind students that observation includes the ability to describe something using the five senses.
  C. Have students brainstorm activities that could promote the development of skills for observing, classifying, measuring, and communicating.
  D. Have students list materials that could be placed on a science table to encourage science processing skills.

Planning Science Activities

8. Have students discuss ways to make unplanned activities a part of classroom science curriculum.
9. Have students discuss reasons why having children use science equipment themselves would be more effective than demonstrating science experiments to children.
10. *Science Activities,* transparency master 23-1. Use the master as a basis for discussion of the opportunities that science activities should offer children.
11. Have students describe the optimum location and contents of a science area.
12. Have students create a collection of materials that could be placed on a science table.
13. Have students draw a sketch of a science center including equipment.
14. Have students brainstorm a list of sources of science supplies and equipment.
15. *Sources of Science Supplies and Equipment,* reproducible master 23-2. Have students investigate the costs of items listed or prospects of getting items listed for free. Students should also add three items that could be used for science activities available from each source.

Role of the Teacher

16. Have students observe a teacher and note how the teacher encourages children to be careful observers. Students should share their observations in class.
17. Have students prepare a list of centerpieces for the lunch table that could be used to foster science concepts.
18. Have students role-play asking open-ended questions about science activities.
19. Have students list and describe the five basic process skills.
20. Have students discuss examples of activities that would help promote the five basic process skills.
21. Have students observe a science activity in a child care program and record their observations.

Developing the Child's Understanding of Senses

22. Have students brainstorm a list of activities that could be used to promote the sense of touch.
23. Have students discuss the importance of developing the sense of smell in relationship to science learning.
24. Have students design an activity to help children build visual observation skills.
25. Have students interview teachers and find out what activities they use to help children become more aware of the sense of hearing. Students should share the activities with the class.

26. Have students create a list of foods that would help children become exposed to different flavors. Students may classify the foods as sweet, tart, spicy, mild, sour, etc.
27. *Science Overview,* Activity A, SAG. Have students answer the questions about science and science-related activities.

Using Color to Teach Science Concepts

28. Have students discuss the relationship of color to science activities.
29. Have students make a chart that categorizes foods by color.
30. Have students create an activity in which colors are mixed to create new colors.

Using Water to Teach Science Concepts

31. Have students list the science concepts that can be taught with water.
32. Have students create a display of water table accessories. Students should label each accessory with the water concepts reinforced by using the accessory.
33. Have students write plans for five activities using water. Choose several activities and have their authors demonstrate them to the class.

Using Foods to Teach Science Concepts

34. Have students review recipes from books and magazines and create recipe files containing activities that children could use to participate in both processing and creating of a product.
35. Have students create a list of themes and foods that could be coordinated with the themes.
36. *Learning Science Through Cooking Experiences,* reproducible master 23-3. Create enough copies for each student to have five recipe forms. On each form, students should write a recipe that could be used for cooking with young children. Students should list supplies needed for and concepts taught by the recipes.

Using the Child's Own Body to Teach Science Concepts

37. Have students practice identifying their own features in pictures of themselves.
38. Have students create an original growth chart.

Using Gardening to Teach Science Concepts

39. Have a group of students plan a seed party for the class. The leaders of the party should encourage the other students to discuss the flavors of each seed. They should also prepare a chart to classify the seeds as grown above the ground or under the ground.

40. Have students make a dish garden using a pineapple, turnip, carrot, and beet top. Students should observe the amount of time it takes for each top to sprout roots.

41. Have students plant bean, corn, and radish seeds and observe how they grow.

Using Air to Teach Science Concepts

42. Have students prepare a bubble solution and practice using it to teach the concept that air takes up space.

43. Have students create a prop that could be used to teach children about the wind.

Using Magnets to Teach Science Concepts

44. Have students list the concepts that children can learn through activities with magnets.

45. Have students make a collection of different types of magnets.

46. Have students make a chart showing the items that magnets pick up and do not pick up.

Using Wheels to Teach Science Concepts

47. Have students list the concepts children can learn from activities involving wheels.

48. Have students plan a science activity using wheels and try it with a group of students in the class.

49. Have students create a display of pictures of items that do and do not have wheels.

Using Field Trips to Teach Science Concepts

50. Have students brainstorm a list of field trips that would supply opportunities for discovery.

51. Have students take technology walks in their own neighborhoods and list all of their observations. Students should share their observations in class.

52. *Planning Field Trips,* Activity C, SAG. Have students complete the chart by preparing a list of field trips that would stimulate a child's curiosity and indicating what children could observe at each site.

Using Animals to Teach Science Concepts

53. Have students explain the value of pets.

54. Have students list the types of animals that can be housed in early childhood centers.

55. *Pet Care,* Activity D, SAG. Have students indicate whether the statements related to animal care are true or false.

56. *Science,* reproducible master 23-4. Have students complete the statements related to science and science activities.

57. *Methods of Teaching Science,* Activity B, SAG. For each method of teaching science concepts listed, have students list three concepts that children could learn through the method.

Care of the Earth

58. Have students plan an Earth Day activity suitable for use with young children.

Additional Resources

59. Guest speaker. Invite a child care teacher to discuss with the class how science is integrated into the daily curriculum.

60. Guest speaker. Invite a science teacher to discuss science activities for young children.

61. Field trip. Arrange for students to visit a discovery center at a local wildlife preserve or arboretum. Have a representative discuss the resources available there to teach children science concepts.

62. Guest speaker. Invite a veterinarian to discuss the selection and care of pets.

Research Topic

63. Have students research materials that have been used to successfully teach science concepts to children. Students should create a catalog of items containing pictures or sketches of each item and a description of how it can be used to teach science concepts.

Answer Key

Text

Review and Reflect, page 363

1. the study of natural processes and their products
2. curiosity, imagination
3. Answers will vary, but may include: enhances curiosity, builds vocabulary and language skills, enhances reading readiness, improves hand-eye coordination, develops small muscle skills.
4. false
5. D
6. Kitchens have sources of heat and water, two sources that are needed in many science experiences.
7. A science table is used to display items related to the science area.
8. true
9. observing objects using the five senses; drawing conclusions from observations based on knowledge gained in past experiences; classifying objects into sets based on one or more observable properties; comparing sets of objects by measuring and counting; communicating by describing objects, relationships, and occurrences
10. Open, close.
11. (List four:) Water, color, food, bodies, gardens (plants), air, magnets, wheels, field trips, animals. (Student response for explanations.)

Student Activity Guide

Science Overview, Activity A

1. Science is the study of natural processes and their products.
2. They begin to see relationships between different events. They start to group their information and make generalizations.
3. Their curiosity is enhanced. They build skill in picking out similarities and differences. Vocabulary improves and reading readiness is enhanced. Language skills improve, and general knowledge improves. Small muscle development and hand-eye coordination improve.
4. For many science projects it is important to be near heat and water sources.
5. You should consider whether the item is safe and whether children have the skills needed to use the item.
6. Observing objects using the five senses. Drawing conclusions from observations based on knowledge gained in past experiences. Classifying objects into sets based on one or more observable properties. Comparing sets of objects by measuring and counting. Communicating by describing objects, relationships, and occurrences.
7. Give children enough time to respond. When children respond, be positive. When a better answer is given, explain how that answer adds to the other answers.
8. (Student response.)

Pet Care, Activity D

1.	T	11.	T
2.	F	12.	T
3.	T	13.	T
4.	T	14.	F
5.	T	15.	T
6.	F	16.	T
7.	F	17.	F
8.	T	18.	T
9.	T	19.	F
10.	T	20.	T

Teacher's Resource Guide/Binder

Science, reproducible master 23-4

1. processes, products
2. observing, measuring, classifying, comparing, predicting, discovering

3. sensitive, curious
4. observation
5. differences
6. physics
7. conclusions
8. questioning
9. respond
10. color
11. fun, educational
12. photographs, drawings
13. weight
14. seeds
15. magnifying
16. balloons
17. curiosity, discovery, interaction

Chapter Test

1.	A	14.	T
2.	D	15.	F
3.	C	16.	C
4.	B	17.	C
5.	E	18.	C
6.	T	19.	B
7.	T	20.	B
8.	F	21.	A
9.	T	22.	C
10.	F	23.	A
11.	F	24.	D
12.	T	25.	D
13.	F		

26. 1. Observing objects using the five senses: seeing, feeling, tasting, smelling, and hearing. 2. Drawing conclusions from observations based on knowledge gained in past experience. 3. Classifying objects into sets based on one or more observable properties. 4. Comparing sets of objects by measuring and counting. 5. Communicating by describing objects, relationships, and occurrences.

27. Close-ended questions require single answers. These questions evoke few decision-making skills and are usually answered in a yes-no fashion. Open-ended questions require more than a one-word response. They promote discussion and require more decision-making skills. (List three:) Water flows when poured; water makes objects wet; some containers hold more water than others; some items float on water; water dissolves some foods; some materials soak up water.

Science Activities

Science activities should offer children opportunities for

- ◆ observing
- ◆ noting differences and likenesses
- ◆ solving problems
- ◆ collecting specimens
- ◆ developing interests and abilities
- ◆ listening to sounds
- ◆ viewing videos
- ◆ looking at books
- ◆ collecting pictures

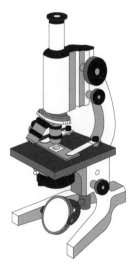

Sources of Science Supplies and Equipment

Name _____ Date _____ Period _____

Many items can be obtained inexpensively or for free for use in science activities. Check with the places listed below to find out if they would be willing to sell or donate the items given. Record the information in the chart. For each location, add three other items that could be used and record information about their availability.

Item	Cost	Available Free?
Farm or Dairy		
Bottles		
Hay or straw		
Leaves		
Gravel		
Seeds		
Garden Supply Store		
Plant bulbs/Plants		
Garden hose		
Soil		
Sprinkling cans		
Seeds		
Service Station		
Ball bearings		
Jacks		
Pulleys		
Wheels		
Maps		

(continued)

Name_____

Item	Cost	Available Free?
Music Store		
Broken string and drum heads		
Pitch pipes		
Tuning forks		
Medical and Dental Offices		
Glass tubing		
Tongue depressors		
Thermometers		
Funnels		
Pet store		
Animals		
Aquariums		
Fish		
Animal cages		
Butterfly nets		
Hardware store		
Cement		
Hammers		
Nuts and bolts		
Yardsticks		
Pulleys		

Learning Science Through Cooking Experiences

Name _____ **Date** _____ **Period** _____

Recipe: _____

Supplies needed: _____
_____
_____
_____
_____
_____
_____

Concepts taught: _____
_____
_____
_____
_____
_____
_____

Science

Name _____ **Date**_____ **Period** _____

Complete the statements below using the words from the list. Write the words in the space provided.

balloons	products	observing	fun
differences	color	respond	physics
magnifying	discovery	conclusions	sensitive
processes	observation	educational	curious
classifying	questioning	photographs	interaction
discovering	comparing	seeds	predicting
measuring	drawings	curiosity	weight

1. Science is the study of _____ and their _____.

2. Science is the process of _____, _____, _____, _____, _____, and _____.

3. Studying science encourages children to be _____ and _____ about their environment.

4. _____ is the beginning of all scientific investigation.

5. Science activities should offer children opportunities to note _____ and likenesses.

6. A teeter-totter is a means of teaching playground _____.

7. Children need to draw _____ from observing.

8. To encourage scientific investigation, the teachers should use effective _____ techniques.

9. During discussions, children need sufficient time to _____ to open-ended questions.

10. Identifying _____ by name is one way children can describe their environment.

11. Science experiments that children can eat are _____ and _____.

12. _____ and _____ of themselves help children understand their own bodies.

13. A chart recording each child's weight can be used to teach the concept of _____.

14. Most five- and six-year-old children can identify common _____ such as apple, peach, and watermelon.

15. A _____ glass can be used to encourage children to view color, size, shape, and texture of seeds.

16. By inflating _____, you can help children understand the concept that air takes up space.

17. Field trips stimulate the child's _____, supply opportunity for _____, and encourage _____ with the environment.

Guiding Science Experiences

Name _____

Date _____ Period _____ Score _____

Matching: Match the following senses and activities that promote sensory development.

_____ 1. Reaching into a box and identifying objects.

_____ 2. Having children identify items with distinct odors placed in small cups.

_____ 3. Naming what is missing from a group.

_____ 4. Matching a child's voice with the correct child.

_____ 5. Blindfolding children and giving them food samples.

A. feeling
B. hearing
C. seeing
D. smelling
E. tasting

True/False: Circle *T* if the statement is true or *F* if the statement is false.

T   F   6. Science is a study of natural processes and their products.

T   F   7. Science encourages the development of curiosity and imagination.

T   F   8. Without data from observations, children often ask questions.

T   F   9. Some of the most successful science experiences will be unplanned.

T   F   10. Most preschool centers do not have a science center.

T   F   11. Equipping a science area is expensive.

T   F   12. Premature input from the teacher can sometimes stifle a child's curiosity.

T   F   13. The best science experiences are teacher dominated and controlled.

T   F   14. All children should be provided materials for learning science in the classroom.

T   F   15. Close-ended questions promote discussion.

Multiple Choice: Choose the best response. Write the letter in the space provided.

_____ 16. This animal is usually chubby and has a shiny coat and bright eyes.
    A. Snake.
    B. Fish.
    C. Hamster.
    D. Frog.

_____ 17. This animal enjoys wood for gnawing.
    A. Dog.
    B. Rabbit.
    C. Hamster.
    D. Frog.

(continued)

_____ 18. This animal needs a cave of small rocks in one corner of the aquarium.
    A. Rabbit.
    B. Guinea pig.
    C. Snake.
    D. Toad.

_____ 19. These pets have a diet of meat, worms, and insects.
    A. Rabbits.
    B. Snakes.
    C. Hamsters.
    D. Fish.

_____ 20. These animals usually sit in water to moisten their bodies.
    A. Toads.
    B. Frogs.
    C. Snakes.
    D. Hamsters.

_____ 21. These pets can be left without attention longer than most pets.
    A. Fish.
    B. Rabbits.
    C. Hamsters.
    D. Guinea pigs.

_____ 22. Fish need to have a water temperature between _____ at all times.
    A. 30° and 40° F
    B. 50° and 60° F
    C. 70° and 80° F
    D. 80° and 90° F

_____ 23. This animal needs much cleaning.
    A. Rabbit.
    B. Frog.
    C. Snake.
    D. Toad.

_____ 24. This pet is easy to handle and enjoys being held and cuddled.
    A. Rabbit.
    B. Toad.
    C. Frog.
    D. Guinea pig.

_____ 25. This pet needs to have large quantities of leafy vegetables and water available.
    A. Snake.
    B. Toad.
    C. Frog.
    D. Rabbit.

Essay Questions: Provide complete responses to the following questions or statements.

26. List the five basic process skills of science.

27. Explain the difference between open-ended and close-ended questions.

28. List three concepts that can be taught with water.

Guiding Social Studies Experiences  24

Objectives

After studying this chapter, students will be able to
- explain the importance of social studies experiences.
- outline the role of the teacher in designing and guiding social studies experiences.
- describe ways to include multicultural, intergenerational, government, ecology, geography, holiday, and current events concepts in the curriculum.

Teaching Materials

Text, pages 365–376
  Terms to Know
  Review and Reflect
  Apply and Explore
Student Activity Guide
  A. *Social Studies Activities*
  B. *Using a Theme in Planning*
  C. *Know Your Resources*
Teacher's Resource Guide/Binder
  Social Studies Themes, transparency master, 24-1
  Halloween Theme, reproducible master, 24-2
  Valentine Theme, transparency master, 24-3
  Goals for a Multicultural Perspective,
    transparency master, 24-4
  Social Studies Terms, reproducible master, 24-5
  Chapter Test
Teacher's Resource Binder
  Current Events Calendar,
    color transparency, CT-24A
  Holiday Concepts Calendar,
    color transparency, CT-24-B
The Observation Guide
Mastering CDA Competencies

Introductory Activities

1. As a class, have students develop a list of concepts that they think should be included in a social studies curriculum.

2. Have students discuss their everyday roles such as student, daughter/son, etc.
3. Lead a class discussion on ways to teach children to respect themselves and others.

Instructional Concepts and Student Learning Experiences

Importance of Social Studies _____

4. Have students discuss the skills that children should acquire from social studies.
5. *Social Studies Activities*, Activity A, SAG. Have students write activities to promote learning in eight areas that are developed by social studies curriculum.

The Teacher's Role in Social Studies _____

6. Have students explain the role of observation in developing a social studies curriculum.
7. Have students discuss the importance of selecting developmentally appropriate materials and activities for a social studies curriculum.
8. Have students discuss developmental characteristics and their implementations for planning a social studies curriculum.
9. Have students develop a checklist for social skills of three-year-olds.
10. Have students identify instructional tools that can be successfully used to teach social studies concepts.
11. *Social Studies Themes*, transparency master 24-1. For the theme ideas given, have students discuss activities that could be used to promote each theme.
12. *Halloween Theme*, reproducible master 24-2. Distribute the master to students and discuss the ideas for various activity areas related to a Halloween theme.
13. *Valentine Theme*, transparency master 24-3. Have students work as a class to develop learning experiences related to a Valentine theme.
14. *Using a Theme in Planning*, Activity B. SAG. Have students plan a theme of their choice. Then have them describe several learning experiences for each of the activity areas listed.

15. Have students prepare a list of community resources, including museums, art galleries, stores, and services, that are available for social studies curriculum.
16. Have students discuss incidental learning that could teach social studies concepts.
17. Have students observe a social studies activity in a child care setting and record their observations. Students should share their observations in class.

Building Social Studies Concepts

18. Have students discuss how concepts are built.
19. Have students discuss the benefits of developing concepts.
20. Have students discuss the aspects of children that affect the formation of concepts.

Multicultural Concepts

21. *Goals for a Multicultural Perspective*, transparency master 24-4. Use the master as a basis for discussion of the goals for a multicultural perspective.
22. Have students explain why parents and other family members are vital resources for promoting a multicultural perspective in the child care setting.
23. Have students give examples of stereotyping and omission in society. Students should discuss ways to avoid these problems in the classroom.
24. Have students plan an activity to promote a multicultural perspective.

Intergenerational Concepts

25. Have students ask children to share their ideas about elderly people. Students should share the comments in class.
26. Have students describe goals for an intergenerational curriculum.
27. Have students brainstorm a list of activities that could be done in conjunction with a retirement home or senior citizen's center.
28. Have students develop a checklist for choosing materials to teach gerontology to children.

Government Concepts

29. Have students talk to children of different ages to find out their concepts of government. Students should discuss these concepts as a class.
30. Have students discuss activities that develop political concepts.

Ecology Concepts

31. Have students find current articles about ecology and discuss them as a class.
32. Have students discuss activities to teach ecology concepts.

Change Concepts

33. Have students explain children's concepts of time.
34. Have students brainstorm a list of ways to teach children about change.

Geography Concepts

35. Have students develop a game to prepare children to read maps.
36. *Social Studies Terms,* reproducible master 24-5. Have students complete the statements related to social studies.

Community Living Concepts

37. Have students bring in various sizes of boxes and create a "box town" of their community to share with young children.
38. Have students list possible field trips throughout the community that would be appropriate for young children.

Current Events

39. *Current Events Calendar,* color transparency CT-24A, TRB. Use this transparency to introduce the concept of using a daily calendar to show current events. You may want to:
    A. Stress that having a predictable procedure is a way of promoting children's feelings of security. As a result, some teachers use a daily calendar at group time each day. The purpose of the calendar is to teach the concept of time.
    B. Have students discuss their experiences with calendars in school.
    C. Ask students to list the benefits of recording individual and group experiences on the calendar.
    D. Remind the students that all teacher-made classroom materials should appear professionally prepared. Discuss the elements of a professionally prepared teacher-made aide.
40. Have students design a bulletin board for current events.
41. Have students brainstorm a list of activities for teaching current events. Then have them plan one activity that focuses on a current event.

Holiday Concepts

42. *Holiday Concepts Calendar,* color transparency CT-24-B, TRB. Use this transparency to introduce a method or teaching children how to use the calendar as a resource. You may want to:
    A. Ask students to brainstorm other symbols that could be included on a calendar.
    B. Discuss why a line calendar is easier to use with young children than the traditional format.

304

C. Ask students to share how the calendar is included in the daily schedule of programs that they have observed.

D. Have the students brainstorm a list of symbols that could be included throughout the year on a calendar.

43. Have students explain precautions that should be followed when introducing holiday concepts to preschool children.

44. Have students select and plan an activity for a holiday or special event.

45. Have students research and compile a list of international holidays.

Additional Resources

46. *Know Your Resources*, Activity C, SAG. Students are asked to identify available community resources that may be helpful in planning a variety of learning experiences.

47. Guest speaker. Invite a child care teacher to share how social studies concepts are integrated into the curriculum.

48. Panel discussion. Invite people representing different cultures to discuss their customs with the class.

49. Guest speaker. Invite a gerontologist or a social worker who specializes in working with the elderly to discuss the benefits of having young children interact with the elderly.

Research Topics

50. Have students survey people of different occupations, asking these people to describe their roles in society. For each role surveyed, students should construct a chart describing the role and ways to introduce the role to children. Students should then compile the charts in a three-ring binder.

51. Have students research the roles of the elderly in different societies and report on their findings.

Answer Key

Text

Review and Reflect, page 376

1. (List three:) Develop self-respect and healthy self-concept, develop self-control and independence, develop respect for others' feelings and ideas, learn to share ideas and materials, learn about the roles people have in real life, develop ways of relating to and working with others.

2. (List four:) Observe children during play, interact with them in a casual way, ask the children's parents to share their children's interests with you, and observe the children's choice of books.

3. Young children are able to plan whom to play with, materials needed for a project, places to visit, people to invite to the classroom, and how to celebrate birthdays and holidays.

4. Learning experiences that happen during the course of a normal day. (Student response for examples.)

5. evaluation

6. perceptions

7. Respect for oneself as a worthwhile and competent human being; acceptance and respect for others' similarities and differences; an appreciation of one's own racial and ethnic background; the skill to interact positively with other children; an understanding that there are many ways to do things.

8. Omission implies that some groups have less value than other groups in our society. This is done by omitting a group's presence in teaching materials.

9. false

10. false

11. (Student response.)

12. (Student response.)

13. (Student response.)

Teacher's Resource Guide/Binder

Social Studies Terms, reproducible master 24-5

1. concepts	9. evaluation
2. social	10. culture
3. children	11. studies
4. difficult	12. omission
5. ability	13. negative
6. checklists	14. intergenerational
7. themes	15. ecology
8. perceptions	16. celebrating

Chapter Test

1. C	12. F
2. E	13. F
3. D	14. T
4. B	15. F
5. A	16. F
6. T	17. A
7. T	18. C
8. T	19. D
9. F	20. B
10. T	21. D
11. T	

22. Young children are capable of planning what materials to work with, who to play with, materials needed for a project, what places to visit, who to invite to the classroom, and how to celebrate birthdays and holidays.

23. The goals of a multicultural perspective are to help a child develop each of the following: respect for oneself as a worthwhile and competent human being; acceptance and respect for others' similarities and differences; the skill to attack tasks, expecting to succeed; an appreciation of one's own racial and ethnic background; the skill to interact positively with other children; an understanding that there are many ways to do things.

24. (Student response.)

Social Studies Themes

I'm Me, I'm Special

Community Helpers

My Feelings

Auto Mechanics

My Family

Bakers

Brothers and/or Sisters

Butchers

My Home

Teachers

My Friends

Farmers

My Grandparent(s)

Seasons

My Neighborhood

Christmas

My School

Hanukkah

The Mail Carriers

Halloween

The Library

Valentine's Day

The Fire Station

Thanksgiving

The Police

Easter

The Doctor

Birthday

The Dentist

Clothes

The Supermarket

Homes

The Post Office

Touch

The Service Station

Sight

The Greenhouse

Sound

The Restaurant

Taste

The Park

Smell

Letters

Newspaper

Halloween Theme

Art
- Use orange and black paint at the easel or for finger painting.
- Use orange tempera or food coloring to tint play dough.
- Use pumpkin seeds for a collage.
- Cut easel paper into the shape of a pumpkin.
- Use Halloween cookie cutters to make prints.

Cooking and Snacks
- Prepare orange gelatin.
- Bake pumpkin pie, bread, and/or cookies.
- Make cut-out sugar cookies.
- Bake pumpkin seeds.
- Prepare vanilla pudding and tint it with orange food coloring.
- Prepare orange juice and cut both ends off a piece of licorice to use as a straw.
- Cut Halloween shapes from cheese slices with a cookie cutter.

Dramatic Play
- Display masks that people use in their work. Include sun glasses, ski goggles, safety goggles, football helmet, motorcycle helmet.
- Display a variety of hats, including cowboy, police officer, mail carrier, baker, and chef's hats.
- Display a variety of costumes including clown, man, woman, bride, etc.

Small Manipulative
- Use puzzles that contain pumpkins.
- Purchase Halloween gummed stickers (at a local store or your school supply catalog) for children to use.
- Construct a lotto game with pumpkins.

Field Trips
- Go to the grocery store to purchase cooking supplies.
- Visit a farm that grows pumpkins.
- Take a walk to discuss fall colors.

Book Center
- Add books that contain a Halloween theme such as *Hi Cat* by Ezra J. Keats.

Games
- Collect several small masks and play, "What's missing?"
- Play "Guess Who?" by making Halloween sounds.

Fingerplay
- Use the following:
  See my jack-o-lantern. (Point)
  Looking at you. (Smile)
  You need not be afraid. (Look afraid)
  It can't holler BOO!

Large Muscle Activity
- Have a costume parade.

308

Valentine Theme

Activity Area	Learning Experiences
Art	
Cooking & Snack	
Dramatic Play	
Field Trip	
Small Manipulative	
Games	
Fingerplay	
Book Corner	
Large Muscle Activity	

Goals for a Multicultural Perspective

Each child should develop

- ◆ respect for oneself as a worthwhile and competent human being.

- ◆ acceptance and respect for others' similarities and differences.

- ◆ the skill to attack tasks, expecting to succeed.

- ◆ an appreciation of one's own racial and ethnic background.

- ◆ the skill to interact positively with other children.

- ◆ an understanding that there are many ways to do things.

Social Studies Terms

Name _____ **Date** _____ **Period** _____

Complete the statements below using the words from the list. Write the words in the space provided.

ability	concepts	evaluation	perceptions
celebrating	culture	intergenerational	social
checklists	difficult	negative	studies
children	ecology	omission	themes

_____ 1. _____ help children to mentally organize, categorize, and order their experiences.

_____ 2. _____ studies includes history, geography, economics, current events, and career education.

_____ 3. Young _____ develop social studies concepts as they experience the world around them.

_____ 4. _____ materials may create disinterest, stress, or pressure.

_____ 5. _____ levels can be determined by observing the children.

_____ 6. Using _____ are one method of evaluating the children's progress.

_____ 7. _____ can be a helpful guide in planning the social studies curriculum because they help combine the learning opportunities of several activities.

_____ 8. _____ are what the child learns about a relationship or object as a result of sensory experiences.

_____ 9. _____ helps you see if goals have been met, what new goals are needed, and whether any current goals need modification.

_____ 10. _____ is a word social scientists use to describe people's whole way of life.

_____ 11. _____ indicate that a child's attitude toward other racial groups begin to form during the preschool years.

_____ 12. _____ is a form of discrimination found in multicultural curriculum materials.

_____ 13. _____ stereotyping is one of the most chronic problems faced by today's elderly society.

_____ 14. _____ programs are valuable for children as well as adults.

_____ 15. _____ is the study of the chain of life.

_____ 16. _____ holidays in a center can help children understand changes.

Guiding Social Studies Experiences

Name _____

Date _____ **Period** _____ **Score** _____

Matching: Match the following terms and identifying phrases.

_____ 1. Programs that provide benefits to both the young and the old.

_____ 2. Before age five, these concepts are bits of information gathered from the radio, home, and school.

_____ 3. Is a form of bias.

_____ 4. Includes exploring space, playing in water, and digging dirt.

_____ 5. Is a study of the chain of life.

A. ecology
B. geography
C. intergenerational
D. omission
E. political concepts

True/False: Circle *T* if the statement is true or *F* if the statement is false.

T F 6. Social studies provides children with a chance to learn useful group living skills.

T F 7. Eating a variety of ethnic foods promotes an understanding of social studies.

T F 8. History is included in the field of social studies.

T F 9. Curriculum planning should be limited to the teacher.

T F 10. Themes can be a helpful guide in planning a social studies curriculum.

T F 11. Children as well as adults benefit from intergenerational programs.

T F 12. Young children's concepts of the aged are always positive.

T F 13. By age three, children can usually identify pictures of the president and the flag.

T F 14. Good observation skills are necessary to develop ecology skills.

T F 15. Holiday celebrations may be used to teach children that change is continuous.

T F 16. Formal geography experiences are usually introduced during the preschool years.

Multiple Choice: Choose the best response. Write the letter in the space provided.

_____ 17. Social studies helps children _____.
  A. develop respect for other people's feelings and ideas
  B. develop dependence
  C. learn about imaginary heroes
  D. develop ways of working alone

(continued)

_____ 18. Thoughtful social studies programs reflect the _____.
- A. teacher's tastes and desires
- B. parents' wishes for children
- C. children's interests and abilities
- D. center's policies

_____ 19. Examples of community resources include _____.
- A. puppets.
- B. paper
- C. crayons
- D. museums

_____ 20. Most children have contact with _____.
- A. a variety of elderly people
- B. their grandparents
- C. elderly people in nursing homes
- D. elderly groups from community centers

_____ 21. Which of the following is not a guideline for including elderly volunteers in a program?
- A. View each person as an individual.
- B. Design and provide training.
- C. Maintain close communication.
- D. Keep roles of volunteers undefined.

Essay Questions: Provide complete responses to the following questions or statements.

22. Describe the ways in which the children can plan their social studies experiences.

23. List the goals for a multicultural perspective.

24. List four recommendations for including the aged in classroom activities.

Guiding Food and Nutrition Experiences  25

Objectives

After studying this chapter, you will be able to
- explain the value of food and nutrition experiences.
- conduct positive food and nutrition experiences for children that promote healthy eating habits.
- give examples of ways to work with parents to best serve children's nutritional needs.
- list nutritional concepts to teach in early childhood settings.
- outline the procedure for conducting cooking experiences.
- select and prepare simple recipes for children to use in early cooking experiences.
- identify various eating problems encountered in young children.
- teach children to set a table.

Teaching Materials

Text, pages 377–384
  Terms to Know
  Review and Reflect
  Apply and Explore
Student Activity Guide
  A. *Teaching Nutrition*
  B. *Collecting Recipes*
  C. *Setting the Table*
Teacher's Resource Guide/Binder
  Nutrition Concepts for Young Children,
    transparency master, 25-1
  Sensory Experiences with Food,
    reproducible master, 25-2
  Guiding Food Experiences Recipes,
    recipe master, 25-3
  Developing Good Eating Habits,
    transparency master, 25-4
  Mealtime Tips Puzzle, reproducible master, 25-5
  Chapter Test
Teacher's Resource Binder
  Chocolate Chip Cookies, color transparency, CT-25
The Observation Guide
Mastering CDA Competencies

Introductory Activities

1. Ask students to list foods that they like. Students should discuss reasons they like these foods such as taste, appearance, etc.
2. Ask students to name foods from other cultures that they have eaten. Students should discuss what they liked or disliked about them.
3. Have students discuss foods that they associate with happy, warm feelings. Students should discuss how the atmosphere in which foods are presented could affect children's acceptance of the foods.

Instructional Concepts and Student Learning Experiences

Working with Parents

4. As a class, have students collect materials that could be placed in a nutrition lending library and organize the materials.
5. Have students write a foods and nutrition newsletter designed for parents.

Nutrition Concepts

6. Have students discuss methods of introducing nutrition concepts to children through food experiences.
7. *Nutrition Concepts for Young Children,* transparency master 25-1. Use the master as a basis for discussion of nutrition concepts that can be taught to children. For each concept, students should discuss appropriate activities.
8. *Teaching Nutrition,* Activity A, SAG. Have students use the form provided to develop a chart that depicts basic nutrition concepts through simple drawings.

Cooking Experiences

9. Have students interview preschool, child care, Head Start, or kindergarten teachers. Students should ask them to share their favorite classroom cooking activities. Students should share their findings in class.
10. *Chocolate Chip Cookies,* color transparency CT-25, TRB. Use this transparency to show

students how a language experience chart can be used to promote food experiences. You may want to:

A. Stress that language experience charts can help children develop an interest in the printed word. They learn that print communicates a message. These charts can also help children develop the left-to-right progression skills necessary for reading in the U.S.

B. Have students state other advantages of using language experience charts.

C. Have students brainstorm additional cooking activities that could be easily charted.

D. Remind students that while preparing language experience charts, use a soft-leaded pencil to first sketch the alphabet letters and symbols. After the letters are correctly formed, a medium felt-tipped marker can be used to trace over all of the figures.

11. Have students brainstorm a list of basic concepts that children can learn by participating in cooking experiences.

12. Have students visit a center and observe snack time. Students should record the activities observed and list the values of the snack time.

13. Have students discuss cooking safety and precautions that need to be taken to maximize learning.

14. Have students observe a classroom cooking experience and record their observations. Students should write a list of tips for conducting cooking activities based on their observations.

15. *Collecting Recipes,* Activity B, SAG. Have students use the forms provided to record two recipes and develop recipe charts for those recipes.

16. Have students plan a classroom cooking activity, conduct the activity with a group of students, and evaluate the results of the activity.

17. Have students read through cookbooks and find five recipes to use with children.

18. *Sensory Experiences with Food,* reproducible master 25-2. Have students list four food activities for each sensory experience listed.

19. *Guiding Food Experiences Recipes*, recipe master 25-3. Use these recipes as you guide children through cooking experiences.

Eating Habits

20. Have students discuss how children learn appropriate food habits.

21. *Developing Good Eating Habits,* transparency master 25-4. Use the master to discuss methods of promoting good eating habits. Encourage students to suggest other tips for promoting good eating habits.

22. Have students describe how a child's activity level may affect eating habits.

23. Have students identify four reasons a child may appear to lack an appetite at mealtime.

24. Have students discuss how a child who is always tired at mealtime should be handled prior to eating.

25. Have students discuss why children may refuse to eat food.

Setting the Table

26. *Setting the Table,* Activity C, SAG. Have students design a place mat for teaching children how to set the table. Students should include a plate, glass, fork, spoon, and napkin on the place mat.

27. Have students prepare a list of centerpieces that could be used as conversation pieces.

28. Have students explain why small serving sizes should be used at meals and snacks.

29. Have students describe how independence should be encouraged at mealtime.

30. Have students describe how and when milk should be served.

31. Have students describe the role of children during cleanup.

32. *Mealtime Tips Puzzle,* reproducible master 25-5. Have students complete the puzzle by filling in the appropriate terms in the statements related to food experiences.

Additional Resources

33. Panel discussion. Have students invite a panel of parents to discuss the likes and dislikes of young children concerning food.

34. Guest speaker. Invite a child care teacher to discuss snack time at the center.

35. Guest speaker. Invite a cook for a child care center to discuss favorite recipes of young children.

Research Topics

36. Have students research methods of handling appetite problems of young children. Students should give an oral report on their findings.

37. Have students find two different cookie recipes to try with children. Students should try each recipe at different times with the same group of children. Then have students write a paper comparing the two experiences, including such factors as ease of preparation, enjoyment of cookies, etc.

Answer Key

Text

Review and Reflect, page 384

1. (List three: Student response.) preparing foods, setting the table, eating snacks and meals, cleaning up.

2. true
3. Schedule quiet, relaxing activities just before mealtimes; provide child-sized tables, chairs, and serving tools; encourage children to serve themselves; expect some accidents.
4. Lending libraries, meetings/workshops/discussion groups, newsletters. (Student response for explanations. See page 378.)
5. recipe cards
6. false
7. B
8. Children learn poor eating habits from people with whom they have contact.
9. C
10. true

Teacher's Resource Guide/Binder

Mealtime Tips Puzzle, reproducible master 25-5

1. mealtime
2. serve
3. tables
4. spills
5. tasting
6. stirring
7. small
8. recipe
9. snack

(Listed tips are student response.)

Chapter Test

1. T	11. T
2. F	12. F
3. F	13. C
4. T	14. A
5. T	15. C
6. T	16. D
7. F	17. C
8. F	18. B
9. T	19. D
10. T	20. B

21. (List three:) schedule quiet, relaxing activities just before mealtimes; provide child-sized tables, chairs, and serving tools; encourage children to serve themselves; expect some accidents and be prepared for them
22. Place a utility cart or small table next to the eating area. After the main meal is completed, have the children take their plates to the cart. If dessert is being served, they may keep their eating utensils and glasses. When dessert is finished they should then take all their dinnerware and eating utensils to the cart.
23. (List three:) hot weather, having just eaten before coming to the center, being fatigued, feeling ill
24. (Student response. See page 377.)

Nutrition Concepts for Young Children

♦ Nutrition is how our bodies use the foods we eat to produce energy, growth, and health.

♦ There is a wide variety of food available. Foods come from both plants and animals. In addition, the same food can be used to make many different dishes.

♦ Foods vary in color, flavor, texture, odor, size, and shape.

♦ Foods are classified into basic food groups:

> Bread, cereal, rice, and pasta group.
>
> Vegetable group.
>
> Fruit group.
>
> Milk, yogurt, and cheese group.
>
> Meat, poultry, fish, dry beans, eggs, and nuts group.
>
> Fats, oils, and sweets group.

♦ A good diet includes foods from each of the food groups.

♦ There are many factors that enhance the eating experience:

> Aesthetics of food.
>
> Method of preparation.
>
> Cleanliness, manners.
>
> Environment/atmosphere.
>
> Celebrations.

♦ We choose foods we eat for many reasons:

> Availability.
>
> Family and personal habits.
>
> Aesthetics of food.
>
> Social and cultural customs.
>
> Mass media.

Sensory Experiences with Food

Name _____ **Date** _____ **Period** _____

Listed below are the five senses. Under each is a sensory experience with food. Think of four other activities that could be included under each.

Sight

1. Watch bread rising.

2. _____

3. _____

4. _____

5. _____

Feel

1. Feel the coolness of ice cream.

2. _____

3. _____

4. _____

5. _____

Hearing

1. Listen to water bubbling.

2. _____

3. _____

4. _____

5. _____

Taste

1. Taste the sweetness of maple syrup.

2. _____

3. _____

4. _____

5. _____

Smell

1. Smell bacon frying.

2. _____

3. _____

4. _____

5. _____

Guiding Food and Nutrition Experiences

Recipes

Bagel Miniatures

½   cup creamy peanut butter
2   tablespoons soft-style cream cheese
2   tablespoons honey
3   whole-wheat or cinnamon-raisin bagels
   fresh fruits, thinly sliced
   lemon, orange, or pineapple juice

In a small bowl, combine peanut butter, cream cheese, and honey; mix well. Cut each bagel in half lengthwise. Toast bagel halves in toaster at medium setting. Place bagels on cutting board; spread with peanut butter mixture. Dip fruit slices in lemon, orange, or pineapple juice to prevent darkening. Attractively arrange slices on top of bagel halves. Using a serrated knife, cut each bagel half into four equal pieces. Makes 24 servings.

Banana Pops

   bananas
   orange juice
   crushed corn flakes, chopped peanuts, or granola
   wooden sticks

Peel one banana for every two children. Cut bananas in half. Dip each banana in orange juice. Roll in crushed corn flakes, chopped peanuts, or granola. Insert a wooden stick in the center. Banana pops can be served frozen or at room temperature.

(continued)

Apple Pinwheels

apples

cheese spread, cream cheese, or peanut butter

Core one medium sized apple for each child. Stuff the opening with cheese spread, cream cheese, or peanut butter. Slice cross-wise and serve.

Easy Nachos

2 to 3 cups	refried beans
14	taco shells, cut into quarters
2	cups of shredded cheddar cheese

Spread refried beans on each taco quarter and then sprinkle with grated cheese. Bake or broil until the cheese melts.

Carrot-Raisin-Cheese Spread

1 cup	plain yogurt
1½ cups	raisins
2 cups	grated carrots
1½ cups	cottage cheese

Blend or mix together until well combined. Spread on bread or crackers.

(continued)

Yogurt Shake

10	medium bananas
5 cups	yogurt
4 cups	apple juice

Place all of the ingredients in a food processor. Blend for 20 seconds. Makes approximately 20 servings.

Watermelon Ice Pops

1	medium sized watermelon

Cut the rind off the watermelon. Remove all of the seeds. Place the fruit in a food processor and blend. After the fruit has been blended, pour into forms or fill 6-ounce juice cans half full and insert sticks. Freeze.

Peanut Butter

2 pounds	unsalted shelled peanuts
2-3 tsps.	vegetable oil
	salt (to taste)

Place the peanuts in a blender with 2 teaspoons of vegetable oil and salt. Blend until smooth. If necessary, add an additional teaspoon of oil. Serve on crackers, bread, or raw vegetables, such as celery sticks.

(continued)

Yummy Peanut Butter Balls

2 cups	peanut butter
1½ cups	dry milk
1 cup	raisins
½ cup	honey

Mix all the ingredients. Roll into small balls. For variety, substitute granola, coconut, or sesame seeds for the raisins.

Cheese Fondue

1 loaf	French bread
1 ounce	cheese per child
	individual paper cups

Cut the bread into chunks. Melt the cheese and pour into individual cups. Dip bread into cheese.

Milkshakes

1 cup	cold milk
½ cup	fruit or fruit juice
1 cup	ice cream, if desired

Blend all the ingredients together. This recipe can be modified:

Orange Milkshake: Add ½ cup orange juice.

Prune Milkshake: Add ½ cup prune juice.

Strawberry Milkshake: Add ½ cup crushed sweetened berries.

Banana Milkshake: Add ½ mashed banana. (Serves two children)

(continued)

Fruit or Vegetable Kabobs

Vegetables: asparagus spears, broccoli florets, carrot sticks, celery sticks, green pepper sticks, radish roses, cucumber slices, cherry tomatoes, mushrooms, turnip sticks

Fresh fruits: apples, apricots, bananas, berries, cherries, grape-fruit, grapes, melon, nectarines, oranges, peaches, pears, pineapple, plums, tangerines

Lemon, orange, or pineapple juice

Cut any of the above fruits and vegetables and thread on a stick or skewer in desired combinations. For fresh fruit, dip chunks into lemon, orange, or pineapple juice to keep from darkening.

For variety, add cheese or meat chunks.

Cottage Cheese Pudding

1 pint	cottage cheese
2 cups	applesauce
1 16 oz. can	coarsely chopped apricots
1½ teaspoon	cinnamon
1 cup	raisins

Combine all ingredients and chill. Any fruit may be substituted for the apricots.

Vegetable Dip

1 cup	small curd creamed cottage cheese
⅓ cup	milk
1 tablespoon	lemon or lime juice

Place all of the ingredients into a blender. Blend until smooth. Serve with fresh, raw vegetables or fruits.

(continued)

Butter

5 pints	cold whipping cream
	dash salt
1	small baby food jar (with lid) for each child

Fill each jar half full of very cold whipping cream. Let the children shake the containers until butter forms. Remove the excess milk. Add the dash of salt. Encourage the children to spread the butter on individual crackers.

Dill Dip

1 cup	sour cream
1 cup	mayonnaise
1 tablespoon	dried minced onion
1 tablespoon	dill weed

Combine and chill. Serve with a variety of raw vegetables.

Guacamole

1	ripe avocado
1	ripe tomato, chopped
1 teaspoon	lemon juice
¼ cup	mayonnaise
	salt and pepper

Peel and mash the avocado. Add the chopped tomato, lemon juice, and mayonnaise. Add salt and pepper to taste. Mix completely.

Developing Good Eating Habits

♦ Schedule a quiet, relaxing activity just before mealtime.

♦ Provide child-sized table, chairs, serving utensils, and pitchers.

♦ Expect children to serve themselves.

♦ Expect some accidents or spills. Be prepared with a sponge at each table.

♦ Encourage children to wipe up their own spills.

Mealtime Tips Puzzle

Name _____ **Date**_____ **Period** _____

Complete the puzzle by filling in the blanks in the statements below.

					M							
1.					M							
2.					E							
3.					A							
4.					L							
5.					T							
6.					I							
7.					M							
8.					E							
9.					S							

1. Before _____, schedule a quiet, relaxing activity.

2. Children should be encouraged to _____ themselves.

3. _____, chairs, and serving utensils should be child-sized.

4. To wipe up _____, be prepared with a sponge at each table.

5. After cooking, _____ provides the children opportunities to learn about new foods.

6. _____, measuring, pouring, and grating are language concepts.

7. Some teachers prefer to schedule cooking activities during _____ group time.

8. Left to right progress skills are taught as children are taught to read _____ charts.

9. The first cooking experiences should involve making simple products that can be served at _____ time.

On the lines below, list four mealtime tips that you think might be helpful. Share your tips with the class.

_____

_____

_____

_____

Guiding Food and Nutrition Experiences

Name_____

Date _____ **Period** _____ **Score** _____

True/False: Circle *T* if the statement is true or *F* if the statement is false.

T   F   1. Cooking experiences provide opportunities for the children to learn language concepts.

T   F   2. Children should choose whether or not to wear an apron during a cooking experience.

T   F   3. The children should premeasure the ingredients before a cooking experience.

T   F   4. Small group time is a favorite time for some teachers to schedule cooking experiences.

T   F   5. If parents, relatives, or peers model poor food habits, the children will imitate them.

T   F   6. The children's eating habits may be affected by their activity levels.

T   F   7. A child always eats the same amount of food every day.

T   F   8. Children who do not feel like eating should be forced to eat.

T   F   9. Instead of refusing, teachers also need to taste all of the foods served.

T   F   10. By setting the table, children can learn counting as well as space relationships.

T   F   11. Centerpieces can be something the class has made.

T   F   12. Milk should only be served after the meal.

Multiple Choice: Choose the best response. Write the letter in the space provided.

_____ 13. It is important that children first learn to serve _____.
A. the teachers
B. the aides
C. themselves
D. classroom volunteers

_____ 14. Regarding spills, children should be encouraged to _____.
A. wipe up their own
B. ignore them
C. tell a teacher to wipe them
D. assist a teacher in wiping them

_____ 15. The table should be set by _____.
A. children volunteering
B. teachers
C. children taking turns
D. cook

(continued)

_____ 16. When setting the table, the glass should be placed _____.
     A. above the plate
     B. on the left side of the plate
     C. on the right side of the plate
     D. above the knife

_____ 17. Serving dishes should be placed on _____.
     A. a cart
     B. a serving table
     C. each table
     D. None of the above.

_____ 18. A serving should usually consist of _____.
     A. only one serving spoon
     B. one or two serving spoons
     C. three or four serving spoons
     D. four serving spoons

_____ 19. A second glass of milk should be provided _____.
     A. never
     B. before the meal
     C. after the meal
     D. after all foods have been tasted

_____ 20. After the meal, responsibility for cleanup for each individual child is taken by _____.
     A. adults only
     B. each individual child
     C. an assigned child
     D. the cook

Essay Questions: Provide complete responses to the following questions or statements.

21. List three rules for providing good food experiences.

22. Describe the cleanup process after a meal.

23. What are three reasons a child may appear to lack an appetite at mealtimes?

24. Explain the value of cooking experiences for young children.

Guiding Music and Movement Experiences  26

Objectives

After studying this chapter, students will be able to
- explain the benefits of music experiences.
- design a music center.
- outline the teacher's role in music experiences.
- demonstrate the use and purpose of rhythm instruments in the program.
- name a variety of rhythm instruments.
- list considerations for scheduling music activities.
- plan a variety of music activities.
- explain how to teach various movement activities.
- describe movement activities that promote children's development.

Teaching Materials

Text, pages 385–404
  Terms to Know
  Review and Reflect
  Apply and Explore
Student Activity Guide
  A. *Musical Truths*
  B. *Rhythm Instruments*
  C. *Fingerplays*
  D. *Teaching Movement*
Teacher's Resource Guide/Binder
  Value of Music Activities, transparency master, 26-1
  Selecting Songs, transparency master, 26-2
  Purpose of Rhythm Instruments,
    transparency master, 26-3
  Educational Value of Fingerplays
    transparency master, 26-4
  Favorite Fingerplays, reproducible master, 26-5
  Movement Activities, reproducible master, 26-6
  Chapter Test
Teacher's Resource Binder
  Teaching Songs, color transparency, CT-26
The Observation Guide
Mastering CDA Competencies

Introductory Activities

1. Ask students to name the types of music to which they like to listen. Have students discuss how they feel when they listen to that music.
2. Gather a collection of a variety of types of music on a cassette tape. Have students discuss the moods created by the different types of music. Students should also discuss which types of music they liked and disliked, and why.
3. Have students brainstorm a list of items that could be used to make instruments.
4. *Musical Truths,* Activity A, SAG. As a pretest to the chapter, have students determine whether the statements given are true or false.

Instructional Concepts and Student Learning Experiences

Benefits of Music Experiences _____
5. Have students discuss how music can be used to introduce vocabulary words.
6. Have students interview parents of young children about their children's reactions to music. Students should share the parents' responses in class.
7. *Value of Music Activities,* transparency master 26-1. Have students discuss the benefits listed and give examples of each. Encourage students to add other benefits to the list.

Music Center _____
8. Have students list the contents of a music center.
9. Have students draw a design for a music center.
10. Have students create an attractive, functional display of music instruments.

The Teacher's Role _____
11. Have students describe how the teacher encourages discovery.
12. *Teaching Songs,* color transparency CT-26, TRB. Use this transparency to introduce the three methods of teaching songs: phrase, whole song, and phrase/whole combination method. You may want to:
    A. Stress that when a new song is introduced, it should be heard in its entirely. Then it can be

taught in sentences, phrases, or short verses. The method used will depend upon the nature and mood of the song.

B. Discuss why the phrase method may be most effective for teaching some songs.

C. Have students share their observations of effective music experiences in child care centers.

D. Remind students that children enjoy songs with clear and simple melodies.

13. Have students discuss ways of encouraging children who do not want to participate in music activities.

14. *Selecting Songs,* transparency master 26-2. Use the transparency master as a basis of discussion of criteria for selecting songs.

15. Have students create a brochure designed for teachers to use when selecting songs for children.

16. Have students create a song using the melody of "Twinkle, Twinkle, Little Star" or "Mary Had a Little Lamb."

17. Have students explain the three methods used to teach songs.

18. Have students select a song and teach it to the class.

19. Have students observe a teacher teaching a song to a group of children and discuss their observations in class.

20. Have students select a song and teach it to a group of children.

21. Have students describe methods of accompanying singing.

Rhythm Instruments

22. *Purpose of Rhythm Instruments,* transparency master 26-3. Use the master as the basis for discussion of the purpose of using rhythm instruments.

23. Have students describe how rhythm instruments should be introduced.

24. Have students construct two or three rhythm instruments.

25. *Rhythm Instruments,* Activity B, SAG. Students are asked to choose a rhythm instrument and to develop and perform a demonstration on how to make and use the instrument.

26. Have students look through child care center supply catalogs and list instruments that can be purchased for use with children.

Scheduling Music

27. Have students discuss when music experiences should occur.

28. Have students discuss suggestions for group music.

29. Have students explain the importance of individual music activities.

Music Activities

30. Have students name four musical activities that are included in a good curriculum.

31. Have students brainstorm a list of sounds that can be taped to teach children listening skills.

32. Have students list two considerations for choosing a fingerplay for two-year-old children.

33. Have students prepare a file of fingerplays.

34. *Educational Value of Fingerplays,* transparency master 26-4. Use this master to point out the value of fingerplays.

35. *Favorite Fingerplays,* reproducible master 26-5. Have students try some of the fingerplays given as a class. Students should be encouraged to use the list for planning future activities with children.

36. *Fingerplays,* Activity C, SAG. Have students use the form to develop a fingerplay that could be taught to a child.

37. Have students describe the term mouthing.

38. Have students recite chants they know.

Movement Experiences

39. Have students list objectives for movement activities.

40. Have students describe body percussion activities.

41. Have students practice a movement activity in front of a full-length mirror.

42. *Teaching Movement,* Activity D, SAG. Have students resolve each situation listed by providing an appropriate solution.

Movement Activities

43. Have students list and describe four types of movement activities.

44. *Movement Activities,* reproducible master 26-6. Have students practice each of the movement activities listed.

45. Have students explain pantomiming as it is used in the preschool classroom.

46. Have students observe a movement activity in a classroom and record descriptions of the feelings and ideas expressed by children during the activity.

47. Have students select a movement activity and introduce it to their class members.

Additional Resources

48. Guest speaker. Invite a dancer to speak to the class about his or her experiences with music.

49. Guest speaker. Invite a musician to discuss with the class the interpretation of music, composition, and other subjects related to music.

50. Field trip. Arrange for the class to visit a child care center and observe a music experience.

Research Topics

51. Have students research articles on the types of songs that are most enjoyed by children. Have them write a paper on the qualities that make a good children's song and include examples of popular songs.

52. Have students develop a videotape on teaching songs to children. The tape should give examples of various methods as demonstrated by teachers in classroom settings.

Answer Key

Text

Review and Reflect, page 403

1. (List four:) builds a sense of community; provides an opportunity to learn and use language concepts and vocabulary; provides an opportunity to practice counting skills; provides a pleasant background for playing, eating, and sleeping; releases tension and energy, and calms angry feelings; can be used to express feelings though movement and dance; can be used to manage behavior; makes learning fun; teaches listening skills; helps build an understanding of musical concepts, including loud/soft, high/low, fast/slow, up/down; helps build an appreciation of different cultural backgrounds

2. true
3. C
4. Your delight in music will be catching.
5. false
6. B
7. phrase method, whole song method, phrase/whole combination (Student response for explanations.)
8. With these instruments, facial expressions and lip movements can be seen by the children. They will feel your involvement in the activity.
9. (List four:) build listening skills; accompany the beat of a sound or recording; classify sounds; discriminate between sounds; project music or mood; experiment with sounds; organize sound to communicate feelings and ideas; develop classification skills by learning the difference between quiet and loud, hard and soft, and other sounds.
10. true
11. Group
12. (Student response.)
13. false
14. Chants
15. Movement experiences should provide children with the opportunity to explore the many ways the body moves; practice combining movement and rhythm; discover that many concepts and ideas can be expressed to others though movement; learn how movement is related to space.

16. (List three:) Choose a time when the children are calm and well rested. Define space limits. Tell children they need to stop when the music stops. For variety in movement experiences, provide props such as paper streamers, balloons, balls, and scarves. Use movement activities involving cassette tapes, rhythm instruments, and verbal instructions. Allow children to get to know activities by repeating many of the experiences. Stop before signs of fatigue appear.
17. Body percussion
18. Auditory discrimination skill is the ability to detect different sounds by listening.
19. dance

Student Activity Guide

Musical Truths, Activity A

1. T	11. F
2. T	12. T
3. T	13. T
4. F	14. F
5. F	15. T
6. F	16. F
7. F	17. T
8. F	18. T
9. T	19. T
10. T	20. F

Fingerplays, Activity C

1. Fingerplays should be short.
2. Words used should be simple.

(Order may be reversed. Student response for original fingerplay.)

Teaching Music, Activity D

1. Demonstrate how to clap by holding up one palm steadily. Refer to this palm as the instrument. The other hand should serve as the mallet. Clap with relaxed arms and wrists and shoulders out.
2. Stand in front of a full-length mirror and practice the movements.
3. A steady beat should be provided for two-year-olds.
4. First, have the children sit in front of you. Then make sure there is enough space between each child so movements can be made freely. Stress instructions with actions.
5. Use descriptive words, such as happy, sad, angry, sleepy, and lazy.
6. It is best for use with four-, five-, and six-year-olds.

Teacher's Resource Guide/Binder

Chapter Test

1. F
2. E
3. C
4. A
5. D
6. B
7. F
8. F
9. T
10. F
11. F
12. T
13. T
14. T
15. T
16. F
17. F
18. T
19. T
20. T
21. T
22. F
23. B
24. C
25. B
26. B
27. C
28. D
29. (Student response. See pages 385–386.)
30. A chant is a song consisting of word patterns, rhymes, and nonsense syllables in one to three tones repeated in a sequence.

Value of Music Activities

Teachers use music with young children for several purposes:

- ♦ To provide an opportunity to learn and use language.

- ♦ To provide a pleasant background for playing, eating, and sleeping.

- ♦ To build a sense of community.

- ♦ To release tension and energy, and to calm angry feelings.

- ♦ To express feelings through movement and dance.

- ♦ To make learning fun.

- ♦ To teach listening skills.

- ♦ To teach differences in sounds.

- ♦ To develop an understanding of musical concepts.

- ♦ Including loud-soft, high-low, fast-slow, up-down.

- ♦ To develop an appreciation of different cultural heritages.

Selecting Songs

The best songs for young children meet the following criteria:

- ◆ Respect the children's age, abilities, and interests.

- ◆ Tell a story.

- ◆ Have frequent repetition.

- ◆ Have a developmentally appropriate vocabulary.

- ◆ Have a strongly defined mood or rhythm.

- ◆ Have moods the children can identify and imitate.

- ◆ Relate to children's specific level of development.

- ◆ Have a vocal range of no more than one octave. Children are usually most comfortable with the C to A or D to B range.

Purpose of Rhythm Instruments

- ◆ Build listening skills.
- ◆ Accompany the beat of a sound or recording.
- ◆ Classify and discriminate between sounds.
- ◆ Project the music or mood.
- ◆ Encourage experimenting with sounds.
- ◆ Organize sounds to communicate feelings and ideas.
- ◆ Help children develop listening skills.
- ◆ Help children develop classification skills such as loud, quiet, hard, soft, fast, and slow.

Educational Value of Fingerplays

♦ Helps develop finger dexterity

♦ Provides experience in dramatization

♦ Helps some children with speech defects

♦ Helps to draw out shy or timid child

♦ Helps to quit group or other activities

♦ Helps prevent quarreling and pushing during waiting periods

♦ Language

♦ Concept for motion

Favorite Fingerplays

Clap Your Hands

Clap your hands 1, 2, 3.   [Suit actions to words.]
Clap your hands just like me.
Roll your hands 1, 2, 3.
Roll your hands just like me.

Teapot

I'm a little teapot,   [Place right hand on hip, extend left hand, palm out.]
Short and stout.
Here's my handle,
And here's my spout.
When I get all steamed up,
I just shout:
"Tip me over, and pour me out."   [Bend to the left.]
I can change my handle   [Place left hand on hip and extend right hand out.]
And my spout.
"Tip me over, and pour me out."   [Bend to the right.]

Clocks

[Rest elbows on hips; extend forearms and index fingers
Big clocks make a sound like   up and move arms sideways slowly and rhythmically.]
T-i-c-k, t-o-c-k, t-i-c-k, t-o-c-k.
Small clocks make a sound like   [Move arms faster.]
Tick, tock, tick, tock.
And the very tiny clocks make a sound   [Move still faster.]
Like tick, tick, tock, tock.
Tick, tock, tick, tock, tick, tock.

(continued)

My Turtle

This is my turtle.   [Make fist; extend thumb.]

He lives in a shell.   [Hide thumb in fist.]

He likes his home very well.

He pokes his head out when he wants to eat.   [Extend thumb.]

And pulls it back when he wants to sleep.   [Hide thumb in fist.]

Three Frogs

Three little frogs   [Hold up three fingers of left hand.]

Asleep in the sun.   [Fold them over.]

We'll creep up and wake them.   [Make creeping motion with fingers of right hand.]

Then we will run.   [Hold up three fingers while right hand runs away.]

This Is My Right Hand

This is my right hand.

I raise it high.   [Suit actions to words.]

This is my left hand.

I'll touch the sky.

Right hand, left hand, Roll them round and round.

Right hand, left hand, Pound, pound, pound.

One, Two, Buckle My Shoe

One, two—buckle my shoe. [Count on fingers as verse progresses. Suit actions to words.]

Three, four—knock at the door.

Five, six—pick up sticks.

Seven, eight—lay them straight.

Nine, ten—a good, fat hen.

Open, Shut Them

Open, shut them.   [Suit actions to words.]

Open, shut them.

Open, shut them.

Give a little clap.

(continued)

Open, shut them.

Open, shut them.

Open, shut them.

Put them in your lap.

Creep them, creep them

Right up to your chin.

Open up your little mouth,

But do not put them in.

Open, shut them.

Open, shut them.

Open, shut them.

To your shoulders fly,

Then like little birdies

Let them flutter to the sky.

Falling, falling almost to the ground,

Quickly pick them up again and turn

Them round and round.

Faster, faster, faster.

Slower, slower, slower.

(Repeat first verse.)

Animals

Can you hop like a rabbit?   [Suit actions to words.]

Can you jump like a frog?

Can you walk like a duck?

Can you run like a dog?

Can you fly like a bird?

Can you swim like a fish?

And be still like a good child,

As still as this.

Apple Tree

	[Hold hands above head, form circles
Away up high in the apple tree,	with thumb and forefinger of each hand.]
Two red apples smiled at me.	[Smile.]
I shook that tree as hard as I could.	[Put hands out as if on tree—shake.]
And down they came,	[Hands above head and lower to ground.]
And h-mmmmmm were they good!	[Rub tummy.]

Five Little Pumpkins

Five little pumpkins sitting on a gate;

[Hold up five fingers and bend them down one at a time as verse progresses.]

The first one said, "My, it's getting late."

The second one said, "There are witches in the air."

The third one said, "But we don't care."

The fourth one said, "Let's run, let's run."

The fifth one said, "It's Halloween fun."

"WOOOOOOOO" went the wind,   [Sway hand through the air.]

And out went the lights.   [Loud clap.]

These five little pumpkins ran fast out of sight.   [Place hands behind back.]

Grandma's Spectacles

These are Grandma's spectacles.

[Bring index finger and thumb together and place against face as if wearing glasses.]

This is Grandma's hat.   [Bring fingertips together in a peak over head.]

This is the way she folds her hands,   [Clasp hands together.]

And lays them in her lap.   [Lay hands in lap.]

Ten Little Ducks

Ten little ducks swimming in the lake.   [Move ten fingers as if swimming.]

Quack! Quack!   [Snap fingers twice.]

They give their heads a shake.   [Shake fingers.]

Bang! Bang! Goes the hunter's gun.   [Two claps of hands.]

And away to their mothers,

The ten ducks run.   [Move hands in running motion from front to back.]

Movement Activities

Listed below are movement activities to do with the children. When these activities are introduced, the teacher should demonstrate for the children. This should be done simultaneously as the directions are given.

Beat the Drum

Fast.

Slow.

Heavy.

Soft.

Big.

Small.

Choose a Partner

Have one partner make a big shape. The other partner should:

Go over him or her.

Go under him or her.

Go through him or her.

Go around him or her.

To Become Aware of Time

Run very fast.

Walk very slowly.

Jump all over the floor quickly.

Sit down on the floor slowly.

Slowly grow up as tall as you can.

Slowly curl up on the floor as small as possible.

To Become Aware of Space

Lift up your leg in front of you.

Lift it up backwards, sideways.

Lift your leg and step forward, backwards, sideways, and around and around.

Reach up to the ceiling.

Stretch and touch the walls.

Punch down the floor.

(continued)

To Become Aware of Weight

To feel the difference between heavy and light, the child should experiment with his or her own body force.

Punch down to the floor hard.

Lift your arms up slowly and gently.

Stomp on the floor.

Walk on tiptoes.

Kick out one leg as hard as you can.

Very smoothly and lightly, slide one foot along the floor.

To Organize Movement into Dance

Combining time, space, and weight, children learn to organize movement into dance.

To do this, organize the children to do the following:

Walk a circle on the floor, fast.

Tiptoe around your circle, slowly.

Jump around the circle, hard and strong.

Draw a circle in the air with your arm, above your head.

Now draw circles everywhere, make up a circle dance.

Play a Word Game

The purpose of this activity is to move the way you might be feeling.

Tell the children to stand up.

Then have them act out such words as:

Angry.

Happy.

Sleepy.

Lazy.

Then have the children make their bodies and faces move.

Tell them to move in the following ways:

I feel sad.

I feel angry.

I feel happy.

I feel lazy.

(continued)

● Moving Shapes

Try to move about like something huge and heavy—elephant, tugboat, bulldozer.

Try to move like something small and heavy—a fat frog, a heavy top.

Try moving like something big and light—a beach ball, a parachute, a cloud.

Try moving like something small and light—a feather, a snowflake, a flea, a butterfly.

Put Yourself Inside Something

You're outside—now get into it.

You're inside of something—now get out of it.

You're underneath something.

You're on top of something.

You're beside or next to something.

You're surrounded by it.

Pantomime

● You're going to get a present.

Shape the box.

How big is it? Feel it.

Hold it.

Unwrap it.

Take it out.

Put it back in.

Think about an occupation.

How does the worker act?

Show me that it is cold (hot).

You're two years old (sixteen, eighty, etc.).

Show me that it's very early in the morning (late in the afternoon).

Show me what the weather is like.

Pretend you're driving (typing, raking leaves, etc.).

Take a partner. Pretend you're playing ball (having a fistfight).

●

(Developed in cooperation with Judy Gifford. Permission granted to reprint.)

Guiding Music and Movement Experiments

Name _____

Date _____ Period _____ Score _____

Matching: Match the following terms and identifying phrases.

_____ 1. These can be constructed from empty oatmeal boxes.

_____ 2. Can be constructed from empty tissue and paper towel tubes.

_____ 3. Frequently the first instruments introduced in the classroom.

_____ 4. They can produce varied tones by hitting the rim, center, or elsewhere.

_____ 5. These instruments periodically need to have the surface covering replaced.

_____ 6. These instruments sound like horses galloping when they are clapped together.

A. bongo drums
B. coconut cymbals
C. rhythm instruments
D. sandpaper sticks
E. shakers
F. tom-toms

True/False: Circle *T* if the statement is true or *F* if the statement is false.

T   F   7. Music should be as restricted as possible for the young child.

T   F   8. The music center should be located in the closed portion of the classroom.

T   F   9. Instruments should be displayed on an open shelf.

T   F   10. Quantity is more important than quality when purchasing musical supplies and equipment.

T   F   11. Children can match the tones of a piano easier than a human voice.

T   F   12. Music should not be restricted to a particular time but should occur throughout the day.

T   F   13. Nonparticipating children need to be handled with patience.

T   F   14. Children enjoy repetition in a song.

T   F   15. Children do not tire of a well-loved song.

T   F   16. The phrase method of teaching a song to children should be used with much older children.

T   F   17. The guitar is easier to learn to play than the Autoharp®.

T   F   18. The Autoharp® is a simple instrument to play.

T   F   19. Rules need to be established for rhythm instruments.

T   F   20. All adults in the classroom should be required to participate at music time.

T   F   21. The voice is a child's primary musical instrument.

T   F   22. Children who stutter should not be expected to sing.

(continued)

Multiple Choice: Choose the best response. Write the letter in the space provided.

_____ 23. The method of teaching songs that is best used with short, simple songs is the _____.
      A. phrase method
      B. whole song method
      C. phrase/whole combination method
      D. part song method

_____ 24. This method of teaching songs often involves stressing key phrases with rhythmic movement or visual props _____.
      A. phrase method.
      B. whole song method.
      C. phrase/whole combination method.
      D. part song method.

_____ 25. This activity consists of word patterns, rhymes, and nonsense syllables _____.
      A. song
      B. chant
      C. flannel board story
      D. musical notes

_____ 26. This activity provides children an opportunity to explore the way their bodies move in space _____.
      A. chants
      B. movement
      C. mouthing
      D. singing

_____ 27. An example of a body percussion activity includes _____.
      A. singing
      B. chanting
      C. clapping the hands
      D. whistling

_____ 28. Pantomiming is most appropriate for _____.
      A. two-year-olds
      B. three-year-olds
      C. infants
      D. five-year-olds

Essay Questions: Provide complete responses to the following questions or statements.

29. List three reasons teachers use music with young children.

30. Describe a chant.

Guiding Field Trip Experiences  27

Objectives

After studying this chapter, students will be able to
- describe the importance of field trips.
- explain points of consideration for first field trip experiences.
- list ways to promote safety on field trips.
  outline the process for selecting a field trip.
- explain the types and purposes of theme walks.
- plan a field trip, from pretrip planning to follow-up activities.

Teaching Materials

Text, pages 405–417
   Terms to Know
   Review and Reflect
   Apply and Explore
Student Activity Guide
   A. *Community Field Trips*
   B. *Planning the Trip*
   C. *Before and After the Field Trip*
   D. *Completing the Trip*
Teacher's Resource Guide/Binder
   Value of Field Trips, transparency master, 27-1
   Resource People, transparency master, 27-2
   Educational Goals, reproducible master, 27-3
   Pretrip and Posttrip Activities,
      transparency master, 27-4
   Field Trip Checklist, reproducible master, 27-5
   Chapter Test
Teacher's Resource Binder
   Community Resource People,
      color transparency, CT-27
The Observation Guide
Mastering CDA Competencies

Introductory Activities

1. Ask students to recall their favorite school field trips. Have students discuss what they liked about the trips.
2. Discuss with students the value of field trips for young children.

3. Have the class brainstorm a list of places in the community that they would take children for a field trip.

Instructional Concepts and Student Learning Experiences

The Importance of Field Trips _____

4. Have students explain reasons for adding field trips to the curriculum.
5. *Value of Field Trips,* transparency master 27-1. Use the master as a basis for discussion of the purpose of field trips.

First Field Trips _____

6. Have students discuss reasons field trips might make children nervous or uncomfortable.
7. Have students explain the importance of emphasizing the daily routine when children are taken on first field trips.
8. Have students list places that would be good for children's early field trips.

Selecting Trips _____

9. Have students describe theme walks.
10. Have students brainstorm a list of possible themes for theme walks.
11. *Community Resource People,* color transparency CT-27, TRB. Use this transparency to help students identify community resource people. You may want to:
    A. Have students brainstorm a list of community resource people.
    B. Ask students to identify curriculum themes or units that could include resource people.
    C. Discuss forms of appreciation that children can share with community resource people.
    D. Review the orientation that resource people need before meeting with children.
12. *Community Field Trips,* Activity A, SAG. Have students complete the chart by listing community field trips that children might enjoy and themes related to these field trips.

13. *Resource People,* transparency master 27-2. Have students discuss ways that resource people listed could be used in an early childhood program.
14. Have students brainstorm a list of resource people.
15. Have students describe how to give an orientation to a resource person.
16. Have students brainstorm a list of unusual thank-you's that children could give to resource people.

Planning a Field Trip

17. Have students explain the purpose of a field trip.
18. Have students describe the relationship between children's age and the appropriateness of field trips.
19. Have students explain the importance of calculating costs of a field trip.
20. Have students discuss the advantages and disadvantages of using public transportation for field trips.
21. Have students explain why field trips should be scheduled for midmorning.
22. Have students discuss the criteria for determining the ideal adult-child ratio.
23. Have students explain the importance of trip rules.
24. Have students list rules for a field trip.
25. Have students discuss methods of keeping the children together in a group on a field trip.
26. *Educational Goals,* reproducible master 27-3. Have students complete the chart by writing goals for the field trips listed.
27. Have students describe when preparation for a field trip should begin.
28. Have students explain methods of preparing parents for field trips.
29. *Pretrip and Posttrip Activities,* transparency master 27-4. Have students determine whether the activities listed would be appropriate for pretrip, posttrip, or both.
30. Have students plan a list of pretrip and posttrip activities for trips to the post office and the bakery.
31. *Planning the Trip,* Activity B, SAG. Have students select a field trip and answer the questions given about the field trip.
32. *Before and After the Field Trip,* Activity C, SAG. Have students brainstorm pretrip preparations and follow-up activities for a trip to the local post office.
33. *Field Trip Checklist,* reproducible master 27-5. Have students plan a field trip using the checklist.
34. Have students attend a field trip with a child care class and evaluate the experience.
35. *Completing the Trip,* Activity D, SAG. Have students complete the given statements by filling in the blanks with the correct words from the list.

Additional Resources

36. Guest speaker. Invite a child care teacher to speak to the class on planning a field trip.

37. Guest speaker. Speak with a child care teacher to locate a resource person who hosted a field trip for his or her class. Invite the resource person to speak to the class on the children's reactions to the field trip and the speaker's feelings on his or her preparation for the trip.

Research Topic

38. Have students survey teachers and parents about places children enjoy visiting and why. Students should choose 10 of these places and write overviews of how a field trip to each location should be planned.

Answer Key

Text

Review and Reflect, page 417

1. (List four:) Children develop keener observation skills, build vocabularies, clarify concepts as new information is gained, learn about their community, participate in multi-sensory experiences, gain new insight into dramatic play, learn about their environment, practice following directions in a group.
2. B
3. true
4. false
5. Select only people who enjoy children. They should represent many cultural groups, both sexes, and people of different ages. Select people who complement your curriculum.
6. (List four:) Teachers have the opportunity to: describe to the tour guide the purpose of the trip; explain the children's interests and their need to use a number of senses; prepare the tour guide for the types of questions the children may ask; locate bathrooms; check for any potential dangers; ask about parking; observe for teaching opportunities; revise trip goals, if necessary.
7. A
8. Public transportation is often crowded and noisy, which can upset children. There is a danger of children being hurt or lost during the trip to the site.
9. The best day for a field trip depends on several factors. First, the behavior and routine of the group is a factor. Some groups are always tired and restless by Friday. For such a group, Friday must be avoided. Second, the attendance schedules of the children is a factor. All children will not attend the center on the same days. The

specific trip being planned is also a factor for choosing the right day.

10. false
11. Children must wear their name tags. Children must speak softly. Children must remain with their assigned teachers.
12. Follow-up activities reinforce the learning of the trip.

Student Activity Guide

Completing the Trip, Activity D

1. curriculum
2. observation
3. concepts
4. community
5. directions
6. machinery
7. fall
8. short
9. familiar
10. theme
11. social
12. file
13. preparation
14. tissues
15. permission
16. crowds

Teacher's Resource Guide/Binder

Chapter Test

1. D
2. C
3. B
4. A
5. T
6. T
7. F
8. T
9. T
10. F
11. T
12. F
13. F
14. F
15. F
16. T
17. T
18. T
19. C
20. C
21. D
22. B
23. B
24. A
25. (Student response. See page 406.)
26. (Student response. See page 410.)
27. name of site; telephone number, address; contact person (tour guide); costs; distance from center in blocks or miles; dangers; special learning opportunities

Value of Field Trips

Some of the reasons for adding field trips to curriculum are to:

- ◆ develop keener observational skills.
- ◆ build vocabularies.
- ◆ clarify concepts as new information is gained.
- ◆ develop career awareness.
- ◆ learn about the community.
- ◆ participate in multi-sensory experiences.
- ◆ gain new insights for dramatic play.
- ◆ enjoy learning about the environment.
- ◆ practice following directions while in a group.

Resource People

- Mail Carrier
- Police Officer
- Highway Patrol Officer
- Musician
- Dancer
- Rock Collector
- Insect Collector
- School Custodian
- Clown
- Magician
- Santa Claus, (when appropriate)
- Fire Fighter
- Storyteller
- Doctor
- Nurse
- Artist
- Hair Stylist

Educational Goals

Name _____ **Date** _____ **Period** _____

To maximize the benefits of a field trip, educational goals must be carefully planned. Listed below are goals for taking a trip to a service station. Study these goals. Write goals for trips to the other locations listed.

Service Station	Hair Salon
♦ To observe technicians at work. ♦ To learn the care of cars. ♦ To see how machinery works. ♦ To learn or review the vocabulary words technician, gas pump, noise, hoist, and tow truck.	
Post Office	**Fire Station**
Bakery	**Florist**
Apple Orchard	**Grocery Store**

Pretrip and Posttrip Activities

Trip	Activities
Apple orchard	• Taste a variety of apples. • Make applesauce or apple muffins. • Read stories about apple orchards. • Serve apple butter, baked apples, or some other form of apple. • Make lotto boards using the different colors and sizes of apples as symbols.
Fire Station	• Place puzzles and stories related to the role of fire fighters in the classroom. • Read stories about fire fighters. • Place fire fighters' clothing in the dramatic play area. • Act out fire safety procedures.
Print shop	• Provide rubber stamps, ink pads, and paper on which to print. • Plan "object printing" art activities. • Place a typewriter or computer in the classroom. • Make games using alphabet letters.
Hair stylist	• Provide a prop box containing hair rollers, combs, towels, brushes, and a hair dryer with the cord removed. • Place dolls with hair and combs in the dramatic play area. • Hang up a mirror and have children compare the ways they wear their hair.
Bakery	• Taste different types of breads. • Decorate cupcakes or cookies. • Prepare muffins.

Field Trip Checklist

Name _____ **Date** _____ **Period** _____

	Date Completed
Select trip.	
Determine costs.	
Consider dangers involved.	
Plan goals.	
Plan and take a pretrip.	
Share trip expectations for children with tour guide.	
Revise goals, if necessary.	
Plan pretrip and posttrip activities.	
Prepare name tags for children to wear on trip.	
Check to see that all children have signed permission slips.	
Inform parents of the trip.	
Prepare a sign for the classroom door.	
Collect first aid kit, paper tissues, and refreshments, when necessary.	
Take trip.	
Send thank-you note or token of appreciation to resource person.	
Make any helpful notes in field trip file that might be used for future trips.	

Name _____

Date _____ Period _____ Score _____

Matching: Match the following terms and identifying phrases.

_____ 1. A short, simple field trip taken in or around the center.

_____ 2. Guests or field trip hosts of interest to children.

_____ 3. Used to prepare for a field trip.

_____ 4. Trip rules that children are expected to follow.

A. behavioral expectations
B. pretrip
C. resource people
D. theme walk

True/False: Circle *T* if the statement is true or *F* if the statement is false.

T   F   5. Children gain firsthand experiences from field trips.

T   F   6. The greater the number of senses involved, the greater the likelihood of learning.

T   F   7. First trips should be all-day excursions.

T   F   8. First trips should be designed to build the child's self-confidence.

T   F   9. Permission slips signed by the parents must be on file for each child before a trip.

T   F   10. A trip to a television studio may be fun and educational for two-year-olds.

T   F   11. Crowds can be overwhelming for some children.

T   F   12. Most field trips are expensive.

T   F   13. Parents should drive to curb field trip expenses.

T   F   14. Field trips should be scheduled for mid-afternoon.

T   F   15. Friday is the best day to schedule a field trip.

T   F   16. Normally a ratio of one teacher to four to six children is sufficient for most field trips.

T   F   17. Trip goals should be shared with the parents.

T   F   18. Resource people need an orientation before meeting the children.

Multiple Choice: Choose the best response. Write the letter in the space provided.

_____ 19. First trips should be limited to _____.
A. the zoo
B. the fire station
C. short trips around the block
D. the grocery store

(continued)

_____ 20. When you take children on first field trips, be sure to _____.
A. start with an interesting location, such as the zoo
B. tell children they are silly to worry about their parents finding them
C. remind children of their daily routine
D. take children to unfamiliar places

_____ 21. Theme walks do not involve _____.
A. sharpening children's observation skills
B. talking about what children will observe
C. choosing a theme such as shapes or people
D. arranging for transportation to the theme walk site

_____ 22. The dentist's office could be visited for a related theme on _____.
A. wheels
B. health
C. foods
D. plants

_____ 23. A good early trip is usually a walk to the _____.
A. bakery
B. grocery store
C. doctor's office
D. dentist's office

_____ 24. During a color walk, three-year-old children may enjoy looking for _____ colors.
A. one or two
B. two or three
C. three or four
D. four of five

Essay Questions: Provide complete responses to the following questions or statements.

25. List five reasons for taking field trips.

26. Describe the purpose of a pretrip.

27. What information should be included in the field trip file for each site?

Programs for Infants and Toddlers 28

Objectives

After studying this chapter, students will be able to
- list the characteristics of a nurturing infant-toddler caregiver.
- state guidelines for proper infant-toddler care.
- design functional and developmentally appropriate infant and toddler environments.
- handle the routines of infants and toddlers.
- select toys that are safe and developmentally appropriate for infants and toddlers.
- plan the curriculum for infants and toddlers.
- maintain the environment to prevent illness.

Teaching Materials

Text, pages 421–438
Terms to Know
Review and Reflect
Apply and Explore
Student Activity Guide
  A. *Caregiver Traits*
  B. *Environment Needs*
  C. *Toys for Development*
  D. *Child Care Procedures*
Teacher's Resource Guide/Binder
Infant Equipment Checklist, reproducible master 28-1
Diaper Check Chart, reproducible master, 28-2
Toy Inventory, reproducible master, 28-3
Chapter Test
Teacher's Resource Binder
Types of Infant-Toddler Toys,
  color transparency, CT-28
The Observation Guide
Mastering CDA Competencies

Introductory Activities

1. Ask students to share any experiences they have had caring for infants or toddlers.
2. Have students discuss how infants and toddlers differ developmentally from older children.

Students should speculate on how these differences would affect child care programs for these children.
3. Have students brainstorm a list of activities that infants may enjoy and a list of activities that toddlers might enjoy.

Instructional Concepts and Student Learning Experiences

Characteristics of Infant and Toddler Caregivers

4. Have students interview parents of infants and toddlers, asking them what qualities they desire in an infant or toddler caregiver. Students should share their findings in class.
5. Have students observe an infant-toddler program and make a list of positive characteristics they observe in the caregiver.
6. Have students discuss the infant-toddler caregiver's role in modeling characteristics for infants and toddlers.
7. *Caregiver Traits,* Activity A, SAG. Have students complete the chart by checking the characteristics they feel infant-toddler caregivers should model. Also have students check the characteristics they feel they model.

Guidelines for Infant-Toddler Care

8. Have students discuss the merits of the guidelines for infant-toddler care given in the text.
9. Have students discuss ways to encourage the curiosity of infants and toddlers while keeping them safe.

Infant Environments

10. *Infant Equipment Checklist,* reproducible master 28-1. Have students use the checklist to evaluate the safety of an infant environment in a child care center.
11. Have students design an infant space on a large piece of tagboard. Students should include space for eating, sleeping, diapering, playing, and observing.

Toddler Environments

12. Have students explain why toddlers need more open space than infants.
13. Have students observe the arrangement of a room for an infant-toddler program. Students should make a sketch of the space and write a short evaluation of how the space is used.
14. *Environment Needs,* Activity B, SAG. Have students choose the best answer for each of the statements related to infant and toddler environment needs. Then have them write an explanation for each answer.

Caring for Infants and Toddlers

15. Have students interview an infant-toddler caregiver about adjusting to rhythms of different children. Students should share the caregiver's comments in class.
16. Have students explain why infants and toddlers require consistent care.
17. Have students discuss differences among babies in crying behavior.
18. Have students define *separation anxiety* and discuss methods of dealing with it as a caregiver.
19. Collect daily record forms from several child care centers. Have students discuss the contents of each.
20. Have each student write a question a caregiver would want to ask the parent of an infant about feeding the infant. Ask students to share their questions with the class. Then have the class compile the questions into a portion of a survey that parents might complete when enrolling their infant at a child care facility.
21. Have students prepare finger foods that would be appropriate to serve to toddlers.
22. *Diaper Check Chart,* reproducible master 28-2. Have students observe an infant-toddler program and complete the chart for the time they observe.
23. Have students practice proper hand washing procedures for diapering.
24. Obtain some petri dishes of agar from the science department. Have students place marks on the lids to divide the dishes in half. On one side, have students press a few of their unwashed fingers. Have students wash their hands using the procedures outlined in Chart 28-8. Then have students press a few of their washed fingers on the other side of the dish. Students should label the dishes and observe for bacterial growth throughout the following week.
25. Have students list considerations in planning a nap time schedule.

Toys for Infants and Toddlers

26. Have students discuss the relationship between toys and physical and intellectual development.

27. Bring in a variety of toys designed for infants and toddlers. Have each student select a toy and point out the features that make it safe for young children.
28. Have students identify criteria for selecting toys for infants and toddlers.
29. *Types of Infant-Toddler Toys,* color transparency CT-28, TRB. Use this transparency to help stimulate discussion about the types of toys suitable for infants and toddlers:
    A. Remind students that safety is the first consideration when choosing toys for infants and toddlers.
    B. Discuss the purpose of toys for infants and toddlers.
    C. Have students brainstorm examples of toys for each of the categories listed on the transparency. (Refer to Chart 28-10, if needed.)
    D. Have the students list ways to prevent overfamiliarity with toys.
30. *Toys for Development,* Activity C, SAG. Have students complete the chart by mounting pictures of toys for infants or toddlers that promote small motor, large motor, and reaching and grasping skills, and that create interesting sounds.
31. *Toy Inventory,* reproducible master 28-3. Have students use the list to take an inventory of toys in an infant-toddler program.

Curriculum

32. Have students describe how curriculum for infants differs from curriculum for toddlers.
33. Have students list sensory materials for toddlers.
34. Have students identify toddler activities that promote small muscle, large muscle, music, and language skills.
35. Have students prepare 10 activities for toddlers for an activity file.

Parent Involvement

36. Have students describe the information that caregivers should share with parents on a daily basis.
37. Have students survey parents of infants and toddlers to find out their goals and concerns for their children. Then have the students discuss how they, as caregivers, might react to these goals and concerns in their daily care of the children.

Record Keeping

38. Have students explain why good record keeping is important.
39. Have students review the daily care record shown in Chart 28-6 and discuss the importance of recording the information shown.

Maintaining the Environment to Prevent Illness

40. Have students explain the purpose of illness policies.
41. Have students find and review your state's rules and regulations regarding illness policies.
42. Collect illness policies from three infant-toddler programs. Have students compare the policies.
43. *Child Care Procedures,* Activity D, SAG. Have students read the given story, *A New Job for Jan.* Students should then write the mistakes Jan made and what Jan can do to avoid making those mistakes in the future.

Additional Resources

44. Invite several parents of infants and toddlers to discuss their children's care needs.
45. Arrange for students to visit the maternity ward of a hospital and have a doctor or nurse speak on the care of infants.
46. Arrange for the class to visit a center for infants and toddlers to observe the room setting and activities.
47. Invite an infant-toddler caregiver to discuss curriculum for this group.
48. Invite a pediatrician to talk with the class about the transmission of illnesses among infants and toddlers in child care facilities.

Research Topics

49. Have the student research to find toys that are safe and developmentally appropriate for infants and toddlers. The student should give a presentation to the class on the value of these toys, showing several of the toys as examples.
50. Have the student research through books, pamphlets, and interviews with parents and health professionals and compile a booklet on the care of infants.

Answer Key

Text

Review and Reflect, page 438

1. (List three. Student response.)
2. Parents bringing food to the center can quickly place it in the refrigerator.
3. receiving, playing, napping, diapering, eating
4. one-third to one-half
5. trust
6. C
7. Separation anxiety is emotional distress that occurs in children nine to twelve months of age who have difficulty separating from their parents.

8. Hold and cuddle the infant during feeding in order to form a bond.
9. Yes. Exploring their food gives toddlers important sensory experiences that promote cognitive growth.
10. Bar soaps, when wet and jellylike, can harbor germs.
11. The inventory is useful for letting teachers know what toys have been used recently and what toys are available. The inventory is also helpful when ordering new toys.
12. They like to see the consequences of their actions.
13. goals
14. (List five: See pages 432–433.)
15. Be objective and factual. Do not be negative or judgmental. State comments in a positive manner.
16. Helps staff and parents decide whether a child is too sick to be brought to, or remain in, the center

Student Activity Guide

Environment Needs, Activity B

1. B	6. A
2. A	7. A
3. B	8. B
4. B	9. B
5. A	10. A

(Student response for explanations.)

Child Care Procedures, Activity D

Jan made the following mistakes: She ignored the crying baby. She woke sleeping babies to check their diapers. Jan did not wash her hands before changing a diaper. She changed the diaper on the floor by the crib rather than in the proper place in the changing area. Jan gave Maria a dirty pacifier. She did not wash her hands after changing the diaper or before she cut up the apples and cheese. She did not place the toddlers in the appropriate type of chairs when she gave them a snack. While Jan took a break and read the magazine, she could not give her full attention to the children. (Student response for ways to avoid the mistakes in the future.)

Teacher's Resource Guide

Chapter Test

1. B	6. F
2. A	7. T
3. E	8. T
4. D	9. T
5. C	10. F

11. F   18. D
12. T   19. C
13. T   20. D
14. F   21. C
15. F   22. A
16. A   23. A
17. C
24. (Student response. See page 422.)
25. Each infant should be assigned to one caregiver. The assigned caregiver should feed the infant leisurely while holding and cuddling the infant.
26. Dispense enough liquid soap to provide a good lather. Add a small amount of water and rub back and forth, providing friction. Work up a good lather. Rinse hands. Use paper towels or an elbow to turn off the faucet and dry hands.
27. Some parents want their child to sleep at the center so he or she is awake and alert at the end of the day. Other parents, who may have to travel some distance to get home, prefer to have a sleepy baby at the end of the day. Their goal is to have the baby sleep on the way home.
28. (List five:) art area, sensory area, small muscle area, large muscle area, music area, language area (List three questions from pages 432–433.)

Infant Equipment Checklist

Name _____ **Date**_____ **Period** _____

Use the following checklist to evaluate the safety of an infant environment in a child care center.

	Yes	No
Changing Table		
1. Table has straps to prevent falls.	☐	☐
2. Table has drawers or shelves that are accessible without leaving baby unattended.	☐	☐
Cribs		
3. Slots are spaced no more than 2 3/8 inches (60 mm) apart.	☐	☐
4. No slots are missing or cracked.	☐	☐
5. Mattress fits snugly—less than two fingers between edge of mattress and side of crib.	☐	☐
6. Mattress support is securely attached to the head and foot boards.	☐	☐
7. No cut outs in head or foot boards to allow head entrapment.	☐	☐
8. Drop-side latches cannot be easily released by a baby.	☐	☐
9. Drop-side latches securely hold side in raised position.	☐	☐
10. All screws and bolts that hold crib components together are present and tight.	☐	☐
Crib Toys		
11. No toys have loops or openings with perimeters greater than 14 inches.	☐	☐
12. No strings or cords longer than 7 inches dangle into the crib.	☐	☐
13. Crib gym has label warning to remove the gym from the crib when child can push up on hands or knees or reaches five months of age, whichever comes first.	☐	☐
14. Components of toys are not small enough to be a choking hazard.	☐	☐
Gates and Enclosures		
15. Openings in gate are too small to entrap child's head.	☐	☐
16. Gate has a pressure bar or other fastener that will resist forces exerted by a child.	☐	☐
High Chairs		
17. High chair has restraining straps that are independent of the tray.	☐	☐
18. Tray locks securely.	☐	☐

(continued)

	Yes	No
19. Buckle on waist strap is easy to fasten and unfasten.	☐	☐
20. High chair has a wide base for stability.	☐	☐
21. Caps or plugs on tubing are firmly attached so they cannot be pulled off and create a choking hazard.	☐	☐
22. Folding high chair has effective locking device.	☐	☐

Pacifiers

	Yes	No
23. Pacifiers have no ribbons, string, cord, or yarn attached.	☐	☐
24. Shield is large enough and firm enough so it cannot fit into child's mouth.	☐	☐
25. Guard or shield has ventilation holes so baby can breath if shield does get into mouth.	☐	☐
26. Pacifier nipple has no holes or tears that may crack or break off in the baby's mouth.	☐	☐

Adapted from *The Safe Nursery,* U.S. Consumer Product Safety Commission

Diaper Check Chart

Name _____ **Date**_____ **Period** _____

Observe an infant-toddler program and complete the diaper check chart for the time you are present. (Fill in the names of the children in the spaces at the top.)

7:00 a.m.								
7:30 a.m.								
8:00 a.m.								
8:30 a.m.								
9:00 a.m.								
9:30 a.m.								
10:00 a.m.								
10:30 a.m.								
11:00 a.m.								
11:30 a.m.								
noon								
12:30 p.m.								
1:00 p.m.								
1:30 p.m.								
2:00 p.m.								
2:30 p.m.								
3:00 p.m.								
3:30 p.m.								
4:00 p.m.								
4:30 p.m.								
5:00 p.m.								
5:30 p.m.								
6:00 p.m.								

S = Sleeping   W = Wet   X = No change needed   BM = Bowel movement

Toy Inventory

Name _____ Date_____ Period _____

Use the chart below to take an inventory of toys at an infant-toddler center. Place a number in the blank beside each type of toy to indicate how many you find. In the spaces provided, list any other types of toys you find.

Toys for Infants

Sensory Toys

____ mobiles

____ metal mirrors

____ picture books

____ rattles

____ squeaky toys

____ audio tapes/CDs

____ stuffed animals

____ dolls

____ _____

____ _____

Small Motor Toys

____ small balls

____ nesting toys

____ blocks

____ busy boxes

____ plastic rings

____ _____

____ _____

____ _____

Large Motor Toys

____ cradle gyms

____ walkers

____ swings

____ _____

____ _____

____ _____

Toys for Toddlers

Art Materials

____ paint

____ paint brushes

____ large crayons

____ chalk

____ markers

____ _____

____ _____

____ _____

Sensory Materials

____ colored and/or scented water

____ soap bubbles

____ shaving cream

____ sand toys

____ floating toys

____ _____

____ _____

____ _____

Small Muscle Toys

____ stacking toys

____ building blocks

____ sorting boxes

____ puzzles

____ stringing beads

____ play dough

____ nesting toys

____ cards

____ _____

____ _____

Large Muscle Toys

____ balls

____ slides

____ tumbling mats

____ pull toys

____ push toys

____ small wagons

____ large blocks

____ climbing tunnels

____ riding toys

____ jungle gyms

____ _____

____ _____

____ _____

Musical Toys

____ audio tapes/CDs

____ musical instruments

____ music boxes

____ videotapes

____ _____

____ _____

____ _____

Language Toys

____ puppets

____ books

____ pictures

____ posters

____ unbreakable mirrors

____ dolls

____ _____

____ _____

____ _____

Programs for Infants and Toddlers

Name _____

Date _____ Period _____ Score _____

Matching: Match the following areas in an infant-toddler environment with their descriptions.

_____ 1. This area is usually located near the entrance to the center.	A. diapering area
_____ 2. This area should be located next to a sink.	B. feeding area
_____ 3. Ideally, this area should be next to the diapering area.	C. play area
_____ 4. This area should contain a bulletin board and lockers or hooks.	D. receiving area
_____ 5. This area should have low dividers and short pile carpeting.	E. sleeping area

True/False: Circle *T* if the statement is true or *F* if the statement is false.

T   F   6. Infants and toddlers need caregivers who provide inconsistent guidance.

T   F   7. Too many new experiences at one time can overwhelm young children.

T   F   8. Studies show that when an infant's cries are answered promptly, the frequency of crying will be reduced.

T   F   9. Separation anxiety is a sign that the child is learning and developing a special relationship with someone.

T   F   10. It is unusual for an infant to be placed on a special diet.

T   F   11. Infants should be fed when it is convenient for the caregivers.

T   F   12. Children may object to having their diapers changed.

T   F   13. Some toys contain a special plastic that will show up clearly on an X ray.

T   F   14. In the progression of hand movement skills, most children develop the pincer pick-up motion first.

T   F   15. Curriculum for infants requires more planning than curriculum for toddlers.

Multiple Choice: Choose the best answer and write the corresponding letter in the blank.

_____ 16. Which of the following foods would be the best choice to serve to toddlers?
A. Cooked green peas.
B. Macaroni and cheese.
C. Mashed potatoes.
D. Spaghetti and meatballs.

(continued)

_____ 17. What type of soap should be used for hand washing?
  A. Powdered.
  B. Bar.
  C. Liquid.
  D. Flakes.

_____ 18. After each use, the seat of a potty chair needs to be sprayed with _____.
  A. warm water
  B. cold water
  C. liquid soap
  D. a disinfectant solution

_____ 19. Which of the following toys would most promote a toddler's language skills?
  A. Building blocks.
  B. Play dough.
  C. Puppets.
  D. Tumbling mats.

_____ 20. About what portion of time do toddlers spend staring?
  A. One-half.
  B. One-third.
  C. One-fourth.
  D. One-fifth.

_____ 21. Which of the following pictures would be most worthwhile to include in a picture collection for infants and toddlers?
  A. An apple.
  B. A chair.
  C. A puppy.
  D. A rose.

_____ 22. Which of the following would be *least* important to find out from parents when children are first enrolled in an infant-toddler program?
  A. Clothing size.
  B. Favorite toys.
  C. Food preferences.
  D. Routines at home.

_____ 23. Rattles and teething rings must be cleaned _____.
  A. daily
  B. biweekly
  C. weekly
  D. bimonthly

Essay Questions: Provide complete responses to the following questions or statements.

24. List four guidelines for effective infant-toddler programs.

25. Describe how an infant should be fed.

26. Describe proper hand washing.

27. Why should the child's parent be consulted in planning a nap time schedule?

28. List five activity areas for toddlers and three questions caregivers should ask themselves when planning the areas.

Programs for School-Age Children  **29**

Objectives

After studying this chapter, students will be able to
- describe the three basic program models used in school-age child care.
- identify the characteristics of an effective teacher in a school-age program.
- discuss how to arrange indoor and outdoor space in a school-age child care environment.
- explain ways to assess children's interest for curriculum planning.
- list the components of a typical daily schedule in a school-age child care program.

Teaching Materials

Text, pages 439-450
Terms to Know
Review and Reflect
Apply and Explore
Student Activity Guide
A. *Quality School-Age Programs*
B. *My Ideal Environment*
C. *Design a Survey*
D. *Games for Fostering Development*
Teacher's Resource Guide/Binder
Equipping Interest Centers, reproducible master, 29-1
School-Age Child Care Advice,
reproducible master, 29-2
Chapter Test
Teacher's Resource Binder
School-Age Program Models,
color transparency, CT-29
The Observation Guide, Chapter 29
Mastering CDA Competencies

Introductory Activities

1. Ask students to explain why there is a need for school-age child care programs.
2. Have students discuss ways they think school-age programs might differ from preschool programs. List their responses on the chalkboard.

3. *Quality School-Age Programs,* Activity A, SAG. Have students answer the yes-or-no questions about quality school-age programs. You may wish to use this exercise as a chapter pretest. You could also choose to have students complete this activity as they read the chapter or use it as a review before taking the chapter test.

Instructional Concepts and Student Learning Experiences

Quality School-Age Programs _____

4. Have the students develop a brochure on factors to consider when selecting a program for school-age children.
5. *School-Age Program Models,* color transparency CT-29, TRB. Use this transparency to introduce the three program models used as curriculum formats in school-age child care programs:
   A. Have students explain why good school-age programs would include aspects of all three program models.
   B. Have students divide a sheet of paper into two columns headed Strengths and Weaknesses. Have them list what they consider to be the strengths and weaknesses of each of the three school-age program models.
   C. Have students identify the age, interests, and abilities of school-age children they think would be most compatible with each of the three program models.
   D. Have each student write a one-page opinion paper about which program model he or she would prefer if teaching in a school-age program.
6. Have students work with partners to brainstorm a list of curriculum themes that would appeal to school-age children enrolled in a unit-based program. Have students explain why each theme would be appealing.
7. Have students discuss why the quality of school-age programs is enhanced when the adult-child ratio is low.

Characteristics of Staff _____

8. Go around the room, asking each student to complete the following statement: "High-quality programs are staffed by teachers who . . ."
9. Have students make posters illustrating characteristics of well-trained staff in a school-age program.
10. Have students write a paragraph describing one way they could act as facilitators to teach a unit on Martin Luther King, Jr. Day or Presidents' Day in a school-age program.
11. Have students describe how teachers can promote prosocial behaviors, such as taking turns, helping, cooperating, negotiating, and talking through interpersonal problems.
12. Have students list potential rules for social living appropriate for school-age programs.
13. Have students role-play a discussion between a teacher and a school-age child about planning curriculum and choosing activities.
14. Invite each student to bring in an item from another culture. Examples might include art, clothing, currency, magazines, dolls, jewelry, musical instruments, cooking utensils, games, and toys. Ask each student to suggest a way his or her item could be used to teach respect for cultural diversity to school-age children.
15. Show students several examples of children's storybooks, videotapes, posters, and puzzles showing people from different cultures in a variety of positive roles. Ask students to explain how each of these examples might help school-age children develop respect for cultural diversity.
16. Have students play some active games that might be used in a school-age program.
17. Have students write a one-page paper discussing how the role of a teacher in a school-age program can be challenging and rewarding.

The Environment _____

18. Have students interview a teacher in a school-age program about how he or she prepares the environment to reflect the children's interests, ages, needs, and abilities. Ask students to share what they learned in the interview with the rest of the class.
19. Show students pictures of different classroom arrangements for school-age programs, including some in facilities designed for other purposes. Discuss the advantages and disadvantages of the different arrangements.
20. Have students write a list of suggestions for preparing the environment in a library, cafeteria, gym, or church basement to house a school-age program.

21. Divide the class into small groups. Instruct each group to visit a store or find a catalog that offers business furnishings. Have groups take photographs, draw sketches, or clip pictures of storage units, furniture, carpeting, curtains, and other items that would be appropriate for a school-age program. Each group should also prepare a summary of the features, quality level, and price of each item they select. Have groups display their pictures and summaries in class.
22. Have students survey several directors of school-age child care programs to find out how they prefer to arrange the indoor space at their facilities. Students should ask directors to give reasons for their preferences. Ask students to summarize their findings as a class.
23. Have each student draw a floor plan of the indoor space for a school-age child care program. Display the floor plans in your classroom. Ask students to note the similarities and differences.
24. *Equipping Interest Centers,* reproducible master 29-2. Have students list items that might be included in each of the following interest centers: hobby, block, cooking, science, math, game, music, dramatic play, and arts and crafts.
25. Have students visit a local library and prepare a list of books they might choose for the quiet area of a school-age environment.
26. *My Ideal Environment,* Activity B, SAG. Have students pretend that they are 10 years old. Ask them to describe their ideal environment for an after-school program.

Planning Curriculum _____

27. Have students explain why children, parents, and staff should all be included in planning the curriculum for a school-age program.
28. Have students visit a school-age child care program and lead a group discussion. Ask them to share with the class what they learned about the interests of the school-age children.
29. *Design a Survey,* Activity C, SAG. Have students design a survey they could use to assess the interests of school-age children.

Scheduling

30. Bring in sample schedules from three or four school-age programs. Ask students to explain why similarities and differences might occur.
31. Have students brainstorm greetings and comments teachers could use when school-age children enter a classroom. Write students' responses on the chalkboard.
32. Have students bring in simple recipes for foods

from different cultures that school-age children can prepare during mealtime.

33. Have students make a list of low-key activities that would be appropriate to make available to school-age children during rest time.

34. *Games for Fostering Development,* Activity D, SAG. Have the students break into small groups and brainstorm a list of board, card, indoor, and outdoor games that would foster development of school-age children.

35. *School-Age Child Care Advice,* reproducible master 29-2. Have students pretend they are columnists who write a "Teacher Hot Line" column for a professional journal. Have them answer letters from teachers of school-age programs about their concerns.

Additional Resources

36. Invite two or three parents of school-age children to class to discuss the criteria they used when selecting child care programs.

37. Invite a licensing specialist to class. Ask him or her to discuss regulations related to school-age child care programs.

38. Invite a school-age child care teacher to class. Ask the teacher to share curriculum planning techniques.

Research Topic

39. Have the student survey four directors of school-age child care programs. The student should find out what characteristics these directors look for when hiring teachers. Have the student write a paper comparing the directors' responses with the characteristics discussed in the text. The student should provide possible explanations for any differences noted.

Answer Key

Text

Review and Reflect, page 450

1. latchkey
2. loneliness, unhealthy fears, lack of physical exercise, poor nutritional habits
3. child-centered program model, adult-centered program model, unit-based program model (Descriptions are student response. See pages 440-441.)
4. Children can get adult help when they need it. Adults can provide the constant supervision needed to create a safe environment. While supervising, adults can use observation to gain information about the interests, needs, and abilities of each child.

5. act as facilitators, use positive guidance, involve children, promote respect for cultural diversity, enjoy physical activity

6. A quality school-age child care environment provides appropriate space, materials, and equipment. The environment reflects the children's interests, ages, abilities, and needs. The environment also allows children to have fun, learn, and thrive as they move at their own pace.

7. You need to begin by assessing the children's interests.

8. get-acquainted interviews, group discussions, self-reports, surveys

9. recreational, academic

10. Mixed groups reduce competition. These groups give older children an opportunity to develop leadership skills. Older children can help younger children with such activities as board games and crafts. The younger children learn by observing and interacting with the older children.

Student Activity Guide

Quality School-Age Programs, Activity A

1.	Y	11.	Y
2.	Y	12.	N
3.	N	13.	N
4.	N	14.	N
5.	Y	15.	Y
6.	N	16.	Y
7.	Y	17.	Y
8.	N	18.	Y
9.	N	19.	N
10.	Y	20.	Y

Teacher's Resource Guide/Binder

Chapter Test

1.	B	16.	T
2.	A	17.	T
3.	C	18.	F
4.	A	19.	T
5.	C	20.	T
6.	F	21.	C
7.	T	22.	D
8.	T	23.	B
9.	F	24.	B
10.	T	25.	C
11.	F	26.	D
12.	F	27.	C
13.	F	28.	C
14.	F	29.	D
15.	T	30.	A

31. family child care homes, for-profit child care centers, programs offered by nonprofit organizations

32. Children can get adult help when they need it. Adults can provide the constant supervision needed to create a safe environment. While supervising, adults can use observation to gain information about the interests, needs, and abilities of each child.

33. He or she may use moveable carts to store games, art supplies, books, and other program materials. He or she may have the children help by including setup and cleanup in the children's daily schedule.

Equipping Interest Centers

Name _____ Date _____ Period _____

Complete the following chart by listing items that might be included in each of the interest centers shown.

Hobby Center	Block Center	Cooking Center
Science Center	**Math Center**	**Game Center**
Music Center	**Dramatic Play Center**	**Arts and Crafts Center**

School-Age Child Care Advice

Name _____ **Date** _____ **Period** _____

Pretend you are a columnist who writes a "Teacher Hot Line" column for a professional journal. Answer the following letters from teachers of school-age programs about their concerns.

Dear Teacher Hot Line:

I am teaching in a school-age program with too many children and too few adults. On Monday, I am meeting with the program director. How can I convince him that this is not an ideal environment?

Dear Teacher:

_____

_____

_____

Dear Teacher Hot Line:

At a recent parent conference, a parent openly criticized me. She said I am not doing enough to help the school-age children in my class appreciate cultural diversity. I have introduced different cultural foods at our holiday celebrations. What else can I do?

Dear Teacher:

_____

_____

_____

Dear Teacher Hot Line:

When I took the position of a school-age teacher last fall, I assessed the children's interests. Throughout the year, I developed curriculum based on this assessment. However, the children no longer seem interested. What did I do wrong?

Dear Teacher:

_____

_____

_____

Dear Teacher Hot Line:

My school-age program is not working. When the children arrive after school, I try to provide structured activities similar to those they experience during the school day. The children seem bored and restless. What am I doing wrong and how can I improve the program?

Dear Teacher:

_____

_____

_____

Programs for School-Age Children

Name _____

Date _____ **Period** _____ **Score** _____

Matching: Match the following school-age program models with their descriptions. (Models may be used more than once.)

_____ 1. This model includes a high level of adult direction.

_____ 2. This model allows children an opportunity to self-select activities.

_____ 3. This model revolves around curriculum themes that reflect the children's interests.

_____ 4. Staff members encourage children's involvement by serving as facilitators and resource persons.

_____ 5. Staff members offer a variety of cooking, science, music, and art activities related to a theme.

A. child-centered program model
B. adult-centered program model
C. unit-based program model

True/False: Circle *T* if the statement is true or *F* if the statement is false.

T   F   6. There is a decreasing demand for school-age child care.

T   F   7. Even a mature child can benefit from attending a school-age child care program.

T   F   8. A quality school-age program provides companionship, supervision, a safe environment, and activities to promote development.

T   F   9. Staff should help school-age children avoid the stress of problem-solving activities.

T   F 10. Foods, games, toys, and holiday celebrations can be used to teach children about different cultures.

T   F 11. Teachers who are well suited for school-age programs should be athletic to direct physical activities.

T   F 12. For safety reasons, most interest center supplies should be stored in locked cabinets to which only staff have access.

T   F 13. In open areas, children can do homework, use computers, read, and relax.

T   F 14. One area of the outdoor space at a school-age facility should be reserved for running, climbing, swinging, and organized sports.

T   F 15. Children, parents, and staff should all be involved in the curriculum planning process for a school-age program.

T   F 16. Some suggestions offered during a group planning session may need to be eliminated due to expense, location, or safety.

T   F 17. Mealtimes in a school-age program should be used as a learning experience. *(continued)*

T   F   18. Rock music may help children relax during rest time.

T   F   19. A good program does not duplicate activities that take place at school.

T   F   20. Participating in cleanup activities helps children develop a sense of pride.

Multiple Choice: Choose the best answer and write the corresponding letter in the blank.

_____ 21. Many school-age children are left to care for themselves because of the _____.
A. low cost
B. inconvenience
C. lack of quality programs
D. curriculum

_____ 22. A general guideline is that parents should not regularly leave a child in self-care until _____.
A. kindergarten
B. first grade
C. third grade
D. fifth grade

_____ 23. A high-quality school-age program has _____.
A. high adult-child ratios
B. parent involvement
C. rigid scheduling
D. All of the above.

_____ 24. Staff in school-age programs act as _____.
A. rulers
B. facilitators
C. decision makers
D. judges

_____ 25. Which of the following is *not* a prosocial behavior?
A. Helping.
B. Taking turns.
C. Forcing.
D. Negotiating.

_____ 26. A quality school-age child care environment should provide appropriate _____.
A. space
B. materials
C. equipment
D. All of the above.

_____ 27. The minimum indoor space available for each child in a school-age program should be _____.
A. 10 square feet
B. 25 square feet
C. 35 square feet
D. 50 square feet

_____ 28. The minimum outdoor space available for each child in a school-age program should be _____.
A. 25 square feet
B. 50 square feet
C. 75 square feet
D. 100 square feet

(continued)

_____ 29. Which method of assessing children's interests is particularly effective with nonreaders?
   A. Self-reports.
   B. Surveys.
   C. Get-acquainted interviews.
   D. Group discussions.

_____ 30. The largest part of a school-age program schedule should be devoted to _____.
   A. activity time
   B. homework
   C. mealtime
   D. rest time

Essay Questions. Provide complete responses to the following questions or statements.

31. Name three options outside a child's home parents might choose for after-school child care.

32. Why should low adult-child ratios and small group size improve program quality.

33. Describe creative strategies a teacher might use to get a church basement ready each day for a school-age program.

Guiding Children with Special Needs  30

Objectives

After studying this chapter, students will be able to
- contribute to the development of an Individualized Educational Plan for a child with special needs.
- develop individualized learning objectives and teaching strategies for a child.
- explain the role of the teacher in working with children who have special needs.
- describe methods for identifying and working with special needs that may be encountered in the early childhood program: hearing, speech, language, vision, physical, health, cognitive, and behavioral disorders.
- describe methods of integrating children with special needs into a typical program.
- explain the special needs of children who are gifted and how these needs can be met.

Teaching Materials

Text, pages 451–470
  Terms to Know
  Review and Reflect
  Apply and Explore
Student Activity Guide
  A. *Special Needs Match*
  B. *Special Communication Needs*
  C. *Physical and Health Disorders*
  D. *Helping Children Who Have Special Needs*
  E. *The Child Who Is Gifted*
Teacher's Resource Guide/Binder
  Identifying the Gifted Child, transparency master, 30-1
  Identifying Children with Learning Disabilities, transparency master, 30-2
  A Child with Special Needs, reproducible master, 30-3
  Chapter Test
Teacher's Resource Binder
  Allergy Symptoms, color transparency, CT-30
The Observation Guide
Mastering CDA Competencies

Introductory Activities

1. Ask students to discuss any experiences they may have had with children (or adults) who have special needs.
2. Ask students to define the term *special needs*.
3. Have the class brainstorm different types of special needs.
4. *Special Needs Match*, Activity A, SAG. As a chapter pretest, have students match the terms and definitions. This activity can also be used as a chapter review.

Instructional Concepts and Student Learning Experiences

Individualized Educational Plans

5. Have students list and explain the six components of an IEP.
6. Have students practice writing IEPs based on children with various special needs.

Teachers' Roles

7. Have students discuss the teacher's role in guiding children with special needs.
8. Have students describe three techniques of collecting observational data on children.
9. Have students observe a teacher working with a child who has special needs. Have them record the teacher's actions.
10. Have students discuss the possible effects of labeling children with special needs.

Hearing Disorders

11. Have students describe the behavior of a child with a hearing loss.
12. Bring to class an example of the most popular type of hearing aid for children. Demonstrate how the hearing aid works.
13. Have students list suggestions for working with hearing-impaired children.
14. Have students practice speaking to a person in the way they would speak to someone who is hearing impaired.

15. Have students bring to class a book that would be appropriate for a hearing-impaired child.

Speech and Language Disorders

16. Have students explain how to observe and identify children with speech disorders.
17. Have students review figure 30-6, *Developmental Order for Speech Sounds.* Discuss possible reasons for sound skills developing in the order presented. Students should also discuss how knowing the order can help prevent concern when children who are too young cannot pronounce certain sounds properly.
18. Have students identify the common sound substitution for *s.*
19. Have students practice modeling effective listening and speaking skills to a child with a speech and language disorder.

Vision Disorders

20. Have students list common visual impairments and describe their symptoms.
21. Have students discuss methods of identifying vision disorders.
22. Have students discuss methods of teaching children with vision disorders.
23. *Special Communication Needs,* Activity B, SAG. Have students answer the questions related to hearing, speech, language, and vision problems.

Physical Disabilities

24. Have students explain the differences among severe, mild, and moderate physical impairments.
25. Have students describe cerebral palsy and spina bifida.
26. Have students select a type of physical disorder and list adjustments that would be made to the facility to accommodate that disorder.

Health Disorders

27. *Allergy Symptoms,* color transparency CT-30, TRB. Use this transparency to discuss common allergies in young children:
    A. Stress that the most common health problem of young children is allergies. Up to 50 percent of all people have mild to severe allergies.
    B. Discuss the four categories of allergenic substances that promote allergy symptoms: inhalants, ingestants, contactants, and injectables. Have students name examples of each type.
    C. Review and discuss how the airborne, allergenic substances that trigger allergy symptoms in young children can be controlled in a child care center.
    D. Have students list the symptoms of common allergies.

28. Have students prepare a list of items found in a child care center that could cause an allergic reaction in children.
29. Have students make a chart describing the symptoms, special needs, and care for the health disorders: allergy, arthritis, asthma, ADD, cystic fibrosis, diabetes, epilepsy, hemophilia, and leukemia.
30. Have students discuss special concerns and responsibilities for teachers when caring for children with diabetes or epilepsy.
31. *Physical and Health Disorders,* Activity C, SAG. Have students complete the chart by explaining the symptoms and problems related to each physical and health disorder listed.

Integrating Children with Special Needs

32. Have students create a list of resources available to help teachers successfully integrate children with special needs into a child care program.
33. Have students practice methods of informing children about children with special needs who are in their programs.
34. *Helping Children Who Have Special Needs,* Activity D, SAG. Have students use the form to report on an article or book that relates to handling children with special needs in a regular classroom.

Gifted Children

35. Have students discuss the six areas in which children may be gifted.
36. *Identifying the Gifted Child,* transparency master 30-1. Use this transparency to review the characteristics that might identify a gifted child.
37. Have students compare and contrast acceleration and enrichment.
38. Have students brainstorm a list of activities that could be used in an enrichment program for a four-year-old.
39. Have students interview the parents of gifted children to find out problems their children face. Students should discuss their findings in class.
40. *The Child Who Is Gifted,* Activity E, SAG. Have students use the form to record information from an interview with the parent or teacher of a child who is gifted.

Learning Disabilities

41. Have students define the term learning disabilities.
42. *Identifying Children with Learning Disabilities,* transparency master 30-2. Use this transparency to help students identify common traits of children with learning disabilities.
43. Have students observe children with learning disabilities in a classroom setting.

Additional Resources

44. Panel discussion. Invite parents of children with special needs to discuss their experiences with the class.

45. Guest speaker. Invite a teacher of children with special needs to discuss methods of adapting the classroom and teaching techniques for children with special needs.

46. Guest speaker. Invite a speech therapist to discuss stuttering with the class.

47. Field trip. Arrange for students to visit a child care center that has a program for children with special needs. Students should observe special equipment and techniques that are used with the children.

48. Guest speaker. Invite a dietitian to explain diabetes and discuss procedures for caring for a diabetic child.

Research Topic

49. *A Child with Special Needs,* reproducible master 30-3. Have the student research one of the special needs listed in the text using written resources and interviews with parents and health professionals. The student should fill out the form giving the causes, symptoms, problems, treatment, care, etc.

Answer Key

Text

Review and Reflect, page 470

1. Communication
2. Inclusion
3. (1) A description of the child's current level of performance. (2) Annual goals for the child. (3) Short-term goals. (4) A statement outlining the involvement of the child in the regular educational program. (5) Educational services that will be provided with a time line noting the dates services will begin and end. (6) Criteria that will be used to decide if educational goals are met.
4. hearing
5. false
6. p, b, m, w
7. omissions, distortions, substitutions
8. stuttering
9. visually
10. Amblyopia
11. Nearsightedness is an inability to see things that are far away. Farsightedness is an inability to see objects that are close by.
12. Consult with the child's parents, a speech clinician, and possibly a physical therapist. Supply eating utensils and play items that can be used

even with poor fine motor skills. Possibly adapt some toys such as putting large wooden knobs on puzzle pieces.

13. Spina bifida
14. (Student response. See page 462.)
15. A
16. false
17. Hemophilia
18. (List six:) early speech, advanced vocabulary for age, keen observation skills, attention span is unusually long for age, inquisitive nature, flexible, persistent, responsible for age, self-critical, strive toward perfection, good memory
19. (List four:) trouble following directions or poor memory skills; trouble storing, processing, and producing information; trouble identifying numbers and letters; poor eye-hand coordination; trouble reproducing letters and numbers
20. true

Student Activity Guide

Special Needs Match, Activity A

1. S
2. C
3. I
4. Q
5. M
6. L
7. R
8. D
9. N
10. H
11. F
12. P
13. B
14. J
15. A
16. E
17. O
18. K
19. G

Special Communication Needs, Activity B

1. Lack of vocabulary compared to average children.
2. A hearing aid worn in the ear or a Y-shaped hearing aid worn over the chest.
3. (Student response.)
4. Omissions, distortions, or substitutions of vowels or consonants or both.
5. (Student response.)
6. (Student response.)
7. It is sometimes called lazy eye. It is the result of a muscle imbalance caused by disuse of an eye.
8. A patch is placed over the stronger eye. If this does not work, surgery may be required.
9. A condition caused by failure of the eye fluid to circulate in the proper way. Lack of fluid results in increased pressure on the eye. Over time, this pressure can destroy the optic nerve.
10. It can be treated with eye drops if diagnosed early. This will prevent loss of vision.

11. Nearsightedness, or myopia, exists when a person is unable to see things that are far away. The eye focuses in front of the retina. Farsightedness, or hyperopia, exists when a person has difficulty seeing close objects. The visual image focuses behind the retina.

12. It is also called color blindness and involves the inability to see a color. It is hereditary, mostly affects males, and is caused by a recessive gene.

13. (Student response.)

Teacher's Resource Guide

Chapter Test

1. I	9. D		
2. J	10. F		
3. B	11. T		
4. G	12. F		
5. E	13. T		
6. H	14. F		
7. A	15. T		
8. C	16. T		

17. T	25. F		
18. F	26. F		
19. T	27. B		
20. T	28. D		
21. F	29. A		
22. T	30. C		
23. T	31. A		
24. F	32. D		

31. This child may miss as much as half of what is communicated. As a result, the child's vocabulary will not be as extensive as that of the other children. Also, this child may have difficulty during stories, group activities, and field trips.

32. (Name five:) excessive rubbing of the eyes; clumsiness and trouble moving around the classroom; adjusting the head in an awkward position to view materials; squinting; adjusting materials so they are close to the eyes; being cross-eyed; having crust on the eye; swollen, red lids

33. inhalants, ingestants, contactants, injectables. (Student response for example of each.)

34. (Name three: Student response.)

Identifying the Gifted Child

In general, the gifted child

- ◆ speaks at an early age.
- ◆ has an advanced vocabulary for his or her age.
- ◆ may learn to read on his or her own at age 2 or 3.
- ◆ is more observant than other children.
- ◆ has a long attention span.
- ◆ is very inquisitive and asks many questions.
- ◆ remembers many details.
- ◆ adapts easily to new situations.
- ◆ is persistent.
- ◆ acts responsibly for his or her age.
- ◆ is self-critical and strives for perfection.
- ◆ is aware of other's feelings.

Identifying Children with Learning Disabilities

In general, children with learning disabilities may

- have trouble following directions.
- have poor memory skills.
- have trouble storing, processing, and producing information.
- have problems identifying or making numbers and letters.
- have poor eye-hand coordination skills.
- have poor spatial orientation.
- seem awkward or clumsy.
- be overactive.
- act disorderly.
- be inflexible.

A Child with Special Needs

Name _____ **Date** _____ **Period** _____

In the space below, provide information on one specific area of special need. This may be a specific type of disability, health disorder, learning disability, or giftedness. You may choose one of those discussed in the text, or another special need of interest to you. Use library resources, special education teachers, or community agencies that work with children who have this special need to find more information.

Area of special need: _____

Causes: _____

_____

_____

Traits or symptoms of children with this special need:

_____

_____

_____

_____

Method of identification or diagnosis, such as special tests:

_____

_____

_____

Possible problems:

_____

_____

Treatment and care:

_____

_____

(continued)

Name_____

Teaching suggestions:

_____

_____

_____

_____

_____

_____

Special services needed:

_____

_____

_____

_____

Programs, agencies, associations, or other resources available for assistance:

_____

_____

_____

_____

Other information related to this special need:_____

_____

_____

_____

_____

_____

_____

_____

_____

_____

Guiding Children with Special Needs

Name _____

Date _____ Period _____ Score _____

Matching: Match the following terms and identifying phrases.

_____ 1. Repetitions, hesitations, and prolongations in the child's speech.

_____ 2. Harshness, hoarseness, and breathiness are examples.

_____ 3. This condition is a result of muscle imbalance caused by disuse of the eye.

_____ 4. A condition caused by failure of the fluid on the eye to circulate properly.

_____ 5. A nonprogressive condition that is a result of damage to the brain.

_____ 6. Results when the bones of the spine fail to grow together.

_____ 7. A sensitivity to something.

_____ 8. A condition that results from the inflammation of joints and surrounding tissue.

_____ 9. A disease characterized by a recurrent shortness of breath.

_____ 10. A hereditary disease that occurs almost from birth that involves serious lung infections.

A. allergy
B. amblyopia
C. arthritis
D. asthma
E. cerebral palsy
I. cystic fibrosis
G. glaucoma
H. spina bifida
I. stuttering disorder
J. voice disorder

True/False: Circle *T* if the statement is true or *F* if the statement is false.

T F 11. Inclusion allows normal and exceptional children to gain skills in interacting with each other.

T F 12. The Individualized Educational Plan needs to include monthly goals for the child.

T F 13. Any developmental deviation in social, cognitive, emotional, or physical development could signal the possible existence of special needs.

T F 14. The ear hearing aid is the one most commonly used with children.

T F 15. Informal observations are the most common method for identifying children with speech problems.

T F 16. Most defects in the eye are correctable.

T F 17. Auditory clues are important for children with visual impairments.

T F 18. A chronic health need is one that persists for a lifetime.

T F 19. Allergies are the most common health problem among children.

(continued)

T   F   20. A person can become desensitized to an irritant by having small amounts of the allergens injected over a period of time.

T   F   21. Hemophilia is a major heart condition in young children.

T   F   22. Leukemia is sometimes called cancer of the blood.

T   F   23. Cerebral palsy is characterized by lack of control of voluntary movements.

T   F   24. Physical disabilities are divided into two classifications: severe and mild.

T   F   25. Children who are considered ambulatory are unable to move from place to place.

T   F   26. Children with ADD are hostile and impulsive.

Multiple Choice: Choose the best response. Write the letter in the space provided.

_____ 27. Federal law requires teachers to _____.
A. include at least two children with special needs in each class
B. take part in identifying children with special needs
C. work alone to design individualized programs
D. remove children with special needs from the regular classroom

_____ 28. Identification does *not* include _____.
A. close observation
B. informal observation
C. alerting the center director
D. labeling

_____ 29. A child with a mild hearing loss _____.
A. may miss as much as half of what is being communicated
B. will have little understandable speech
C. does not need a hearing aid
D. is seldom placed in regular child care programs

_____ 30. Taking a child's mispronounced words and correctly including them in sentences is called _____.
A. referral
B. inclusion
C. expansion
D. augmentation

_____ 31. A congenital defect is one that _____.
A. is caused before birth, but is not hereditary
B. occurs after birth, but is not hereditary
C. is an inherited defect that occurs before birth
D. occurs after birth as a result of heredity

_____ 32. Which of the following is *not* a hereditary disease?
A. diabetes
B. cystic fibrosis
C. hemophilia
D. asthma

(continued)

Essay Questions: Provide complete responses to the following questions or statements.

33. Describe the behavior of a child with a mild hearing loss.

32. Name five symptoms that may suggest a vision problem.

33. Name the four categories of allergenic substances and give one example of each.

34. Name three characteristics commonly observed in gifted children.

Parent Involvement 31

Objectives

After studying this chapter, students will be able to
- list objectives for parent involvement.
- cite advantages and disadvantages of various methods for involving parents in the center.
- describe the importance of a positive caregiver/family alliance.
- design a center newsletter.
- write a letter to parents.
- plan, conduct, and follow up on a parent-teacher conference.
- explain how to conduct a discussion group.
- describe the process of recruiting and orientating parent volunteers.

Teaching Materials

Text, pages 471–488
   Terms to Know
   Review and Reflect
   Apply and Explore
Student Activity Guide
   A. *Getting Parents Involved*
   B. *Parent Letters*
   C. *Parent Discussion Groups*
   D. *Teacher Hotline*
Teacher's Resource Guide/Binder
   Parent Relationships, reproducible master, 31-1
   Parent-Teacher Conference Summary Form,
      reproducible master, 31-2
   Checklist for a Good Conference,
      reproducible master, 31-3
   Class Problem-Solving File,
      reproducible master, 31-4
   Suggestions for Parent Volunteers,
      reproducible master, 31-5
   Chapter Test
Teacher's Resource Binder
   Happy-Gram, color transparency, CT-31
The Observation Guide
Mastering CDA Competencies

Introductory Activities

1. Ask students to give reasons why parents should be involved in child care programs.
2. *Parent Relationships,* reproducible master 31-1. Have students consider how much communication they will want with parents when they are teachers by completing the form. Students should discuss their responses.
3. Have students discuss their ideas on the differences and similarities between parent education and parent involvement.
4. *Getting Parents Involved,* Activity A, SAG. As a chapter preview, have students fill in the blanks in the statements using the words listed. This activity can also be used as a review of the chapter contents after the students have read the chapter.

Instructional Concepts and Student Learning Experiences

Objectives

5. Have students discuss the value of the objectives for parent involvement listed in the text.
6. Have students discuss ways of building positive relationships with parents.

Written Communication

7. Have students write a parent letter using the active voice.
8. Collect newsletters from several centers. Have students analyze them for content.
9. Have students create a newsletter for an imaginary center.
10. *Parent Letters,* Activity B, SAG. Have students write a parent letter using the instructions provided.
11. Have students brainstorm a list of occasions or special events that could be communicated to parents using the daily news flash.
12. *Happy-Gram,* color transparency CT-31, TRB. Use this transparency to illustrate one method of sharing a child's accomplishments with his or her parent(s):

A. Stress the importance of communication for informing parents about their child's accomplishments.
B. Ask students to discuss the writing style that would be most effective in communicating with parents using notes, newsletters, or letters.
C. Have students brainstorm a list of accomplishments that could be shared with a child's parent(s).
D. Discuss how a "Happy-Gram" can promote verbal communication between parent and child.

Parent-Teacher Conferences

13. *Parent-Teacher Conference Summary Form,* reproducible master 31-2. Have students complete the form using children they have observed or by interviewing a teacher about one of the children in his or her class. Students should discuss how this information would affect the content of the parent-teacher conference.
14. Have students discuss the questions parents most frequently ask at conferences.
15. Have students list and discuss five ways of scheduling time for parent conferences.
16. Have students role-play situations in which teachers work with timid, worried, egotistical, and critical parents.
17. Have students explain how a parent-teacher conference could be ended.
18. *Checklist for a Good Conference,* reproducible master 31-3. Have students work in pairs to conduct mock parent-teacher conferences. Students should use the checklist to critique their actions.

Discussion Groups

19. Have students state the purpose of parent discussion groups and discuss the advantages and disadvantages of this technique.
20. *Parent Discussion Groups,* Activity C, SAG. Have students evaluate the value of parent discussion groups by completing the chart and answering the questions.
21. Have students explain techniques for helping parents relax at a discussion meeting.
22. Have students list the steps in preparing for a parent discussion group.
23. Have students brainstorm a list of parent discussion topics.
24. Have students conduct a mock parent discussion meeting by having assigned personalities of their own and their "child."

Other Methods of Involvement

25. Have students create a bibliography of books that would be appropriate for a lending library.

26. Have students explain how a traveling backpack can promote parents' involvement in their children's education.
27. Have students develop a list of equipment and materials for a four- to five-year-old child's traveling backpack.
28. Have students list materials that could be included in a file for each of the topics given in figure 31-12 of the text.
29. *Class Problem-Solving File,* reproducible or transparency master 31-4. As a class project, have students create a problem-solving file. Use the form to assign students topics for which they are to gather materials to include in the file.
30. Have students design a parent bulletin board.
31. Have students discuss guidelines for talking to parents on the phone.

Volunteers

32. *Suggestions for Parent Volunteers,* reproducible master 31-5. Review the suggestions listed for parent volunteers. Why are each of the suggestions included? Ask students what they would add to the list.
33. Have students describe characteristics that parent volunteers need.
34. *Teacher Hotline,* Activity D, SAG. Have students answer the questions as if they were writing for a teacher hotline.

Additional Resources

35. Guest speaker. Invite a center director to discuss parent letters and parent education involvement.
36. Panel discussion. Invite a group of parents to discuss their views on ideal parent involvement in early childhood programs.

Research Topic

37. Have the student research studies on the effects of parent involvement on teachers, parents, or children. The student should write a report on his or her findings.

Answer Key

Text

Review and Reflect, page 487

1. regular communication
2. (List four:) Parent involvement helps parent: develop an understanding of child growth and development; gain confidence in their parenting roles; learn about their children's experiences at the center; understand their children by observing other children; learn new ways of interacting with

their children; become informed about community resources; foster the children's and parent's ability to interact with each other; extend learning from the center into the home; understand how a center-home partnership can promote the children's development.

3. Use the active voice; write towards the parent's educational level.
4. A
5. planning, conducting the conference, follow-up
6. false
7. why, what, how, when, and where
8. This allows time to record any important information and also allows time if the conference runs slightly longer than planned.
9. true
10. A. needs to learn to share with others
    B. tries to get others' attention
    C. is capable of doing more
    D. is not physically well-coordinated yet
11. answer
12. C
13. true
14. (List two:) Group discussions are useful for studying new ideas; they allow several people to take part; individual thinking is challenged.
15. B
16. A lending library is a useful way to share parenting information.
17. problem-solving
18. D
19. The best volunteer is a person who is interested in working with young children.
20. thank-you

Student Activity Guide

Getting Parents Involved, Activity A

1. sunshine call
2. educational
3. parent involvement
4. planning
5. reinforcement
6. active
7. problem-solving
8. orientation
9. daily news flash
10. theme
11. letters
12. positive
13. debating
14. professional
15. newsletters

Teacher's Resource Guide

Chapter Test

1.	D	17.	F
2.	A	18.	T
3.	B	19.	F
4.	C	20.	T
5.	F	21.	F
6.	E	22.	T
7.	F	23.	C
8.	F	24.	D
9.	T	25.	D
10.	F	26.	B
11.	T	27.	D
12.	F	28.	D
13.	T	29.	C
14.	T	30.	C
15.	T	31.	A
16.	T	32.	A

33. (Name four. Student response.)
34. Useful for studying new ideas; allows several people to take part; individual thinking is challenged; individuals have the chance to study and review their own experiences; they are made to think through their positions.
35. Plan the conversation by carefully choosing what to say; keep the call to about five minutes in length; begin the conversation by asking the parent if it is a convenient time to talk, if not, arrange a time to call back; put the parent at ease immediately by telling the reason for the call; share positive statements about the child; whenever possible, also give the parent a word of praise or thanks.

Parent Relationships

Name _____ **Date** _____ **Period** _____

As a teacher, how often do you feel that you would take the actions listed below?

	Always	Sometimes	Never
1. Listen to parents' concerns.			
2. Encourage parents to visit.			
3. Give parents an opportunity to volunteer in the classroom.			
4. Write newsletters for parents.			
5. Encourage parental input during a conference.			
6. Call parents to share a child's success.			
7. Learn about interests and special abilities of the parents.			
8. Show parents examples of the child's work.			
9. Try to be open and honest with parents.			
10. Send notes home with children.			

Why is communication with parents important? _____

_____

_____

_____

_____

Parent-Teacher Conference Summary Form

Name _____ **Date**_____ **Period** _____

Choose a child you have observed or work with a teacher to complete the form. Write comments that reflect a child's usual behavior.

Date _____ Name of child_____

                                                      (first)   (last)

Birth Date _____ Age _____ Years _____ Months _____

1. Child's Relationships

    A. Child's response to being left at center_____

        _____

        _____

        _____

    B. Choice of companions _____

        _____

        _____

        _____

    C. Child plays best when_____

        _____

        _____

        _____

    D. Relationship to adults _____

        _____

        _____

        _____

    E. Degree of participation _____

        _____

        _____

        _____

(continued)

Name_____

F. Acceptance of group routine_____
_____
_____
_____

2. Child's Activity Preferences

_____
_____
_____

3. Child's Emotional Status

_____
_____
_____
_____

4. Child's Behavior at Meal Time

_____
_____
_____

5. Child's Toilet Behavior

_____
_____
_____

6. Observations of Child's Health

_____
_____
_____

7. Child's Physical Abilities

_____
_____
_____

8. Child's Problem-Solving Behavior

_____
_____
_____

(continued)

Name_____

9. Child's Cognitive Characteristics

A. Attention span _____

_____

_____

B. Memory _____

_____

_____

C. Curiosity _____

_____

_____

D. Awareness _____

_____

_____

10. Child's Cognitive Development

A. Color perception _____

_____

_____

B. Number concepts _____

_____

_____

C. Usually communicates through _____

_____

_____

D. Talking frequency _____

_____

_____

E. Enunciation _____

_____

_____

F. Language mastery _____

_____

_____

(continued)

Name_____

11. Summary:_____

_____

_____

_____

_____

_____

_____

_____

_____

_____

_____

_____

_____

_____

_____

_____

_____

_____

_____

12. Parents' participation and reaction: _____

_____

_____

_____

_____

_____

_____

_____

_____

_____

_____

_____

_____

_____

_____

_____

_____

_____

_____

Checklist for a Good Conference

Name _____ **Date** _____ **Period** _____

Choose a partner with whom you can conduct a mock parent-teacher conference. Use this checklist to record and evaluate your actions.

_____ 1. Carefully prepare by writing comments.

_____ 2. Begin the conference on a positive note.

_____ 3. Encourage the parent to talk by asking questions or acknowledging his or her input.

_____ 4. Listen attentively.

_____ 5. Encourage the parent to make suggestions.

_____ 6. Summarize points covered at the end of the conference.

_____ 7. Plan together for future progress.

_____ 8. Thank the parent for sharing.

Comments:_____

_____

_____

_____

_____

_____

_____

_____

_____

_____

_____

_____

_____

_____

_____

Class Problem-Solving File

_____	Allowances
_____	Bedwetting
_____	Blended families
_____	Childhood diseases
_____	Child abuse
_____	Children's clothing
_____	Crying
_____	Emotional development
_____	Death
_____	Divorce
_____	Food
_____	Gifted children
_____	Handedness
_____	Identity
_____	Intellectual development
_____	Language development
_____	Large muscle development
_____	Lying
_____	Mental retardation
_____	Nightmares
_____	Play
_____	Personality development
_____	Reading readiness
_____	Selecting toys
_____	Self-esteem
_____	Separation anxiety
_____	Small muscle development
_____	Social development
_____	Stealing
_____	Speech problems
_____	Teething
_____	Television
_____	Thumbsucking

Suggestions for Parent Volunteers

General Participation

♦ Provide praise with such statements as "I like your painting," or "Thanks for hanging your coat on the hanger," or "You're good at helping with clean-up."

♦ State your suggestions positively by telling what the child should do. For example, instead of saying, "Don't put the puzzle on the floor," tell the child where to place the puzzle.

♦ When talking with the children, get down at their level by squatting or sitting. As the child speaks, give him or her your full attention.

♦ Speak with other adults only when necessary.

♦ Never do for a child what he or she can do for himself or herself. That is, always stress independence. Let the children put on their own coats, boots, etc. Assist only when absolutely needed.

♦ Avoid discussing the children outside of the classroom.

At Storytime

♦ Sit in the circle with the children.

♦ Allow interested children to crawl onto your lap.

♦ Show your interest in the story by listening attentively.

♦ If you are asked to read, hold the book so all the children can see.

At the Easel

♦ Children need to wear a smock while painting.

♦ Only one child should use each side of the easel at a time.

♦ Encourage the children to replace the brushes in the proper color. (There is one brush for each container of paint.)

♦ Show an interest in the children's work, but do not interpret it for them. Likewise, do not ask children what they have made.

♦ After children finish painting, write their names in the bottom right-hand corners of their work. Capitalize only the first letter of each name.

♦ Hang finished paintings on the drying rack.

♦ At the end of the day, encourage the children to take their paintings home.

At Music Time

♦ Participate with the children.

♦ Reinforce the head teacher's actions.

♦ Show your enjoyment of the music.

Parent Involvement

Name _____

Date _____ Period _____ Score _____

Matching: Match the following terms and identifying phrases.

_____ 1. Used to share with the parents something outstanding or interesting the child has done recently.

_____ 2. Provides information about the center at the parents' convenience.

_____ 3. Helps parents and teacher better understand the child.

_____ 4. Helps parents with specific problems they face.

_____ 5. Children take home a few favorite books or games from the center for a short time.

_____ 6. Used for teaching parents how to promote children's learning at home.

A. newsletters
B. parent-teacher conferences
C. problem-solving file
D. sunshine call
E. theme bags
F. traveling backpack

True/False: Circle *T* if the statement is true or *F* if the statement is false.

T   F   7. Parent involvement refers to any activity that parents do in relationship to their parenting roles.

T   F   8. Teachers and parents have always viewed each other favorably.

T   F   9. The child's strengths should be communicated to his or her family.

T   F   10. Parents should only be welcomed at the school for special celebrations.

T   F   11. Parent involvement helps parents gain confidence in the parental role.

T   F   12. Discussion is the most popular method of parent involvement.

T   F   13. Teachers who are confident of their skills are more dedicated to including parents.

T   F   14. Many parents prefer a newsletter to attending frequent parent conferences.

T   F   15. Home learning activities for parents to do with their children should be included in parent letters.

T   F   16. The teacher sets the tone for parent conferences.

T   F   17. Always end a conference with advice for the parents on how to improve their child's behavior.

T   F   18. If a parent appears uncomfortable during a conference, provide reassurance that all information will be confidential.

T   F   19. Open-ended questions result in yes or no answers.

T   F   20. Parents like straightforward "how-to" approaches.

(continued)

T   F   21. Studies show people remember names better than faces.

T   F   22. Parents always enjoy positive references to their children.

Multiple Choice: Choose the best response. Write the letter in the space provided.

_____ 23. Newsletters should be written _____.
            A. giving detailed information
            B. at a college reading level
            C. using the active voice
            D. using the passive voice

_____ 24. A newsletter should *not* contain _____.
            A. a review of classroom activities
            B. upcoming special events
            C. nutritious recipes
            D. articles praising one or two children

_____ 25. Personal notes in the blank section of the newsletter should be _____.
            A. the same for all parents
            B. lengthy
            C. negative
            D. positive

_____ 26. Parent letters are usually sent _____.
            A. weekly
            B. monthly
            C. bi-annually
            D. annually

_____ 27. The best way to schedule parent-teacher conferences is _____.
            A. to have morning conferences
            B. to have evening conferences
            C. to have weekend conferences
            D. to ask parents what is most convenient for them

_____ 28. The best setting for a parent conference is _____.
            A. with the teacher at a desk and the parents on the other side of the desk
            B. at the back of the classroom so the teacher can supervise the children
            C. in the teacher's office so the phone can be answered easily
            D. chairs in a grouping in a private room

_____ 29. At the beginning of a conference, a timid parent may _____.
            A. seem self-confident
            B. brag about his or her child
            C. be afraid to speak
            D. ask many questions

_____ 30. An advantage of parent group discussion is _____.
            A. the time it takes
            B. misinformation can be pooled
            C. individual thinking is clarified
            D. emotions may be aroused

(continued)

_____ 31. To make a sunshine call, you should _____.
   A. plan the conversation carefully
   B. keep the call to ten minutes in length
   C. make some casual small talk before stating the reason for the call
   D. share areas that need improvement as well as positive statements

_____ 32. To get the most from volunteers, do *not* _____.
   A. skip training sessions to spare volunteers' time
   B. share staff expectations of them
   C. explain the importance of volunteers
   D. use the volunteers' names often in conversation with them

Essay Questions: Provide complete responses to the following questions or statements.

33. Name four ways parents benefit from parent-involvement activities.

34. Describe the benefits of group discussions with parents.

35. Describe guidelines that must be followed when calling parents by telephone.

A Career for You in Child Care  32

Objectives

After studying this chapter, students will be able to
- rank their job preferences.
- compile their resumes.
- write letters of application.
- list various methods for seeking employment.
- compute salary ranges on which they could live.
- list questions to ask during an interview.
- prepare teaching portfolios.
- explain the basic interviewing process.
- discuss illegal questions and how to respond to them.

Teaching Materials

Text, pages 489-504
  Terms to Know
  Review and Reflect
  Apply and Explore
Student Activity Guide
  A. *Know How to Job Hunt*
  B. *Career Preferences*
  C. *A Job Application*
  D. *The Bottom Line*
Teacher's Resource Guide/Binder
  Resume Outline, reproducible master, 32-1
  Resume Checklist, reproducible master, 32-2
  Guidelines for Cover Letters
    reproducible master, 32-3
  Interview Inventory, reproducible master, 32-4
  Preparing for Interviews, reproducible master, 32-5
  Chapter Test
Teacher's Resource Binder
  Resume Writing, color transparency, CT-32
The Observation Guide
Mastering CDA Competencies

Introductory Activities

1. Have students discuss any previous experiences they may have had looking and interviewing for jobs. Students should try to describe how the process may differ as they seek a job in child care.
2. Prepare a fashion show focusing on how to dress and groom, and how not to dress and groom, for a job interview. Use students or fellow teachers as models.
3. Ask students to give their ideas about what a resume should be like. Students should list information they think should be included.
4. *Know How to Job Hunt,* Activity A, SAG. As a chapter introduction, have students determine whether the statements about job hunting are true or false.

Instructional Concepts and Student Learning Experiences

Ranking Job Preferences

5. Have students discuss the types of personality traits, skills, and interests that affect a person's job preferences.
6. Have students discuss how knowing their job preferences can help their efforts to find a job.
7. Have students make a job preference list using illustration 32-2 in the text as a guide.
8. *Career Preferences,* Activity B, SAG. Have students rank the job preferences listed and answer the questions that follow.
9. Have students find articles or other resources listing current teacher salaries in your community and other communities.
10. *The Bottom Line,* Activity D, SAG. Have students complete the form to determine their rock-bottom and desired salaries.

Resumes

11. Have students list the components of a resume.
12. *Resume Writing,* color transparency CT-32, TRB. Use this transparency to help students learn the key information that needs to be included on a resume:
    A. Have students list the purposes of a resume.
    B. Have students prepare a list of helpful hints for preparing a resume.

C. Have students prepare sample resumes using the information on the transparency.

D. Stress the importance of asking another individual to proofread a cover letter and resume before sending it to a prospective employer.

13. *Resume Outline,* reproducible master 32-1. Use the master to go through the process of writing a resume as a class. Students should suggest information based on their backgrounds.

14. Have students interview child care directors to find out what they look for in a resume. Students should share their findings with the class.

15. Have students start a collection of resumes written by child care professionals. Students should review the resumes noting features they would like to include in their resumes.

16. *Resume Checklist,* reproducible master 32-2. Have students write resumes and use the checklist to evaluate them.

17. *A Job Application,* Activity C, SAG. Have each student complete the job application form. Then have students evaluate the completed forms in small groups.

Avenues for Seeking Employment

18. Have students clip and study newspaper ads for child care positions.

19. *Guidelines for Cover Letters,* reproducible master 32-3. Have students write a cover letter in answer to an ad using the master as a guideline for writing the letter.

20. Have students use the Internet to find information about openings for child care positions. Ask students to share their findings in class.

21. Have students write ads to place in the "positions wanted" section of a newspaper to indicate their availability for child care positions.

22. Have students describe the purpose of college or school placement agencies.

23. Have students investigate how membership in professional organizations can help them in their job searches.

24. Have students survey child care professionals to find out how they found their current jobs. Students should share their findings in class.

25. Have students make a list of meetings and events at which they would be able to network with child care professionals.

26. Have students discuss the importance of good record keeping during a job search.

Preparing for an Interview

27. Have students discuss methods of building a positive attitude as they prepare for job interviews.

28. *Interview Inventory,* reproducible master 32-4. Have students record the information about themselves requested on the master in preparation for interviewing.

29. *Preparing for Interviews,* reproducible master 32-5. Have students list their strengths and weaknesses on the forms. Students should then divide into small groups and discuss how this information might be used to each student's advantage in an interview.

30. Have students list questions they might ask during an interview.

The Interview

31. Have students come to class as they would dress and groom for an interview. Students should practice conducting themselves appropriately in interview situations.

32. Have students prepare answers to each of the interview questions listed in the text. Students should practice stating their answers aloud with a partner.

33. Make a grab bag containing sample items that might be included in a teaching portfolio. Ask each student to draw one item from the bag. Then have the student identify the item, describe where it might be placed in a portfolio, and explain what prospective employers might discern from it.

34. Have students discuss what constitutes a legal or an illegal question.

35. Have students role-play interview situations in which they must handle illegal questions.

36. Have students write a thank-you note that would be an appropriate follow-up to an interview.

On the Job

37. Have students discuss what it means to "observe, listen, and gently question."

38. Have students brainstorm a list of questions they might ask their coworkers about how to improve job skills and employee relationships.

Additional Resources

39. Invite a guidance counselor to discuss resume writing with the class.

40. Invite a panel of child care directors to discuss what they look for and what questions they ask during a job interview.

41. Invite two or three child care directors to conduct mock interviews with a few volunteers from the class. The volunteers should supply resumes and cover letters to the interviewers in advance. The class should view and discuss the mock interviews.

42. Invite an experienced child care professional to speak to your class about how to prepare a

teaching portfolio. Ask the speaker to share examples from his or her portfolio with the students.

43. Invite a psychologist or counselor to discuss how to positively deal with rejection during a job search.

Research Topics

44. Have the student research the topic of resume writing through interviews with employers and written resources. The student should then compose a pamphlet on how to write an effective resume. The pamphlet should include a list of additional resources.

45. Have the student conduct an experiment to find out what communication methods are most effective during an interview. (Such factors as posture, eye contact, and tone of voice should be considered.) The student should give an oral report to the class on his or her findings.

Answer Key

Text

Review and Reflect, page 504

1. B
2. resume
3. true
4. by listing all unpaid work experience, such as lab work, volunteer work in field of study, involvement in professional groups
5. Placing an ad in the position wanted section of the newspaper is a passive job search technique that requires the employer to seek you out. This usually works best for those people who have a great deal of experience.
6. jobs that are advertised informally through word of mouth
7. contact center directors personally, join local chapters of professional organizations, network
8. A
9. B
10. true
11. B
12. portfolio
13. true
14. Sending a thank-you note will make you stand out. Your letter will serve as a reminder to those you have met.

Student Activity Guide

Know How to Job Hunt, Activity A

1. T	11. F
2. F	12. T
3. F	13. T
4. T	14. F
5. T	15. F
6. F	16. T
7. T	17. F
8. T	18. F
9. T	19. F
10. T	20. T

Teacher's Resource Guide/Binder

Chapter Test

1. C	14. T
2. D	15. F
3. E	16. T
4. A	17. F
5. B	18. F
6. T	19. T
7. T	20. T
8. T	21. B
9. F	22. D
10. F	23. C
11. F	24. D
12. T	25. C
13. T	

26. (Student response. See Chart 32-11 on page 499.)
27. (Student response. See pages 499-500.)
28. (Student response. See Chart 32-13 on page 501.)

Resume Outline

Name _____ **Date**_____ **Period** _____

_____ (Name)

_____ (Address)

_____

_____ (Telephone number)

Objective (if seeking a specific position)

Education

Teaching or Work Experience

Professional Activities (if any)

Other Qualifications

Interests

Resume Checklist

Name _____ **Date** _____ **Period** _____

Write a resume. Then use the following checklist to evaluate it.

	Yes	No
1. Is my job objective specific, providing a focus for the resume?		
2. Are my specific work experiences highlighted?		
A. Have I included my related work experience?		
B. Are the titles and names of my previous employers included?		
C. Are my responsibilities included?		
D. Are there gaps in my work history?		
3. Are professional memberships mentioned to add to my credibility?		
4. Have I listed extracurricular activities to display leadership traits and motivations?		
5. Is my resume free of errors?		
A. Typographical errors?		
B. Misspelled words?		
C. Grammatical mistakes?		
6. Have I avoided the use of "I," "me," "my," etc.?		
7. Is my resume visually inviting?		
A. Printed on cream, white, buff, or pale gray paper?		
B. Printed on 8½- by 11-inch paper?		
C. Printed on one side of page?		

Guidelines for Cover Letters

Name _____ **Date**_____ **Period** _____

Your address: _____

_____

Date: _____

Person to contact: _____

Contact person's title: _____

Name of center: _____

Address:_____

_____

Dear _____:

First Paragraph. This paragraph should state your reason for the letter. Include the specific position for which you are applying. Also, include from which source you learned of the opening. It may be from a friend, the news media, placement center, or instructor. If you are inquiring whether an opening exists, state this. For example, you may say, "I am moving to Minneapolis and am interested in employment as a teacher. Do you have any positions available?"

Second Paragraph. Tell why you are interested in the position. In addition, explain how your background qualifies you for the position. Share any experience you have had. However, avoid repeating the information the reader will find in the resume.

Third Paragraph. Finally, in the closing paragraph, indicate your desire for an interview. If your schedule is flexible, state that you are available at the convenience of the interviewer. If your schedule is not flexible, state that you would like to arrange to interview on a certain date, if possible.

Closing. Close your letter with a statement that will encourage a response. For instance, you may say, "I am looking forward to hearing from you."

Sincerely yours,

(Signature)

Name: _____

Enc. (Typed to indicate that a resume or other additional items are enclosed.)

Interview Inventory

Name _____ **Date** _____ **Period** _____

Use this form to record information you will need to prepare for an interview.

Dates and location of previous employment:

Reasons for leaving last place of employment:

Previous job responsibilities:

Motivation for teaching:

Evaluation of teaching (strengths):

Ability to work with people:

Attendance:

Information about the employer:

Preparing for Interviews

Name _____ **Date**_____ **Period** _____

This exercise is to prepare you for interview questions such as, "Tell me your strengths and/or weaknesses." You should be able to support your strengths. You should also be aware of your weaknesses and how you are working to improve in those areas. List six of your strengths and six of your weaknesses below. Then with a partner, practice expressing these strengths and weaknesses in an interview situation.

Select six positive traits that you think describe you best.

1. _____

2. _____

3. _____

4. _____

5. _____

6. _____

List six of your weakest traits.

1. _____

2. _____

3. _____

4. _____

5. _____

6. _____

Comments on how to present this information in an interview:_____

_____

_____

_____

_____

_____

_____

_____

_____

(continued)

A Career for You in Child Care

Name _____

Date _____ **Period** _____ **Score** _____

Matching: Match the following avenues for seeking employment with their descriptions.

_____ 1. May be listed under different areas, such as child care teacher or preschool teacher.

_____ 2. Most effective for people with a great deal of experience.

_____ 3. Require job seekers to prepare files concerning themselves.

_____ 4. May be accessed through membership in professional organizations.

_____ 5. Provides information through home pages, chat rooms, and message boards.

A. hidden job market
B. Internet
C. newspaper ads
D. positions wanted ads
E. school placement offices

True/False: Circle *T* if the statement is true or *F* if the statement is false.

T　F　6. Determining minimum net income requirements should be part of a job search.

T　F　7. One purpose of a resume is to inform a potential employer of a job applicant's qualifications and experience.

T　F　8. Gaps in employment dates on a resume should be explained in a cover letter accompanying the resume.

T　F　9. When an applicant has been out of school for several years, emphasis on nonjob factors should be stressed.

T　F　10. Grammatical errors on a resume will not reflect unfavorably on an applicant for a child care position.

T　F　11. Salary requirements should always be included in a cover letter.

T　F　12. Positions wanted ads can help job seekers make their availability known when moving to another area.

T　F　13. A filing system can help a job applicant quickly retrieve information about job openings.

T　F　14. In almost every interview, an applicant is given the opportunity to ask questions.

T　F　15. Job applicants should overdress for interviews so they look their best.

T　F　16. It is often a mistake in an interview to quickly answer a question without previous thought.

T　F　17. A teaching portfolio is a child care teacher's scrapbook of amusing anecdotes and fun activities.

(continued)

T   F   18. In an interview, women may be asked if they are planning to have a family.

T   F   19. Job applicants should always write thank-you notes to the people who interview them.

T   F   20. As a new employee, the best way to get along with others is to observe, listen, and gently question.

Multiple Choice: Choose the best answer and write the corresponding letter in the blank.

_____ 21. Successful job applicants _____.
    A. have their resumes written by professional services
    B. commit themselves to the job hunting process 100 percent
    C. treat job hunting as a part-time job
    D. do not need a plan

_____ 22. Pay deductions do *not* include _____.
    A. federal and state income taxes
    B. health insurance
    C. social security
    D. housing expenses

_____ 23. A resume includes _____.
    A. two paragraphs on the kind of job being sought
    B. letters of recommendation
    C. past job experiences
    D. a list of strengths and weaknesses

_____ 24. What percentage of positions is found through some type of networking?
    A. 10 percent.
    B. 25 percent.
    C. 50 percent.
    D. 80 percent.

_____ 25. During a job interview, an applicant should _____.
    A. ask questions about vacation time
    B. volunteer negative information about former employers
    C. greet the employer with a firm handshake
    D. chew gum to feel more relaxed

Essay Questions: Provide complete responses to the following questions or statements.

26. Give five tips for a successful interview.

27. What are five questions commonly asked by employers during an interview?

28. List eight items that might be included in a teaching portfolio.